GENDER, TRANSPORT AND EMPLOYMENT

Oxford Studies in Transport

Series editor: P.B. Goodwin

This series incorporates reports of research work undertaken at or in association with the Oxford University Transport Studies Unit, in the fields of travel behaviour and transport operations and policy. In addition, from time to time appropriate conference proceedings and other related work will be published.

To Chris, Anne and Ravi
who gave time, space and support
throughout the duration of this
venture.

Gender, Transport and Employment

The Impact of Travel Constraints

Edited by
MARGARET GRIECO and LAURIE PICKUP
Transport Studies Unit
University of Oxford

and

RICHARD WHIPP
Centre for Corporate Strategy and Change
University of Warwick

Avebury

Aldershot · Brookfield USA · Hong Kong · Singapore · Sydney

Published by

Avebury

Gower Publishing Company Limited
Gower House, Croft Road, Aldershot,
Hants. GU 11 3HR, England.

Gower Publishing Company,
Old Post Road, Brookfield, Vermont 05036
USA

British Library Cataloguing in Publication Data
Grieco, Margaret
   Gender, transport and employment: the impact of
   travel contraints.- (Transport Studies Unit series).
   1. Great Britain. Women. Employment. Influence of
   transport services
   I. Title II. Pickup, Laurie, 1953- III. Whipp,
   Richard, 1954- IV. Series
   331.4'0941

ISBN 0-566-05555-4

Printed and Bound in Great Britain by
Athenaeum Press Ltd., Newcastle upon Tyne.

Contents

1 Introduction
Time, task and travel: budgeting for interdependencies

RICHARD WHIPP and MARGARET GRIECO

1.   Perspectives

The major purpose of this book is to draw attention to the complex activity patterns of women in our society and to examine the role and significance of transport in their accomplishment. Typically, women's employment, unlike that of men, is undertaken in the context of, and in combination with, a complex set of domestic and household responsibilities (Oakley, 1974; Mackenzie, 1988; Pickup, 1985a, 1985b). The scheduling compatibilities / incompatibilities (Pleck, Staines and Lang, 1980) of female domestic and employment tasks take place within specific spatial and temporal arrangements which are socially determined (Thrift, 1983; Giddens, 1985), for instance, the proximity of residence to workplace. The perspective adopted in this editorial chapter is one which focuses on time, task and activity management; a perspective which finds substance for its approach within the materials presented in this volume.

In order to design appropriate transport policies for our society, there is a need to identify the relationships between gender, transport and employment. That there are major differences in travel behaviour which are gender based is not in question. There are a good many, well documented case studies and numerous reviews speaking to this difference (Pickup, 1983; Jones, 1979; Stuart Chapin, 1974; Hanson and Hanson, 1981). The question of why such differences exist has, however, received less attention.

Similarly, the consequences of lesser mobility on the part of women has relevance for other areas of existence; and, most particularly, for employment.

Attention must focus, initially, upon the relationship of gender to the distribution of household tasks and co-ordination responsibilities and, subsequently, upon the relationship of these **task sets or bundles** to travel behaviour. Within this chapter, a number of linkages between gender, transport and modern society are outlined which are not immediately apparent but have, nevertheless, important consequences for the **intensification** of gender definitions and stereotypes (Collinson, 1988). For instance, the technologising of transport has served to generate and accentuate differences in travel behaviour between the genders; males typically have better access to the higher technological modes of transport (Hamilton and Jenkins, Ch.2) and improvements in transport technology have permitted the geographical separation of residence and workplace (Gillespie, 1979), a situation which disproportionately disadvantages female access to employment. These differences are both a result of, and serve to compound, other dimensions of social disadvantage, one of which is access to superior categories of employment.

Daily behaviour may be seen as a series of activities. The time taken to undertake such activities does not arise arbitrarily but rather is allocated by individuals, within constraints imposed or pre-determined by a host of outside agencies (Pickup, 1983; Carlstein, Parkes and Thrift, 1978). People undertake various types of activities (e.g. work, education or leisure) and each can make competing claims on their time (Thrift, 1983; Gershuny and Thomas, 1980; Jones, Ch.3): such actions, and their consequences, have to be **budgeted and managed**. The act of management does not take place in isolation but in the context of important inter-dependencies between the individual and the household. In the case of women within a male dominated society, the linked management of time, task and related activities, such as travel - especially in the context of paid employment - has been shown to be a considerable feat (Rosenbloom, Ch.4: Jones, Ch.3).

Out of the complexity of the relationship between the dense set of task demands and scheduling responsibilities carried by women and the constraints on the resources available to service them, there emerges a number of key issues:

1) The female role in travel is a cultural phenomenon; female patterns and levels of mobility are rooted in the values and assumptions of 'family' and 'community' (Pickup, Ch.11; Rhodes, Ch.5).

2) Travel is a gendered activity; male and female patterns are divergent. Moreover, strong local female

patterns of activity exist which have been under-recorded or missed because of the tendency to give non-local male movement e.g. commuting to employment, primacy in policy making (Buchanan et al., 1980; Focas, Ch.8; Hamilton and Jenkins, Ch.2) and in the recording of travel behaviour (Clarke et al., 1981).

3) Yet females have specific needs based on their own travel activity patterns (Goodwin, Ch.7; Hamilton and Jenkins, Ch.2).

4) Due to the strength of prevailing stereotypes which construct women's co-ordinating behaviour as instinctual nurturing (Beckett, 1986), there is a danger of missing the unrecognised but positive, creative management of time, task and travel by women (Rhodes, Ch.5; Hosking, Ch.6).

2. Historical evidence on female accessibility to sources of employment: progress or paradox?

a) The death of the factory hooter

The perception that modern society is more accommodating of women working than was historically the case is a very deep-rooted one, despite an abundance of evidence that demonstrates that women's contribution to the world of work has been greatly under-represented (Roberts, 1988; Tilly and Scott, 1978; Yans Maclaughlin, 1971). Yet there are a number of factors which require closer scrutiny before such judgement can be passed. Looking at the work of Whipp on the U.K. pottery industry (Whipp, 1987c, 1988), a very important fact which emerges is that of the **proximity of residence to workplace.**

Indeed, it is argued that such proximity was crucial to the enabling of women's working. The proximity of workplace to residence permitted female pottery workers to run the home and earn an income. The evidence is that it was not uncommon for female workers to make use of breaks in the production routine for domestic purposes. The general point being made here is that where occupation and residence are contiguous, then there is a **lesser dependence on transport** in the securing and retaining of employment.

Historically, the proximity of workplace and residence was more commonplace, partly as a consequence of the greater prevalence of company housing. Clearly, part explanation of the prevalence of this practice were the limitations imposed upon wider geographical labour markets by the contemporary state of transport technology. For instance, there is a substantial body of evidence on the localness of London labour markets in the nineteenth century (Stedman Jones, 1971; Gillespie, 1979).

3

There is an extensive occupational community literature which remarks the relationship between residential proximity and hiring practices. Casual employment practices on the docks (Hill, 1977; Whipp, 1987a) and in the local fish processing industry required the close residential proximity of their labour force (Grieco, 1987a). The continuation of casual employment practices depended upon the continued residential proximity of the work force.

Residential proximity to the workplace was not confined solely to casual sources of employment but was also common for the more stable and regular sources of work (see also Hareven, 1982). It is this relationship that the now defunct practice of sounding the factory hooter signalled. Workforces lived within earshot of employment. Travelling to work is now a more integral part of employment life.

What produced this difference and what are the consequences for gender? Improvements in transport technology can be viewed as important in this move away from very narrow local labour markets, as can changes in housing legislation and provision. Company controlled housing is no longer a norm. The ability of companies to preserve contiguous space for the use of their workforces and thus reduce employee lateness and enforce other aspects of worker reliability (Hareven, 1982; Mackinley, 1987) is now severely constrained (with a few notable exceptions, such as Corby, (Grieco, 1985b). The consequences for gender are perhaps less immediately apparent.

Research, as we argue more fully later in this chapter, has shown that organisation within the household results in women undertaking more of the household tasks, even when the domestic role is combined with external earning or paid employment, and that women often have markedly inferior access to the transport resources commanded by families (Focas, Ch.8). Because of the greater range and number of tasks conducted by women, frequently their need for access to superior transport is greater, yet typically their perceived entitlement is less.

Considering the issue of women's paid employment, the range of domestic tasks undertaken by women means that women have greater problems of co-ordination of time and task, if work and domestic roles are to be combined. In order to meet the normal demands of scheduling, and most importantly critical demands, the quality of transport facility required by women is greater - yet the on-the-ground provision is indeed poorer, both in terms of public and private transport organisation.

Gender stereotypes play a great role in determining who has the use of the car. Similarly, employers frequently hold strong negative stereotypes of women's mobility behaviour (though it should be noted that these are not only grounded in but also contribute towards a material reality) which discourage them from the employment of women. Scheduling and co-ordinating tasks which in a modern society are set at a geographical distance from one another requires a superior quality of access to transport than that conventionally possessed by the typical female multi-task member of the household. Not to possess such access, where the role responsibilities are manifold and separated in space, is to possess a **profile of actual or potential unreliability** (Wells, Ch.10), in the absence of other support systems, which operates against **employability**.

Household practices of discrimination with regard to access to transport facilities are contributed to and compounded by the behaviour of extra-household agencies. Take for instance, the issue of access to company cars. In recent research conducted on the Docklands (Grieco, 1986; Potter and Cousins, 1983), of those employers offering company cars to employees not one was presently in the possession of a woman. This to a great extent reflects the occupational status of women within these companies, and indeed within the society as a whole, but lesser physical mobility in itself contributes towards processes of **blocked occupational mobility**. Similarly, the dependence of women on public transport is widely reported and their needs have received recognition in a number of public documents. Yet the problems of current public transport design and **unreliability** occupy a low priority in policy circles. The unreliability of public transport, most especially of buses (Buchanan et al., 1980), given the dependence of women on this travel mode, leads to negative public profiles and perceptions which directly affect the employability of women.

Taking this approach, it can be seen that (if we confine our analysis to the **local accessibility of employment**) the historical period - in which there was a lower dependence on transport - favoured the wage earning of women in the lower income classes.

Significantly, and along a somewhat parallel reasoning, a recent World Bank policy document issued the advice that the appropriate transport policy for the developing world was to ensure that employment was locally available to the poorer income categories and thus reduce their dependence on transport (World Bank, 1986). This policy direction, with its focus on the requirement for the **geographical adjacency of employment** to disadvantaged social groups, is of considerable relevance for the development of women's employment opportunities. In contemporary society, women's working is highly dependent upon their **mobility**, access to employment is dependent upon access to transport; historically, the **accessibility** of female employment was greater because of the local nature of the residence/ employment equation.

b)   Transported lives: female migrant labour

Whilst the balance of articles in this book, and the
arguments within this chapter, correctly stress the local
character of women's mobility patterns, there are important
and interesting exceptions to this pattern. Two such
exceptions are found in the historical involvement of
female labour in the migratory occupation of **fish
processing** (Buchan, 1977) and in the seasonal occupation of
hopping (Grieco, 1987b, 1989); both of which practices
persisted until as recently as the 1950s. The 'herring
girls' followed the herring catch throughout its season
from Stornoway, through the Shetlands, down to Hull. Labour
was recruited from a number of locations, with the Western
Highlands and the north east coast of Scotland making
substantial contributions to this labour force. Hopping
labour for southern England was likewise recruited from a
number of geographical locations, with urban London making
a significant contribution.

Importantly, from the perspective of this book, both of
these occupations routinely recruited **married** female
labour. Elsewhere, within this volume, a number of authors
have talked to the importance of women's household role as
carers. The extent to which other members of the household
are dependent on the mother/wife or **central carer** has
consequences for the scheduling of both her activities and
those of the others in the household. There are, as Jones
has shown (Ch.3), a high level of **travel interdependencies**
amongst household members anchoring on this key individual.

The importance of women in this role is usually
identified by means of noting the extent to which such
**patterns of dependency and interdependency constrain
women's mobility** to the local arena. However, within both
the seasonal and migratory occupations identified here,
women were active in organising household activities so
that they were able to fulfil their dense domestic budget
of responsibilities and obligations whilst, simultaneously,
meeting the strenuous responsibilities of employment
outside of their regions of residence. Children frequently
accompanied these working mothers on their travels, sharing
both the tasks and the hutted accommodations of their
elders (Butt, 1983).

In order to understand adequately this pattern of
combined motherhood and migrant employment, it is important
to move beyond focussing purely upon the household and to
focus upon the role of the community (Whipp, 1987a;
Roberts, 1988) in facilitating and constraining household
social practices. These patterns of seasonal household
migration should be understood as communal practices; both
the wider kinship structure and the neighbourhood were
involved in the securing of and travelling to these distant
places of employment. This is not to suggest that there is
no space for incorporating household decision models, but
rather to suggest that the decision model approach often

fails to take account of the importance of the social structures and practices which support specific patterns of travel behaviour. Next, we wish to draw attention to the importance of these complex **travel/employment arrangements** from the perspective of **family survival strategies**.

In discussing the contribution of women and children to the household budget, it is important to recognise that this seasonal contribution is frequently under-recorded in official statistics and official accounts of household organisation (Roberts, 1988). Such under-recording has received wider recognition within the new American labour history, where similar practices of female seasonal migration from urban residence to rural employment have been identified (Yans Maclaughlin, 1971). The casual or seasonal character of this employment results in its exorcism from the official account yet its repeated character makes it an important aspect of household budgeting. The materials collected to date on female fish workers and hopping labour demonstrate the importance of women in the social organisation of employment. There is considerable evidence of women being responsible for **determining** the particular **destination** of the family group, which members should go and which stay behind, for the **organising of transport** (Grieco, 1987b, 1989) and for the organising of the seasonal accommodation necessary to the employment.

In terms of wage employment strategies, it is important to recognise that hop and fish processing earnings were largely controlled by women. This seasonal earning was an important part of the annual budgeting. Many accounts of working class life characterise it as having short term budgeting and accounting horizons, typically the focus is upon the absence of savings habits and long term thrift. Paying attention to the seasonality of the various sources of London labour's earning and employment leads to an understanding of the complexity of organising employment and earnings over the annual schedule. Within the popular information sources, there are many references to the dependence of households on this money for winter clothing and shoes. It was money which could be depended upon once the initial contract with the employer was made and represented an important component in an organised and scheduled annual budget.

Following the recent developments in the literature on the distribution of power within the households, it is 9worth noting the contribution that this annual earning opportunity gave women to organise household budgeting. It provided a source of income which could be relied upon independent of the economic activities of the males. Securing this income, however, depended on the annual **transportation of the household** to the place of employment, with all that entailed in terms of the transportation of household goods as well as dependents.

The main thrust of the arguments presented here is that modern practices are not uniformly progressive in terms of female employment opportunities. Historical relationships may actually have, in one aspect (residential / workplace proximity) or another (fewer state controls on the seasonal mobility of children), been more suitable to women's ability to hold certain types of paid employment.

3.   Woman: the household manager

Recent contributions in the social geography of gender (Women and Geography Study Group of the I.B.G., 1984) have correctly focussed upon the individual in the environment (Thrift, 1983) but have been erroneous in their concentration on the passive and subordinate aspects of women's existence. In general, such approaches over-determine the powerlessness of women. Elsewhere, we have argued that this is the case in the field of employment (Whipp and Grieco, 1985; Grieco and Whipp, 1986; Grieco and Hosking, 1987); here, our intention is to demonstrate, that within the household itself, women are organising and managing complex sets of activities. Whereas the conventional and naturalistic understanding is of the head of household, unambiguously male, being the decision taker, in fact and in practice, major decision sets are routinely undertaken by women. Similarly, prevailing images of women as sedentary fail to recognise the number and range of tasks which necessarily take the central household carer out of the home. Functions which historically were firmly seated in domestic space now take place in a range of institutions which are themselves widely **geographically dispersed** (Mackenzie, 1988; Gershuny, 1983). The co-ordination of time and space necessary to the servicing of domestic requirements is now more complex than in the past.

Women perform a number of co-ordinating tasks within the household. These include the handling of sources of constraint (e.g. income), crises (e.g. illness) and a host of variable demands which the family faces. Most importantly, routines and crises are coped with simultaneously. The combination of domestic and paid employment means (as the Rosenbloom chapter shows) that the degree of complexity **embedded** in women's task co-ordination exceeds that of comparably situated men (Pickup, 1983; Hanson and Hanson, 1981). Further, the linking of intra-household needs often generates the necessity for inter-household co-ordination, as in, for example, child minding. Given that the institutions necessary to household functioning are dispersed in space (e.g. schools, shops, hospitals and other services) and have set times of opening, the sequence of travel activities cannot be freely chosen and, thus, adds to the overall complexity of co-ordination and to the demands for skilled performance (Hosking, Ch.6).

At the very least, therefore, any analysis of women and their transport requirements has to proceed from an appreciation of these features of scheduling and sequencing complexity and how they are strategised and managed. The **management of travel** is an integral part of the general household co-ordinating process. Yet, within the general sociological and social policy literature, even the most sympathetic observers of women's role in society have failed to recognise its importance in the structuring of women's lives. Travel and transport are typically hidden or invisible in the sociological analysis of household behaviour (Roberts, 1988; Glendinning and Millar, 1987). Ironically, where sociology and social theory have become concerned with time-space considerations, the analysis has remained, despite the weight of academic and popular evidence, **ungendered** in its analytical thrust (Gregory and Urry, 1985).

Note that parallel acts of activity-space-time co-ordination performed in the sphere of paid employment are labelled 'organised' and are given formal recognition as 'management' (Davidson, 1987); the opposite is true in the domestic sphere, where complex organising activity is taken for granted as a natural and routine state of the world. This latter perspective fails to recognise the important organisational point that present **routine is an outcome of past decision making** and strategies of adaptation. Only the strength of conventional and entrenched imagery (Gilligan, 1982) conceals the competence of the household manager in the execution of a highly complex task set.

The stresses associated with such complex role sets are well documented (Williams, 1977). Single women are typically healthier than married women, caring for others is documented as damaging women's health (Archer and Lloyd, 1982). Depression is associated with low income, heavy child care commitments and lack of employment (Archer and Lloyd, 1982). Anxieties around the use of the transport system would, from the evidence on hand (Atkins, Ch.9; Reale and Di Martino, 1987), seem to contribute towards such patterns of stress. It is an area worthy of further empirical investigation.

The articles contained within this volume amply reflect the complexity of women's activity patterns with their related travel behaviour. In particular, the chapters of Rosenbloom, Jones, Hosking and Rhodes demonstrate the complexities of household co-ordination within the transport domain. That this is not simply a feature of low income status but is also of relevance to professional women is illustrated by the interesting case study of mobility requirements and constraints in an international agency provided by Wells.

9

4.   Social   networks: their   relevance   for   travel
      behaviour

Recently, the fields of both social policy (Abrams, 1980;
Warren, 1981) and social geography (Knox, 1984) have
developed an awareness of the relevance of social networks
to the understanding of social activity. Whereas
previously, the concern was with outcomes or end states,
currently the emphasis is upon the processes and structures
which shape and pattern outcomes (Massey, 1985). Parallel
developments in transport studies are to be found in the
adoption of time-geographic methods (Hagerstrand, 1974) and
the activity approach developed by Jones et al. (1983) at
Oxford. Whilst this latter approach as presently
constituted does not explicitly harness the social network
concept or its associated technical apparatus, it clearly
has its major arguments set in precisely this same
direction. Indeed, there is a natural linkage between the
concept of inter-dependency, crucial to the activity
approach, and social network analysis (Mitchell, 1969).
Within this short section, our intention is to point up the
extent to which the network intuition is currently embedded
in transport thinking and practice. Furthermore, it is our
object to demonstrate the utility of formalising this body
of thought so that the essential elements of social, and,
therefore, travel behaviour are revealed.

One of the best examples of this approach perhaps - (and
a particularly important feature emerging out of the work
contained in this volume) - is the significance of **escorts**
in women's travel behaviour (Rhodes, Ch.5; Atkins, Ch.8).
Much of the existing literature on escorting concentrates
upon the activity of the central household carer in
accompanying the young, the elderly and the infirm on trips
outside of the household, primarily to institutional
venues.

Within this collection, however, attention is also drawn
to the escorting of the able bodied, adult carer on
journeys outside the home as a mechanism for modifying the
hostile character of the **transport environment**. This
practice of organising an escort on trips can be most
usefully examined within the framework of social network
analysis. Those individuals with active and extensive
social networks are better able to journey outside of the
immediate locality as a consequence of their greater access
to a source of escorts. (From a policy perspective, it may
be important to identify those groups in the community
least able to generate their own escort service in this
way, i.e. kinless elderly, and provide compensatory
measures). The generation of escorts frequently depends on
inter-household co-ordination and this increases the
complexity of household scheduling processes. Note also
that the request for an escort typically generates an
obligation to reciprocate on a subsequent occasion, in
accordance with the norm of reciprocity identified by
Sahlins (1965). In effect, such an exchange of services,

made necessary by the perceived hostility of the external environment, may be viewed as an exercise in community building and re-inforcement.

Recent developments in social psychology (Gilligan, 1982; Brown and Hosking, 1986; Grieco and Hosking, 1987) and social history (Di Leonardo, 1987; Ross, 1983) have revealed the extent to which women **invest** in the development of **extensive patterns of social relations** and networks as compared with men. Clearly, from the material presented in this book we can see why, in travel terms at least, there should be such a functional imperative to invest in social relations on the part of women. Safety in mobility often depends on an escort, in other words, the existence of a reliable social relation. Indeed, this is of particular concern for black and Asian women (Rhodes, Ch.5; Focas, Ch.8; Atkins, Ch.9). The **synchronisation of travel behaviour** by women may be of deeper interest, therefore, to those involved in researching processes of community development, urban renewal and the general operation of social networks. Further and future research in each of these areas would certainly benefit from a deeper consideration of the issues outlined above; the essays collected here provide a useful starting point.

The utility of the social network approach is not confined ot the consideration of escort provision alone but has relevance in other important areas of transport organisation and behaviour. Recent qualitative work by TSU (Pickup and Grieco, 1988) in Liverpool revealed a situation where radical changes in bus design (i.e. the introduction of mini-buses on shopping routes) and changes in manning arrangements (i.e. the abolition of bus conductors) (see Goodwin on a similar situation in London, 1985) made shopping journeys considerably more complex for mothers with young children. Here, households combined their personnels or memberships to modify the negative impact of these policy changes.

This was achieved by:

1) separating out the shopping and child care tasks

2) allocating the shopping tasks of both households to the central carer of one household and

3) the child caring tasks of both households to the central carer of another

Clearly, the **flexibility** inherent in the possession of an effective and local social network is important to the scheduling activity of the individual household (Pickup and Grieco, 1988). At the same time, it should be appreciated that the flexibility gained on one occasion is obtained at the expense of **rigidity** or **constraints** on another. The requirement to return favours places constraints on the free scheduling of time by the individual within the

household. The general point arising from this discussion
is that the social pattern of co-ordination simultaneously
enables and constrains individual scheduling. It imposes
rules of **turn taking** which play an important part in
governing travel behaviour or those individuals enjoying
the benefits of strong social support.

Another important dimension of the social network
approach lies in the consideration of inter-household
linkages in the context of the provision of general social
support. For instance, women's caring responsibilities
are, it has been remarked by a number of authorities and
lobbying groups (such as MENCAP), not confined to the home.
Wives are frequently involved in servicing the needs of not
only their own elderly kin but also those of their husband.
This may be particularly important in those situations
where the pattern is one of male only employment; here
differences in male/ female time budgets are likely to
produce a situation where **sociability requirements** to both
kinship lines are met primarily by the female (Grieco,
1987).

Typically, where low income residential dispersal occurs
and where sociability patterns are maintained (English,
Madison and Norman, 1976), there are major travel
implications ensuing for women. Geographical separation of
kin through re-housing projects or schemes may
significantly increase local mobility requirements where
caring continues to be within the framework of kin (Pickup,
1981). Note that whilst the visiting of elderly relatives
is frequently described as a leisure activity both by
observers and by the women involved, as Hamilton and
Jenkins (Ch.2) point out, the description of this activity
as 'social' conceals the extent of **caring work** which is
routinely involved in such social visiting.

Recent policy initiatives which 'return' the function of
care to the 'community' assume and depend upon the
existence of active social networks and an **orientation
towards care** (Gilligan, 1982) within the community for
their operation. The shift towards patient treatment on a
short stay or day bed basis, with its associated practice
of greater use of out patient facilities (and thus of
transport), in the health service provides one such
example. On occasion, social research into the presence of
strong local social networks has been built into the
hospital design process - the decision to experiment with
short stay practices at the new District General Hospital
at Bury St. Edmunds occurred precisely on this basis
(Grieco, 1982). Whilst short stay hospital care practices
simplify treatment from the point of view of the health
service, they may very well complicate household
organisation, travel and activity patterns. Within this
new relationship between, on the one hand, the health
institution and, on the other, the household and social
network, the function of caring falls primarily upon the
shoulders of women.

Lastly, a much missed feature of the relationship of social networks to time, task and travel budgeting is the property of **time storage** that social networks can provide. Currently, many disciplines have devoted space and energy to 'time'; these discussions range from the new geography's focus on 'space-time' in social relations (Gregory, 1982) to recent historical and sociological work on the multiplicity of possible time frames (Grossin, 1983; Lewis and Weigert, 1981; Whipp, 1987b). All are agreed on one issue, however, that is the **non-storability** of time. Yet by exchanging services, individuals are in fact storing and saving time in a relatively predictable and certain fashion and often in ways which can be used to combat crises and create opportunities (Hosking, Ch.6).

5.   Gendered travel patterns and transport disadvantage

Both within this volume and, in a more fragmented form, in the general transport literature (i.e. Buchanan et al., 1980), it has been shown that women experience considerable transport disadvantage both in terms of the **density of their task bundles** and the implications this has for travel, i.e. **trip-chaining** (Rosenbloom, Ch.4). That there is a strong gender dimension to travel is now indisputable. The consequences of such gender differences, with some notable exceptions (Pickup, 1983), are only now beginning to be explored - a situation which is hardly surprising given that the first official U.K. survey explicitly concerned with gender and transport did not take place until the mid-1980s (Focas, Ch. 8).

The evidence which now exists shows that, taken together, the formidable task of household co-ordination and severe constraints on women's access to transport resources, as compared with men, produce a situation of profound structural disadvantage. Transport disadvantage both reflects and compounds other forms of resource disadvantage, i.e low income (Pickup, Ch.11) and has considerable consequences both for levels of stress and, indeed, for their employment prospects. It is ironic that those with the greatest functional need for flexibility have the least access to the most flexible resources.

Case study work in London's Docklands (Grieco, 1986) highlights the point that the difficulties encountered by women in relation to transport (even in a growth area) are a disadvantage not only to themselves but also to potential employers. Dockland firms have had problems in attracting female clerical and secretarial labour precisely because poor quality public transport provision has deterred women from seeking employment in such poorly served locations. Furthermore, the absence of **proximate shopping facilities** also operates to deter female labour from employment in such locations. While individual employers often make private arrangements for transporting their female labour to local shopping centres during the lunch hours, it should be appreciated that the absence of proximate shopping facilities is a considerable deterrent to female employment in a general context where women have **dual roles,** one of which involves the provisioning of the household (Focas, Ch.8). A clear policy implication is that the provision of shopping facilities, either within commercial and business districts or at points of interchange, is important to the development of new office districts. It should be emphasised, therefore, that transport disadvantage is not a problem for women alone but also has consequences for the general economic well-being of areas.

The last decade has seen the emergence of a number of projects, centres and schemes charged with the responsibility for skilling women in traditionally male occupations (Grieco, 1985). The ruling assumption is that the female workers so skilled will be automatically picked up by the market, especially where training is targetted on areas of known skilled labour shortage. There are a number of problems with this model, not least of which is its failure to recognise the entrenched character of many labour market practices of **discrimination** (Collinson, 1988). Women, possessing skills, still have complex and lengthy processes of job search to undertake in order to convert the possession of a skill into commensurate wage earning. Many training centres provide some assistance with travel arrangements and costs during the training period, and the more radical, such as the Charlton Training Centre in south east London (Grieco, 1985a) even provided child care facilities, but this assistance all too frequently either does not continue into the period of job search or is not of sufficient duration for the securing of the desired job.

A situation is occurring where problems of women's mobility are given formal recognition during the training or skilling period, and are compensated for by financial and institutional supports, but this practice of compensating for transport difficulties is not carried into either the job search or job holding stages of the process. At the very least, such a discrepancy in practice will generate lower success rates for these centres than would otherwise have been the case.

A number of contributors to this volume make the point that in the context where women's dependence on public transport is known to be significantly greater than that of men, **governmental investment** in and encouragement of **private means of transport,** i.e. increased funding of road building, etc. accompanied as it has been by disinvestment in public modes of transport, generates and accentuates **distributional inequities** and compounds the transport disadvantage experienced by women. Simply put, present policies improve the transport advantage of men.

We have spent some time noting the deficiencies of public transport and the limitations that nuclear household composition pose for access to transport resources on the part of women. But what are the prospects for the future given the impact of **multi-task constraints** on private transport co-ordination? Recently, an extensive and thorough review of the field (Perez-Cerezo, 1986) drew attention to the problems that the need for flexibility in scheduling posed for the prospect of car pooling amongst women. There is, of course, space here for all sorts of formal modelling but this example serves to make the integral and central point that those most in need of flexibility have the least access, within the U.K., to the resources which best provide it.

The policy options, at the level of the household and at the level of the local authority, are clear: either a) enhance the transport access of those most in need ('dial-a-ride', more equitable access to the household car), and provide adequate routine and critical support services within geographically compact areas, or b) build into general social policy the initiatives and incentives designed to shift the burden of **domestic responsibility** towards a more **gender equitable** balance.

A comprehensive coverage of the state of the art with regard to gendered travel patterns and transport disadvantage is offered by the combined content of the chapters presented by Focas, Hamilton and Jenkins, Pickup and Rosenbloom.

6. **Transport environment: the issue of personal security**

Reference has already been made to the concept of **transport environment** in relation to the relevance of social networks for travel behaviour. The usefulness of the concept of transport environment is given by the need to analyse not just the mode of transport but the social and environmental context in which it operates (Hosking, Ch.6). From the evidence presented here (Atkins, Ch. 9; Focas, Ch. 8) clearly, **trips** are frequently **suppressed** not because of the physical or social characteristics of the transport system itself but because of the 'spaces' which have to be crossed before joining the formally organised transport system at all.

The thrust of this analysis is that improvements in services of themselves will not necessarily lead to increased usage if other contextual factors are neither taken into account nor remedied. Atkins talks persuasively of the impact of such visual signals of danger as graffiti, vandalised transport hinterlands, etc. on the suppression of female trips. Similarly, other research (Grieco, 1986) has pointed to the inadequacy of street lighting and poor road signing in re-development areas and the ways in which, contrary to planning intentions, such factors generate feelings of insecurity and uncertainty in the transitional period and, therefore, negative images of renewal areas.

Such configurations inhibit exploratory travel behaviour and tie women more firmly into local travel patterns and the local area (Hosking, Ch.6). It seems probable that they seriously and adversely affect women's search for employment. At the most extreme level, these factors can result in the confinement of women to the domestic space alone. Such negative physical features of the urban environment have increased potency in a context where general social and gendered perceptions are of women as more physically and psychologically vulnerable.

7.   Conclusion

To date, sociology has underestimated the importance of travel and transport for the understanding of social behaviour; similarly, transport studies have, on the whole, failed to engage in any depth with the sociological models necessary to the understanding of travel behaviour. The focus on time-space co-ordination adopted in this volume provides a useful vehicle for the integration of these two fields.

In conclusion, this volume represents one of the first attempts in the field to provide a general sociological analysis of gender, transport and employment. The purpose of this introduction has been to demonstrate the general relevance and significance of the contents of the book as a whole rather than to lead the reader through the detailed content of the particular chapters. We have sought to show how the understandings on gender, transport and employment contained here relate to other disciplines and fields as well as to demonstrate the importance of gender for future work in the fields of transport studies and transport policy.

Our suggestion is that there are a number of ways of theorising this set of relationships which are not only interesting in their own right, but are important for the development of concrete and equitable transport policies. Our intention in putting these essays together was to correct the existing invisibility of gender in transport studies. We feel that these essays, taken together, do precisely that.

2 Why women and travel?

KERRY HAMILTON and LINDA JENKINS

1.   Introduction

Transport is an essential aspect of women's lives: it
determines our access to a wide range of resources in
society, including employment, child care, education,
health and the political process. And yet the women's
movement has been slow to see the relevance of transport as
a feminist issue and one which has a vital role to play in
the struggle for equality. Conversely, the transport world
has been slow to see the relevance of women, women's needs
or women's issues to the plans and decisions which they
make. It is almost as if 'women and transport' are
implicitly regarded as a ludicrously incongrous
combination. When we tell people that we are doing
research into 'women and transport', the response is one of
bafflement or bemusement. People are often perplexed as to
why women's transport needs should have been singled out
for investigation. The roots of this response may lie in
the close association of transport with the male gender.
Not surprisingly, then, the transport world is dominated by
men to an even greater extent than most aspects of the
public world in our society.

Yet women have travel needs which are as significant as
those of men, though radically different in many respects.
As consumers of transport provision, however, women's needs
have too often been assumed to be identical with men's, or
simply to be unworthy of note. A wider point, however,
needs to be made at the outset. The concept that transport

provision should be geared to people's needs in the same way as, for instance, education and health provision is a minority view in this country: public transport has been excluded from Welfare State thinking. The readings collected together in this book represent the first attempt in this country to begin an analysis of **gender inequalities in transportation**, and to link this to the wider structural divisions in power and wealth which exist in our society. As such, we sincerely hope that it will put 'gender and transport' on the map as a recognised area of study, and also develop a number of debates about women and transport.

In this chapter we will consider, firstly, the ways in which women's transport patterns, needs, problems and options differ from those of men, and, in our summing up, we will place this differentiation in a historical context by looking at the decline in public transport and the rise of the private motor car since World War Two. Secondly, we will make links between the **mobility differential** of men and women and gender inequality at several different levels; the sociological, the psychological and the biological. Our main analysis will focus on women's position in the social structure, but we will also consider the role played by socialisation and physical characteristics.

In order to avoid painting too simplistic a picture, it is perhaps as well to begin by looking in an overall way at factors which affect travel behaviour. For example, in the diagram from Lester and Potter (1983), which has been reproduced below, it can be seen that only one category, 'household and individual characteristics', seems directly relevant to the gender divide, and that gender is only one of these characteristics. On the other hand, many complex statistics begin to make better sense if gender differences are given primacy in the analysis. Here, for instance, gender is an important correlate of at least two other factors - income and vehicle ownership, and in turn, there is an obvious relationship between these two, as the arrows in the diagram indicate. This constellation of gender, income and vehicle ownership/ use will receive particular attention in this chapter.

Figure 2.1. Influences upon travel and travel method

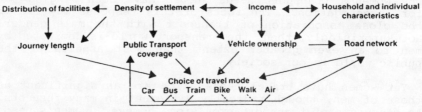

Source: Lester and Potter (1983:7)

Throughout this overview we make some references to (and have footnoted a few examples from) our current research programme, which includes a qualitative empirical study of women's transport needs in West Yorkshire. The research includes a study of the impact of the deregulation of bus services on women's lives, and it should be noted that this is the context in which our research was carried out.

We end this preface to the chapter with some notes on terminology.

Gender: While 'sex' refers to the biological characteristics of maleness versus femaleness, 'gender' refers to the social meanings attaching to this fundamental categorisation.

Work: We have tried wherever possible to avoid the term 'work', since this has been equated with paid employment, with the implication that the socially and economically vital activities for which women continue to be primarily responsible - notably caring and the organisation of domestic life - are not 'work'. The term 'economically inactive' is equally misleading and dismissive.

Household: The use of the 'the household' as a unit of analysis has done much to perpetuate the invisibility of women and their needs. There are assumptions, often unwarranted, that the household is an income sharing unit consisting of a male 'head' and economically dependent women and children. As we shall see, the assumption that 'the household' functions as a transport sharing unit is even more questionable. While 'the household' is a useful unit of analysis for many consumer durables, such as fridges, it is much less appropriate for private motor vehicles.

Housewives: The term 'housewife' obscures women's multiple roles and is dismissive in character ('only a housewife') as well as implying that women are married to houses. We avoid the use of the term, but take it to mean women with full-time caring and domestic responsibilities.

People: We have noted that reportage of transport statistics often refers to 'people' when it would be more accurate to say 'men'. This is particularly the case where household car-ownership figures are being discussed.

Since most official statistics use terms such as these as an integral part of their frame of reference, they tend to obscure or distort women's activities and should, therefore, generally be regarded with caution.

2.   Gender differences in travel patterns

The major problem in attempting to analyse transport and travel in gender terms is, of course, that transport statistics are often not broken down by gender at all. Our knowledge about gender differences in travel behaviour, therefore, remains fragmentary at this stage. A partial picture has emerged from a small number of regionally based surveys, notably that carried out on behalf of the GLC in 1985. In many cases, however, there are no readily available national statistics.

In this section, we will draw on these available sources of data and supplement them with references to some local statistics relevant to our own study in West Yorkshire. The aim is to offer a synopsis of the main differences between travel patterns of men and women, to highlight the communalities in women's travel experience, while at the same time drawing attention to examples of differences between women and to the varying regional contexts which may affect gender divisions in transport.

In terms of **total number of journeys made**, available information indicates a fairly even split between men and women (1). When the travel indicator is **mileage** rather than **trips**, however, a very different pattern emerges. In every age group, men make substantially longer journeys on average than women, and this differentiation is most marked for people in the 30-59 age range (2) (3). Journey length varies markedly by journey purpose, and here gender is an important covariant. For instance, 40% of shopping trips and 39% of 'escort and other' trips, compared to only 17% of journeys to the place of paid employment, were under a mile in length (4). Correspondingly, as Table 2.1 below shows, journeys to 'work' tend to account for a higher proportion of men's journeys while shopping and personal business trips and 'escort and other' trips account for a higher proportion of women's, at least in the 20-60 age range (5) (6).

Table 2.1. Percentage of journeys made by men and women for various purposes, broken down by age

Journey purpose		Age 16-20	Age 21-29	Age 30-59	Age 60-64	Age 65 and over
Journeys to work	Men:	25	31	35	33	5
	Women:	25	19	22	10	2
Shopping/ Personal business	Men:	20	22	24	29	53
	Women:	26	35	40	55	62
Escort & other	Men:	1	3	6	4	2
	Women:	1	11	8	1	1

Source: National Travel Survey, 1978/79, Table 3.4, p.21.

Leaving aside for the moment the rather complex inter-relationship between journey length, journey purpose, transport mode and gender (7) (8) (9), we will focus now on the very central issue of gender differences in the kinds of transport used (10). Generally speaking, women make proportionately more journeys by bus and on foot and as car passengers than men do (11), while men make markedly more journeys as car drivers (12) and motorcyclists and also more by bicycle and train (13). The national statistics are corroborated by more recent regional ones, with some variations, which indicate that there is a strong need for both more local studies, encompassing a wide range of geographical locations, and also for more research at a national level (14) (15).

In addition, there are differences between men and women in terms of the way in which they use public transport. For instance, the preponderance of women passengers is even greater in the off-peak period, as compared to peak-time bus services (16).

So far, we have talked only of gender 'differences' in travel patterns, almost as if the fundamental differences between men and women in terms of journey length and purpose and transport mode were a matter of choice, a case of 'separate but equal'. However, in the case of travel mode in particular, the choices clearly are not equal. The 'great divide' may be seen primarily as being between those who have and those who do not have the use of a car. The availability of a car for personal use has major effects on travel patterns. The more cars that are available within the household, the more people travel by car rather than by any other means of transport (17). Car availability also increases the extent of travel generally. For instance, members of households in which there are not vehicles make an average of 32 journeys per week, compared to an average of 102.5 by households with three or more cars (18).

Since travel is rarely an end in itself, but almost always a means of reaching particular facilities, it follows that car ownership dramatically increases the level of access to resources. The extent of travel generally, and car travel in particular, are strongly related to income and socio-economic status (19). All the statistical indications are that owning and driving a car, and the ability to travel far and often, go hand in hand with wealth, status and power. Conversely, not holding a driving licence and not having the use of a car are major aspects of **transport disadvantage**. Transport disadvantage is not equally or randomly distributed throughout society, but follows the well established lines of structural social inequality. Gender is a major dimension of structural inequality, but there are others: working class people, black and ethnic minority groups, those with disabilities and the very old and very young are also disadvantaged. There are also, of course, important **regional variations** on a number of indicators of prosperity and advantage.

'Women' can be abstracted as a category for analysis and be shown to be receiving a less than equal share of resources, but they are far from a homogenous group.

Having made these qualifying statements, the fact remains that the gender imbalance in car availability and licence holding is dramatic. Statistics based on the 'household' as a unit of analysis have done much to mask the full extent of the inequality. In 1980, 31% of women and 68% of men were qualified to drive (20). That is, over two thirds of men and less than one third of women held a full driving licence (21).

Furthermore, the number of women having both a full driving licence and substantial access to a car is even smaller, though more difficult to assess. In the GLC Women and Transport Study, 34% had a driving licence, but only two thirds of these (i.e. 23% of the whole sample) had primary access to a car (compared to 88% of male licence holders), while 11% had no access to a car at all.

Some West Yorkshire figures can be offered here for comparison. Firstly, the West Yorkshire Metropolitan County Council Transportation Survey of 1981 indicates that, for instance, among manual workers, only 9% of women have both a driving licence and sole access to a car, whereas 47% of men do. 'Economically inactive' women of working age ('housewives') are also very unlikely (11%) to have the sole use of a car as a driver. Graham Read (1983) provides a more detailed analysis of the same data base (22). In the sample of 11,420 men and 12,113 women he found that 36.4% of men had sole and unrestricted access to a car compared to only 9.2% of women. Read (1983:78) comments:

"a high proportion (64%) of male licence holders in one car owning households are the sole driver, as opposed to 20.7% of female licence holders ....Among shared vehicle users, males are far more likely to be priority users than females."

This provides ample confirmation that all household members do not benefit equally from the presence of the car. Consequently, it is not surprising that even where there is a car, or cars, in the household, women are still inclined to be more dependent on public transport than men are. For instance, the General Household Survey reveals that, in 1982, among those living in one car households, the percentage of men using buses dropped markedly to 41% while the percentage of women remained high at 69%. Where there were two or more household cars, only 20% of men used buses, compared to almost half (48%) of the women (23).

To the extent that a contracting public transport system fails to meet the needs of the population in general and women in particular, access to private transport becomes essential for access to a range of resources. Employment is a case in point; the indications are that there is a strong association between having access to a car and having access to employment. Those in employment are more likely to be able to afford a car and those with cars have a better chance of finding a job.

For example, the GLC Women and Transport Survey found that 'for those women who are in paid full-time or part-time work, the most commonly used method of travel to work is as a car driver' (24% compared to 21% travelling by bus and 21% walking; 8% used British Rail; 13% the Underground and 9% as a car passenger), and this in a context where car travel accounts for a smaller proportion of the modal split than the national average.

3.   The position of women in the social structure

The Department of Employment's recent Family Expenditure Survey states that in 1985, it cost an average of £11.28 a week to maintain and run a motor vehicle, and the figure of £8.68 for the purchase of the vehicle, spares and acessories must be added to this, giving a total cost of £20.48 per week (24). Although income is not the only determinant of access to car travel, there is obviously a clear link between women's relative poverty and their low car ownership.

Even after many years of Equal Pay Legislation, women's pay lags far behind that of men (25). This economic inferiority has much to do with women's labour being less highly valued than men's (26). Additionally, women's job tend to be concentrated in the badly paid 'service sector' of the economy (27). Regional diferences in wage levels compound the inequality. For example, since almost 60% of full-time women workers in West Yorkshire earned less than the Council of Europe's 'decency threshold' of '£125.60 per week in 1986, it is little wonder that car ownership is an option for so few (28).

The scale of inequality runs much deeper than this. The dramatic increase in women, especially those with young children, in paid employment has been one of the most important structural changes in the labour market over the last twenty five years (29). However, although women now comprise 46% of employees, almost half work part-time (30). Women's earnings as part-time workers tend to be low, not only because of the pro-rata reduction, but also because part-time workers generally are in a vulnerable position in the labour market. In West Yorkshire, for example, in 1985, 84% of women part-time workers were low paid (31). Even these figures may represent an underestimate of the scale of the problem, since they are based on recorded figures. Much of women's part time employment is 'casual' and, therefore, not reflected in the official statistics.

Why are women so badly paid and why do they work part-time when the rewards are so low? Apart from the low valuation of women's labour, generally speaking, women have fewer employment options than men. **Domestic responsibilities** heavily restrict women's choice of employment. What is often overlooked, however, is that transport options also have a very strong bearing on whether a woman can take up a job or not. Where women live is often determined by the workplace of the male partner, who is defined, for the most part, as the main 'bread winner'. Such are the restrictions on employment opportunities for women that it is common for a woman returning to work after a period of full-time child care to take a less skilled and more poorly paid job than she originally had, e.g. qualified secretaries working as shop assistants or cleaners. **Homeworking**, mainly done by women and the lowest paid of all types of employment surveyed by the West Yorkshire Low Pay Unit, is probably the clearest and most extreme example of the way in which women's bargaining position in the labour market is reduced by transport and child care constraints (32).

Women's economic understanding cannot, however, be fully explained without an understanding of the institut-ionalisation of the economic dependence of women upon men. Historically, the male dominated trades unions have played an active role in promoting wage inequality by supporting the idea of the 'family wage', i.e. that wages paid to the male earner include an element for a non-earning wife and dependent children. Apart from the perpetuation of women's economic dependence on men, this system also penalises the very large number of members of female headed households and overlooks the vital contribution of women's earnings to domestic finances (33) (34).

Despite the well documented diversity of household and kinship formations in contemporary Britain, the systems of social welfare and taxation also continue to be based on inaccurate normative assumptions about the prevalence of the male bread winner / female homemaker / dependent children ideal. In addition, there are myriads of more subtle ways in which the cultural ideal of marriage based on male bread winner / economically dependent, female child carer pattern is disseminated and upheld (35). This ideology of the family has been shown by contemporary sociologists to form a corner stone of the major institutions of society, such as religion, law, education- and, of course, it is also widely promulgated by the mass media, and forms the mainstay of soap operas and advertising alike. This is so strong and pervasive that to many it seems 'only natural' that women get married, give up paid employment to look after their children at home, and receive no direct payment (apart from the £7.25 child benefit) for the massive and vitally important job of reproducing the labour force. It is little wonder then that women's domestic and child care labour has only recently, after a long battle by feminists, been defined as 'work' at all.

Despite the movement of women into the paid employment market, the sexual division of labour within the household persists. The result has been an expansion of women's roles rather than the achievement of gender role equality. Women's activities may reflect any combination of roles, as for example, paid employee; student; unpaid domestic labourer; carer of children, sick or elderly people. Women continue to be primarily responsible for housework, including shopping and child rearing. For instance, the GLC Women and Transport study found that 96% of the women in their sample said that no one else in the household besides themselves regularly did grocery shopping. Probably less visible is the unpaid work which women do caring for sick and elderly adults. Because of changes in the age structure of the population, there are now more dependent old people who need to be looked after, and the carers, whether paid or unpaid, are almost exclusively women (36).

All of these types of 'invisible' work have important transport implications. Some, such as the high proportion of shopping and escort journeys made by women, are fairly obvious. Escorting elderly and infirm relatives on public transport journeys to hospitals, doctors, and sometimes also on shopping trips, as well as escorting children to nurseries, childminders, schools and a whole range of social and leisure activities tends to be carried out by women, particularly when the escort journey is by bus or on foot. Others, such a women's greater reliance on off-peak services for both access to part-time employment and for trips related to their domestic and caring responsibilities, are less obvious. Additionally, the traditional classification of journey purposes is based on male assumptions about the nature of 'work'. Many journeys to friends and relatives which are categorised as 'social' may, in fact, include a significant amount of **socially necessary caring** work (37).

4. Socialisation and psychological gender differences

It can be argued, quite justifiably, that some aspects of women's position in the social structure are shared by other disadvantaged groups in society. For instance, economically dependent or low paid young people, low paid men, and black and ethnic minority groups are also economically disadvantaged and, hence, are likely to be more dependent on public transport than other groups in the population. Additionally, a minority of women have neither significant caring responsibilities nor multiple roles while a minority of men do, precisely because 'gender' is socially rather than biologically constructed. However, even the single, high earning female and the child caring, shopping carrying, role-reversed male are constrained by their location within a deeply patriarchal society.

Men and women do not merely 'play different roles' (note this term implies a high degree of choice), they also tend to be different kinds of people. Gender differences in attitudes and behaviour at adulthood are largely the result of environmental, learning or 'socialisation' factors (38). To understand the full extent of gender inequality, we need to appreciate that socialisation begins at birth and is a continuing process throughout the life span.

The inter-relationships between gender, personality and travel behaviour appears to be an area which is wide open for research. For instance, women's relationship to the private motor car is in general somewhat different to that of men's. The discrepancy in incidence of licence holding can not be accounted for solely in terms of economic inequality. Socialisation antecedents of men's greater interest in things mechanical, in general, and the motor car, in particular, date back to the days of Dinky toys, Meccano and train sets for Christmas.

The important point is that women's access to private motor transport is likely to be severely constrained by a variety of psychological factors such as lesser interest in and ego involvement with cars, less developed mechanical confidence and ability, and perceptions of roads as a hostile, threatening, perhaps even alien environment. In addition, it can be argued that women's lesser mobility, transport options and hence access to resources plays an important role in maintaining the existing imbalance of power.

Preliminary results from our research in West Yorkshire supports this point of view. We have found that women's attempts to learn to drive are often (expensively) spread over a period of years (in some cases decades) and that negative attitudes and experiences in relation to both cars and driving persist long after the driving test is passed. Opportunities for driving practice, both as a learner and as a full licence holder, were often found to be constricted by the attitudes of male relatives, notably husbands. We feel that we are only beginning to scratch the surface as far as uncovering these car related patterns of dependence and control are concerned, and we anticipate that this area will continue to be a major focus of our research.

5 Anatomy is destiny?

While subscribing to the view that the 'biological' is itself socially defined and mediated, we believe that it serves little purpose to deny that there are observed physical differences between men and women, whatever their origins, or to refuse to consider the ways in which these differences may be relevant to any particular issue.

For instance, there are well documented average differences between men and women in height, weight and shape. These ought to have important implications for vehicle design, although this would appear to have seldom been the case. It seems likely that physical differences in size at least partly account for the legendary popularity of the Mini car among women. Again, seat belt design takes no account of the shape of women, particularly in pregnancy. With regard to bus design, if women and children constitute a majority of passengers, should buses be designed primarily with their physical specifications in mind? This would have particular relevance for step height, seating design, positioning of push bells and grab rails, for example.

Gender differences in physical size and strength and mobility are also relevant to women's greater vulnerability to attack and harassment and, hence, greater concern with **personal security as a transport issue.** (The roots of male violence against women, however, have much to do with the relative powerlessness of women, rather than with size or strength). Again, women's footwear and clothing often restrict their mobility, making it more difficult to escape or fight off an attacker. For reasons more complex than they might at first appear, therefore, women are more likely to feel vulnerable to and less able to physically deal with a variety of forms of assault. Women's perceptions of the likelihood of encountering assault, abuse or harassment while travelling by various transport modes therefore merits detailed investigation since this is likely to act as a restriction both on their own mobility and access, and on their uptake of public transport provision.

6. Defining women's transport needs: the implications for transport planners

The 'invisibility' of women's work, referred to above, is only one of the wider problems of the invisibility of women. Hopefully the readings in this book will begin to make visible some aspects of women's transport needs which have been over-looked in the past. As a first step, the relevance for those involved in transport policy of the aspects of gender inequality outlined above may be summarised as follows: women, as a socially-defined category of people, compared to men have:

* primary responsibility for child care and domestic work

* multiple roles: combining paid employment with the unpaid work of domestic labouring and caring

27

* more constrained opportunities for paid employment and a much greater likelihood of being engaged in part-time and/ or casual employment, usually local (40)

* a socialisation history which is qualitatively different from that of men, the transportation implications of which have yet to be studied

* a smaller physical size

Taken collectively, the transport implications of these major features may be outlined as follows:

i) women are less likely to be able to afford private transport and hence are more dependent on walking and public transport. Even when women can drive and there is a car in the household, only a minority have primary access to a car for their own use. Furthermore, social-psychological as well as economic factors place limitations on the feasibility of car-driving as a transport option for many women.

ii) women make around the same number of journeys as men, but a higher proportion of these are local or short distance. As Finch (1984:12) comments:

".. the small local area is essentially women's territory because, while most men live significant parts of their lives away from their place of residence, most women (even if they do some paid work) live most of their lives in the area bounded by the local shops, the school and the bus stop."

The provision of short distance local transport is, therefore, of prime importance for women.

iii) because of women's role as carers, a significant proportion of women's journeys are made primarily to accompany a child or elderly or disabled adults. This has important implications for vehicle design and staffing considerations. It has been abundantly clear from our own research that such escort journeys are not well catered for by current public transport provision. Women with young children are the hardest hit in this respect. One-person operation, high step height and inadequate luggage space make buses an even less convenient option than walking in many cases. From the vivid accounts given to us it was evident that these inadequacies cause real distress and hardship. The problems of travelling with young children continue to be underestimated by transport planners.

iv) Shopping for food and other domestic needs is a major component of women's unpaid domestic labour. Shopping accounts for 25% of women's journeys (GLC, 1985). It follows that on a significant proportion of women's journeys they will be carrying heavy loads. Again, design and staffing considerations are apparent. Our research in West Yorkshire indicates that public transport provision is inadequate for women's shopping needs in terms of bus design and staffing, and also often in terms of the routing and timing of services.

v) Since many women have to combine two or more roles, a substantial proportion of their journeys will be **multi-purpose**. This often results in women's travel patterns being highly complex and variable. This does not make them amenable to simple categorisation. It is unlikely, therefore, that conventional survey research will reveal an accurate picture either of women's travel behaviour or of their transport needs.

vi) Since almost half of women in paid employment work part-time hours, it follows that a substantial proportion of their employment related as well as other journeys (e.g. shopping trips) will be made outside of 'peak' travel times. This has implications for the relative frequency of 'peak' versus 'off-peak' services.

vii) The division of both paid and unpaid labour along gender lines in our society has potentially far reaching implictions for gender differences in journey destinations or purpose, and hence for route and service level planning. In addition to obvious consequences such as women being more often responsible for trips to shops, schools and health care facilities (i.e. accompanying or visiting others), there are also less obvious ones. For instance, women have been shown to take more responsibility for the **'emotional work'** of maintaining socially supportive relationships, particularly within kinship groupings. Social visits made to ensure the psychological welfare of elderly relatives can be regarded as as socially necessary in the same way as trips made to provide material support, such as house cleaning, babysitting or shopping. Particular attention therefore needs to be paid in research and planning terms to the nature of the transport needs associated with women's social visiting. Again, our research in West Yorkshire has shown that many of women's travel needs involve movement between two or more suburban areas rather than suburb to centre journeys. At a national level, these tend not to be well served by bus services. Visits to hospitals and to friends and relatives, although these are particularly important to women, are seldom a priority for transport operators.

viii) Women's lower social status and smaller physical size render them more vulnerable to attacks and abuse of all kinds, primarily from men. Available research, including our own, indicates that the fear of harassment, abuse or assault effectively prohibits many

women from moving around freely, especially, after dark
(41). Women feel especially vulnerable while waiting
for public transport and taxis. The frequency and
reliability of bus and train services, as well as
staffing considerations and the design and lighting of
waiting facilities, are therefore particularly
important to women.

7. Identifying women's transport interests: historical and political perspectives

From what has been said so far, we can conclude that all
groups in the population do not benefit equally from
particular kinds of transport policy and provision.
Women's interests can be identified primarily with public
transport provision, especially with buses, with the
pedestrian environment, and with movement within the local
area. Men's interests, on the other hand, can be
identified with car travel, with roads, and with provision
for longer distance travel, such as high speed trains and
motorways.

The polarity between men's and women's transport
interests becomes clearer when viewed from the historical
perspective. Given that disadvantage is almost always
relative, women's transport disadvantage relative to men is
closely linked with the rise of the private motor car, and
the concommitant decline in public transport. Post-war
transport gives an indication of how women have lost out in
transport terms.

At the end of the war, the new Labour government
immediately put into action their plans for a comprehensive
programme of nationalisation. The nationalisation of
transport brought into being the British Transport
Commission with power to implement a policy of the
integration of all forms of inland transport. In addition
to this major re-organisation, the badly over-worked and
run-down road and rail networks also needed a massive
injection of capital. However, the financial stringencies
of the post-war period led to the postponement of plans for
the overhaul of the transport undertaking.

When the Conservatives won the 1951 election with the
slogan "Setting the people free", the socialist priorities
of the previous administration were replaced by an ethic
whose emphasis was on individual consumerism: the predominant spirit of the times seems to have been 'live now,
pay later'. This helped to pave the way for the rise of
mass car ownership and the rapid growth of the trunk road
and motorway network. The cutting of purchase tax on cars
in 1953 accelerated the growth of car ownership, which had
received an earlier boost in 1950 with the end of petrol
rationing. The steepest rise in ownership of private cars
took place during the 1950s. During this decade ownership
figures more than doubled. Growth continued at a rapid

pace during the 1960s before levelling off to some extent in the 1970s (42). The private motor car became an apt symbol of the new affluence which stood in stark austerity to the war years.

The 1950s also saw the formation of the overtly lobbyist British Road Federation, made up primarily of the Society of Motor Manufacturers and Traders and the Road Haulage Association. The rise of the 'road lobby' was rapid both inside and outside of Parliament. It attracted support across a wide range of interest groups, from the multi-national car manufacturers such as Ford to the car unions and the aspiring car owners (43). In addition, in the wider economic context of declining traditional industries, such as coal, car manufacturing assumed a new importance.

The shift in emphasis from public to private and from road to rail transport entered a new phase during the 1960s, following the appointment of Ernest Marples as Minister of Transport in 1959. Marples, a civil engineer, had a firm belief in motorways as the vision of the future, and in car travel as the new key to the 'movement of the masses'. Far from seeing any obstacles to full car-ownership, he actively promoted it. Snags did, however, become apparent, notably road accidents and traffic congestion. Marples appointed Colin Buchanan to investigate traffic problems. The question was: How could traffic flows in the major cities be kept at a level which was congestion free in order to ensure the continued advantage of car travel? Buchanan's report, 'Traffic in towns', indicated nevertheless that there were definite limits on the potential of the private motor car as a form of mass transport. It concluded that any town with more than 300,000 people could not move all its people by car, no matter how many roads were built. Despite this, the report was used as justification for the building of more and more roads, and for reshaping the environment to accommodate the needs of car drivers.

In parallel with the expansion of the road network came the decimation of the rail network. The railway Modernisation Plan which had been initiated in 1955 came to an abrupt end with the appointment of Dr. Richard Beeching as Chairman of British Railways. Marples wanted Beeching to make the railways profitable, and was receptive to the proposed solution of massive cuts in the network. The Beeching Report, the Reshaping of British Railways, made provision for cutting one third of the rail network and closing 2,000 stations.

Public transport in general was caught in a spiral of decline. The low standards of war-time maintenance had been aggravated by materials and staffing shortages in the immediate post-war period. Lack of capital investment exacerbated these problems and, since the majority of the population remained dependent on public transport, overcrowding on both buses and trains was legendary. By

1955 staffing shortages had worsened into a crisis. In a period of 'full employment', public transport jobs were unappealing because of their anti-social hours. The solution of employing women as bus drivers and railway staff failed to materialise as no agreement could be reached between management and unions. The response of both British Rail and London Transport was, therefore, to import staff, mainly from the Caribbean and, to a lesser extent, from Ireland.

Nor was it possible to offer the higher wages which would have been necessary to maintain an adequate and stable workforce. The urban bus companies faced severe financial problems at this time, and these had much to do with increases in car ownership which resulted in traffic congestion leading to higher operating costs. Since bus operations were expected to be self-financing, fares increases were perceived as the only solution to revenue loss. However, this strategy quickly proved to be self defeating, and the vicious circle of higher fares, loss of patronage and decreased revenue was set in motion.

In 1968, the Transport Act instigated by Barbara Castle attempted to reverse the downward spiral. Its effects were limited by its inability to directly address the causes of the decline in public transport by curbing the power and the influence of the by then formidable Road Lobby. Nevertheless, the Act represented a recognition by the Labour government that people's travel needs should influence transport policy. There was also an attempt to reintroduce integration and to arrange regular government subsidies to public transport in an organised way. Large operating units were set up - notably, the Passenger Transport Executives in the provincial conurbations, and these were able to benefit from economies of scale as well as from the new capital and revenue grants and the scope for integrated planning. Further opportunities for integration were provided by the 1972 Local Government Act. The new Metropolitan Councils acted as co-ordinating authorities with responsibility for highway planning as well as public transport provision. While these opportunities were acted upon in different ways and to differing degrees by different Metropolitan Councils, there were clear improvements in public transport provision in many areas, ranging from the creation of the Tyne and Wear Metro to South Yorkshire's famous low fares, and therefore, this was a period of relative gain for women.

However, it was somewhat short lived; with the abolition of the Metropolitan Councils in 1985, the integrating structures of both the 1968 Transport Act and the 1972 Local Government Act were dismantled. Responsibilities for transport are now fragmented, with district and borough authorities, central government and a variety of appointed executives and joint authority committees having separate spheres of influence. The deregulation of bus services in October 1986 further undermined the capacity of the

Passenger Transport Executives for planning transport policy in a co-ordinated way. Preliminary results show that competitive tendering has so far not led to much innovation or improvement in service provision, while many services, particularly those in the evenings and at weekends and in areas of relatively low demand, have actually deteriorated (46). Added to this are the difficulties faced by P.T.E's in trying to provide co-ordinated time-table information and in persuading operators to keep fares steady, exacerbated by cuts in funding from central government. All of this adds up to a great deal of uncertainty about the future of bus services as well as a deepening of previous regional variations in the quantity, quality and price of public transport. Any deterioration in the bus services will hit women harder than men, and the effects could be far reaching.

In making the link between women's transport interests, the decline in public transport and the rise of the car, the central point is to understand how the private car was seen to meet the transport needs of a larger proportion of the population than it actually does. While the erroneous assumptions about a continuing level of 4% economic growth upon which the projections of 'saturation level' car ownership were based played a crucial role in these miscalculations, the problematic aspects of using 'the household' as a unit of analysis in the quantification of car ownership have received less attention. Even if women had no employment related travel needs, one household car can rarely provide for all the travel needs of all the members. While the male breadwinner, who has traditionally had first call on 'the car', has enjoyed the benefits of massive investment in road construction, women have borne the brunt of diminished investment in public transport.

So far we have based our analysis on a needs based approach: we have shown that women's transport needs are distinct from those of menand that they are poorly met by current transport policy and provision. This approach perhaps carries a suggestion that women as a social group are especially 'needy' - a suitable case for charity. The implication then would be that women's social needs outweigh their social contributions: that they were a deserving case but nevertheless a drain on resources. The refutation of this possible implication involves a consideration of the origins and causes of women's economic and social inequality (described above). The first point to be re-emphasised here is that women's labour is underpaid, undervalued and often not recognised. The conventional yardsticks of social worth and contribution, notably taxation, takes no account of women's unpaid labour. Secondly, women's relative deprivation has been reinforced by deliberately market-based policies. These effects are both cumulative and compound each other. For instance, reductions in off-peak services (which incidentally began long before deregulation) reduce women's access to part-time employment which in turn limits their purchasing power in the transport market.

These complications make it difficult as well as inappropriate to develop our gender analysis along traditional cost-benefit lines. However, it is possible to take a wider macro economic approach to the evaluation of 'costs' and 'benefits' than is normally taken when CBA is applied to specific transport projects and policies.

If this wider approach is taken it becomes possible to present examples of ways in whcih women bear the costs of particular transport policies or projects while receiving disproportionately few of the benefits. These indications run directly counter to any suggestion that women are subsidised by current patterns of transport investment and policy. Firstly, the costs, both to the individual and to the nation, of private car travel, which mainly benefits men, are generally underestimated. At July 1979 prices, the cost of road accidents in 1980, in terms of strains on the emergency and health services and loss of production, has been estimated at £1,730,000,000 (47). Even the most readily visible costs of car travel are enormous, and only a fraction of these are met by (predominantly male) motorists through road taxes and taxes on petrol. The remainder is met by the population as a whole via taxation, rates and personal costs incurred through damage to self or property. Thus, women are liable for half of the costs (perhaps more if we take into accoung, for instance, women's primary role in caring for accident victims), but receive only a fraction of the benefits. Public funding of public transport and the pedestrian environment, from which women receive proportionately more benefit, is paltry by comparison.

There is also another way in which transport investment discriminates against women. In the Department of Transport's evaluations of proposed road building schemes, construction costs are weighed against **time-savings** for motorists and others (time delays are also taken into account, but only in a narrow sense). In order to do this, a monetary value must be placed on people's time. Predictably, the time of train passengers and car drivers (mostly men) is taken to be worth around twice as much as that of bus passengers (mostly women) (48)!

Biases in the taxation system, peculiar to Britain, act as a further subsidy on car travel. Companies' expenditure on cars for their employees is eligible for tax relief. These 'company cars' account for somewhere between a half and two thirds of the new cars bought each year, and an estimated one fifth of commuting (49). Altogether, the total value of such tax subsidies to the car owners has been estimated at around two billion pounds per year, i.e. two million times greater than the the government subsidy to the passenger railway. Since the great majority of company car users are men, this subsidy represents another aspect of policy which discriminates against women. Furthermore, company cars make a significant contribution to traffic congestion, particularly in London (50), and heavy demands on parking space, both of which generates costs which are borne by women as pedestrians as well as in general.

In addition, over the last few decades there have been a number of trends in land use planning which have contributed to women's transport disadvantage. These can only be briefly summarised here. Firstly, car use has encouraged the development of sprawling, low density suburbs. These are difficult for public transport to serve and also, by widening the physical separation of homes and paid work places, place additional constraints on women's employment options. This also tends to be a feature of the New Towns which sprang up in the sixties.

Secondly, the seventies were the era of motorway building in cities, a notable example being Leeds, the 'Motorway City of Europe'(51) It seems to have gone largely unnoticed that this process of reshaping the cities to accommodate the car had adverse effects on the pedestrian environment, and hence on women (52). Major roads act as a barrier to movement between areas, whether these are pedestrianised or not, while the precincts which accompany such schemes themselves are often deserted at night, or frequented by gangs of youths, making them a virtual no-go area for women.

Thirdly, car use has encouraged the development of large, out of town shopping centres and hyper markets, to the detriment of existing town centres and local neighbourhood facilities. Not only does this affect public transport, but by having shops, and indeed all facilities, spread more widely, motorised travel has become necessary for more and more journey purposes. Consequently, the range of facilities available for pedestrians has shrunk significantly. Huge new retail developments in out of town locations are not only virtually inaccessible without a car, they are specifically aimed at car owners for marketing reasons. It follows that the majority of women must be dependent on someone else for access to them, despite the fact that they continue to be primarily responsible for shopping.

Fourthly, the eighties have seen continuing trends towards the centralisation and 'rationalisation' of a wide range of essential services such as schools and hospitals. How such reorganisations affect women's access to facilities, and their associated transport needs, has to the best of our knowledge, rarely been studied even after the event, let alone taken into account at the decision stage.

All four of the trends outlined above may be seen as conferring benefits on car users at the expense, in some way, of non car users. All may, therefore, be seen as having a polarising effect on existing transport facilities along age, class and ethnic as well as gender lines.

Currently, the indications that gender inequalities in transport may be reduced are not hopeful. While relatively more, mainly younger, women are obtaining driving licences, the vast majority of car drivers are still men (53). Meanwhile, sales of new cars, having levelled off to some extent during the seventies, are expected to reach a record level of 1.95 million this year. While public transport faces the uncertainties of the deregulation era, this looks like being another 'Year of the Car', a cause for celebration for some, but cold comfort for many women waiting at the bus stops.

Notes

1.   For instance, the GLC/ LRT Travel Diary
        Survey for Autumn 1984 indicated that women
        and men in the greater London area made an
        average of 18.6 and 19.9 trips per head per
        week respectively. What this means is that,
        on average, men make just over one more trip
        per week each than women. These figures are
        congruent with those of the 1978/79 National
        Travel Survey, where the women in the sample
        accounted for 48% of all journeys made.

2.   See Table 4.4b, National Travel Survey,
        1978/79.

3.   However, two points are worth noting here.
        Firstly, a comparison between the 1965 and
        1978/79 National Travel Surveys indicates
        that, in all except the oldest age groups,
        women have shown a greater increase in their
        average weekly mileage than men have,
        suggesting that the gender gap is narrowing
        (see National Travel Survey 1978/79, Table
        2.13, p. 13). Secondly, a footnote in this
        table discretely reminds the discerning
        reader that walks under one mile have been
        excluded from the analysis. Since other
        research has shown that women make a
        relatively high proportion of their journeys
        on foot and over relatively short distances
        this calls into question the validity of the
        comparison.

4.   Transport Statistics Great Britain 1975-1985,
        Table 1.3. p.13 (based on National Travel
        Survey 1978/79 data).

5.   Unfortunately, these statistics do not show
        up the gender-split as clearly as they might
        since shopping has been aggregated with
        'personal business' and 'escort trips' with
        'other trips'.

6.   Employment status is very relevant to this
        pattern of gender differentiation. The
        differences between men and women in full-
        time employment are very slight, whereas
        those between women in full-time employment
        and those with full-time caring and domestic
        responsibilities are marked. Over half the
        journeys of the latter category of women are
        for shopping or personal business purposes
        and 10% of their journeys come under the
        'escort and other' category, compared to 26%
        and 3% for women in full-time paid
        employment, for whom journeys to place of

employment constitute 39% of all their journeys (see National Travel Survey 1978/79, Table 3.4b, p.21)

7. As Lester and Potter (1983) point out:

    "Contrary to popular belief, the majority of travel is very local. Long journeys are the exception rather than the rule. Over 30% of all journeys are under one mile and, of these, 86% are on foot. More than one half of all journeys are under two miles in length. At journey distances above 3 miles, motor transport predominates, especially the car. Car use is at a peak between 25 and 30 miles, after which journeys by rail begin to increase significantly."
    (See Table 4, p.7, Vital Travel Statistics)

8. Gender differences in journey length persist even when the comparison is between men and women in paid employment, at least as far as the journey to work is concerned. For example, in London in 1981, 24% of women's journeys to work, compared to 18% of men's, took less than 15 minutes. (See Greater London Transportation Survey, 1981).

9. For instance, 46% of all shopping trips are made on foot; only 3% of escort and other trips are made by bus (see Table 1.2 'Journey purpose by main mode of transport, 1978-79, Transport Statistics Great Britain 1975-85. In this case, all walking journeys over 50 yards were included in the analysis).

10. These need to be seen in the context of the overall modal split. Nationally, in 1985, buses and coaches accounted for 42 billion passenger kilometres, or 8% of all passenger transport, while cars and taxis accounted for 426 billion passenger kilometres (82%) and rail transport for only 36 billion passengers kilometres or 7% of the total (see Table 1.1, p.12 Transport Statistics Great Britain).

11. In the National Travel Survey 1978/79 sample, women made 63.3% of all journeys by bus, 73.5% of all journeys as a car passenger and 59.1% of all walking journeys, but only 23.7% of all journeys made by car drivers. Correspondingly, of all journeys made by women, the largest proportion, 41%, were made on foot, while 22% were made as car passengers and 16% each were made as car drivers and bus users. (See Lester and Potter, 1983, Vital Travel Statistics, Table

21). Information from the 1984 General Household Survey also underlines the relatively greater importance of bus travel for women. 15% of women over the age of 16, compared to 10% of men, used buses 5 or more days a week, while 19% used them 2 to 4 days a week, compared to 10% of men. 72% of the 3,115 women surveyed had used buses in the last six months, as opposed to only 51% of the 1,557 men. (See Transport Statistics Great Britain 1975-85, Table 2.35, p.102).

12. For men, on the other hand, journeys as car drivers account for almost half of all their journeys (49%), while walking accounts for just over a quarter (27%) and bus use and trips as a car passenger for only 9% and 7% each respectively. (See Lester and Potter, 1983, Table 21, based on National Travel Survey 1978/79 data).

13. Motorcycles, bicycles and trains are, however, relatively little used forms of transport in this country, accounting for 1%, 3% and 2% of all journeys and 1%, 1% and 7% of total passenger kilometres respectively (Transport Statistics Great Britain, 1975-85, Tables 1.1 and 1.2, p. 102).

14. For instance, the results of the GLC/ LRT Travel Diary Panel Survey (Autumn 1984) indicate that walking (24% vs 15%), buses (25% vs 19%) and journeys as car passenger (16% vs 7%) are all more frequently used methods of transport for women than for men. Men, on the other hand, make twice as many journeys as car drivers than women do (39% vs 20%) and also make more use of British Rail and the Underground. Walking and buses again emerge as the dominant modes of transport for women: taken together they account for almost half of all the journeys made by women in the London area. However, there are also some important divergences from the national picture, as represented by the National Travel Survey of 1978/79. Firstly, there is a relatively lower rate of travel by car in this sample. This applies to both sexes and can be understood in terms of the higher population density and relatively high level of public transport provision in the Greater London area, not to mention the negative aspects of prevailing traffic conditions. Secondly, therefore, bus use is a more commonly used form of transport for women than driving is in the London case. Thirdly, walking, though almost as heavily relied upon

as the buses, is actually less commonly resorted to by women in London (24% of all journeys) compared to the national sample average (41%). Fourthly, in the national sample, women made substantially more trips as a car passenger than as a car driver (22% vs 16%); in the London sample, the figures are reversed (16% as car passengers and 19% as car drivers). These variations need to be taken into account when referring to the heavily quoted results of the GLC Women and Transport Survey.

15.   For comparison, some statistics for West Yorkshire can be offered. Two main factors concerning the overall modal split need to be made. Firstly, car ownership in the county, at 53%, is well below the national average. Only Scotland and the North of England have a higher proportion of households without the use of a car. Secondly, in West Yorkshire as a whole, the bus network is far more extensive and complex than the local rail network. Journeys by rail accounted for only 0.3% of all trips made, while buses and coaches accounted for 13.5%. Again, however, women, relative to men, made more journeys by bus (62% vs 38%), on foot (50% vs 41%) and as passengers in household vehicles (71% vs 29%), whereas men made more journeys as drivers of private vehicles (73% vs 27%), on trains (61% vs 39%), by motorcycle (85% vs 15%) and by pedal cycle (83% vs 17%). (See West Yorkshire Passenger Rail Survey).

16.   For example, in Leeds women comprise 60.5% of peak time bus passengers and 64.4% of off-peak passengers. (See Leeds Bus Passenger Survey, 1985).

17.   For example, National Travel Survey data indicates that members of households in which there is one car make 54% of their journeys by car, while, for members of households in which there are two or more cars, the proportion is 68%. (See Tables 7 and 8, pp. 9-10, in 'Vital Travel Statistics', Lester and Potter, 1983).

18.   Source as above.

19.   In 1983, 92% of households headed by employers and managers and 94% of those headed by an unskilled manual worker (General Household Survey 1982-84 combined). Correspondingly, in 1980, 88% of employers and managers and 91% of professionals,

compared to only 22% of unskilled manual workers held full car licences. (Transport Statistics Great Britain, Table 2.12b, p.77). See also Lester and Potter (1983), Tables 19 and 20, p.17.

20. See Transport Statistics Great Britain, 1974-75, Table 2.12a, p.77.

21. However, again there are regional variations. Preliminary results form the recent Panel Survey carried out by West Yorkshire Passenger Transport Executive immediately prior to deregulation (i.e. in September 1986) indicate that only 28% of the women in the sample of 2,194 held a full driving licence.

22. Additionally, Read's analysis threw up another interesting statistic:

"8% of females who are recorded as holding a full driving licence are not recorded as being vehicle drivers at all, as opposed to only 2.3% men." (1983:78)

23. Among members of non-car owning households, however, the gender difference is almost absent; 84% and 86% of women had used buses in the last six months. See Transport Statistics Great Britain 1975-85, Table 2.36, p.103.

24. However, this figure is well below that of around £35 or more per week which is quoted in, for instance, consumer magazines, and which includes an element for the depreciation of the vehicle. The Automobile Association currently gives a figure of 33.9 pence per mile as the running cost of a car with an engine size in the 1000 to 1500cc range. Multiplied by 10,000 miles per year (which is still below the average of 12,000 miles which is the rule of thumb in the motor trade) this gives a figure of £65.19 per week! On this basis, even a car under 1000 cc, with an estimated running cost of 28.26p per mile, would cost £53.80 per week, while one in the 1500-2000 cc bracket, at 40p per mile, would cost £76.92 per week.

25. In 1984, women's gross hourly earnings, excluding overtime, were 73.5% of men's. Additionally, because women's hours in paid employment are, on average, less than those of men, the disparity in weekly take home pay is even greater than this comparison

suggests. For instance, 30.7% of women compared to 11.4% of men in full-time employment worked less than a 36 hour week in 1984, while only 9% of women, compared to 37.6% of men worked more than 40 hours per week in their paid employment.

26. The wage differential cannot be explained in terms of differing levels of education or skill. Discrimination against women per se offers a more parsimonious explanation (Rubenstein, 1984).

27 In September 1984, out of 9,130 women employees, 7,269 were in services, notably 'distribution, hotels, catering and repairs' (2,330), and 3,688 of these were part-timers. This compares with 6,109 male employees in the service sector out of a total labour force of 11,650. The remainder (1,850 women and 5,541 men) were employed in agriculture, manufacturing and other production and construction industries. See Employment Gazette, 1985.

28. West Yorkshire Low Pay Unit (1987) 'Unfair Pay' . Figures based on the 1986 New Earnings Survey. A previous study by the WYLPU ('On the breadline', 1986) showed that in West Yorkshire in 1985 the average weekly earnings of full-time women manual workers were £97.40 compared to £157.20 for their male counterparts. 84% of these women fall below the Low Pay Unit 'threshold' of £115 for a basic 38 hour working week. The average weekly earnings of female and male non-manual workers were £124.80 and £280.30 respectively. Again, 57% of the women fall into the low paid category. (West Yorkshire Low Pay Unit, 1986).

29. However, it is interesting to note that this trend shows signs of beginning to reverse. An Equal Opportunities Commission New Release (20.11.85) reported that women are nearly 52% of the population and 42% of the workforce; that the U.K. has one of the lowest rates of return from maternity leave in Europe; that the labour force participation rate for mothers of children under five is the second lowest in Europe, and that the latest figures showed a decrease in this rate from 34% to 29% in 1983.

30. Of the approximately 9 million female employees in Great Britain, 5 million worked full-time and 4 million worked part-time,

while among men there were 11 million full-time, but only 0.7 million part-time employees (Social Trends, 1985) (4).

31.   In 1985, more than 350,000 workers in West Yorkshire - i.e. almost half the workforce-were low paid in the sense of earning less than the 'decency threshold' of £116 per week set by the Council of Europe. Significantly, two thirds of these low paid workers were women, and 40% were part-timers. In 1985, 'average and gross hourly earnings of part-time women in Yorkshire and Humberside was £2.48...equivalent to a national weekly wage of £94 for 38 hours'. Three quarters of part-time women workers in the region earned less than the equivalent of £100 per week, while 'nearly 40% of the recorded part-time women workers earned less than £2 an hour'. (Out of a total of 150,000 female part-timers, 127,000 or 84% were low paid (WYLPU, 1986).

32.   According to the Department of Employment estimates, there were 400,000 home workers in Britain in 1983, the great majority of whom were women. However, recent research indicates that these figures are an underestimate (See Allen and Wolkowitz, 1987).

33.   See, for example, Barrett and MCIntosh (1982); Himmelweit and Ruehl (1983).

34.   The still prevalent idea that women work for 'pin money' is, in fact, a myth. In 1984, official government statistics estimated that one in ten households were female headed, but 15% is probably now a more accurate figure. Additionally, it has been estimated that, without the earnings of married women, four times as many families would be living below the poverty line. See Martin and Roberts (1984).

35.   See, for example, Rappaport et al, 1982; Gittens, 1985.

36.   The implementation of 'community care' policies, for example, draws heavily on the labour of unpaid women carers (see Finch, 1984).

37.   One notable example of this from our field work in West Yorkshire was a women in an outling Pennine hamlet, herself in her

sixties, who made extensive use of the bus and walking to reach a number of infirm, elderly friends and 'neighbours' who relied on her to fetch their pensions and basic shopping, to help with housework, and, of course, for company.

38. See, for instance, Maccoby and Jacklin (1974); Hoyenga and Hoyenga (1979); Block (1984).

39. 'Driving out aggression', Observer 11th, January 1987.

40. For instance, the GLC study found that 30% of the employed women in their sample could reach their place of employment in less than 15 minutes; only 11% of their journeys took longer than one hour. For a detailed discussion of the relative importance of gender role constraints and travel costs in limiting women's employment options, see Pickup (1984).

41. See, for instance, Block 3 of the 1985 GLC Women and Transport Survey, and Lynch and Atkins (1987).

42. See Wistrich (1983, Table 1.2.

43. See Hamer (1987).

44. For instance, between 1955 and 1965, the number of cars entering London in the morning rush hour rose by 28,000 while the numbe of buses fell by 1,900 (see Hamilton and Potter, 1985).

45. For instance, one 12% fares increase in the 1950s on London Transport resulted in the immediate loss of 60% of bus passengers and a permanent loss of 16% (see Hamilton and Potter, 1985).

46. For some examples of studies of the initial effects of deregulation see Preston (1988), Headicar et al (1987), SEEDS (1987), Guiver and Hoyle (1987), Belcomber et al. (1987).

47. See Dawson (1987:8-9).

48. Dawson (1987:10).

49. See TEST (1984) 'The company car factor'.

50. See TEST (1985) 'The accessible city' and (1986) 'Changing to green'.

51.   See Starkie (1982).

52.   See National Consumer Council (1987) 'What's
       wrong with walking?'

53.   For example in 1980, in the 20-29 age group,
       69% of men and 42% of women held full driving
       licences.   In   the   50-59   age   group,   the
       differentiation is much sharper: 64% of men
       compared   to   18%   of   women   (Transport
       Statistics Great Britain 1975-85, Table 2.12,
       p.77).

54.   'Boom   year   for   car   sales',   Observer,
       25.10.87. p.89.

3 Household organisation and travel behaviour

PETER JONES

1. Introduction

Traditionally, studies of travel behaviour and need have used the notion of a 'trip' (a movement form one place to another by a given mode of travel for a specified purpose) as the basic unit for measurement and analysis. Trip rates, either at the individual, household, or some aggregate level, are related to the socio-demographic characteristics of the traveller, and to various attributes of the transport and land-use system, in order to explain and predict travel patterns.

Although a whole transport planning methodology has been built on this approach, and applied for three decades in many parts of the world, academics and practitioners are increasingly realising the limitations of this conceptualisation of travel behaviour. In terms of understanding travel in the context of household organisation, or the underlying reasons for travel, the approach has a number of limitations:

a) It focuses on individual journeys rather than dealing directly with the complex patterns of **linked trips** that can be observed among some groups of the population (such as working wives).

b) Analysis is usually carried out either at the individual or household level, but there have been few attempts to link the two and look at the **interactions among household members.**

c) Studies recognise important differences between peak and off-peak travel, but do not look in detail at the **timing** of travel and, hence, do not look at the various deadlines or **institutional constraints** which can dominate many people's daily lives.

d) There is no real answer to the question: 'Why do people travel?' Indeed, the approach implicitly assumes that more travel is a good thing, whereas we know this is not always the case (e.g. where people have to travel further because the local post office closes, or make **escort** trips because it is not safe to let children travel alone).

Over the last decade, a number of researchers and practitioners have been involved in the development of an alternative framework within which to study travel behaviour, termed 'the activity approach'.

From this perspective, travel is studied in the context of **daily household activity patterns**, and is viewed as the means by which individuals or groups move about the urban space in order to participate in activities at different locations, and so satisfy basic needs, role commitments or personal preferences. Here, household organisation lies at the heart of an understanding of travel behaviour.

In this short chapter, we first outline the conceptual basis of an activity approach to travel analysis and then look at how household organisation and travel behaviour inter-relate in different **life cycle stages**, first at a broad level, and then looking more closely at the organisational structures. Using such a framework, it is also possible to examine the processes of household adaptation, and some simple examples are given. Finally, conclusions are drawn about the implictions of this work.

2. The conceptual approach

Daily behaviour may be characterised as a series of **activities** that people undertake in order to satisfy basic physiological needs (such as sleeping or eating), role commitments (e.g. work, educational and domestic activities), or personal preferences (e.g. many leisure activities). Together, the activities which a person participates in make up her/his **activity programme** and daily activity **time budget** (i.e. the allocation of time to individual activities within the programme).

Most activities make use of **facilities** that are only available at a few locations in space and which may only be open during certain hours of the day (or certain days of the week). By convention or necessity, participation in certain activities may be subject to space-time constraints on their timing, duration and/ or location (e.g. sleep, work, meals); or they may be restricted through being complementary to other activities (e.g. personal care and sleep; meal preparation / eating / clearing away) and so have to be undertaken in sequence.

A number of activities which a person undertakes on a regular basis are thus fixed in time or space, for institutional (work/ school) or other reasons. These provide anchor points (or 'pegs') around which more optional or flexible activities must be fitted in; on a short term basis, therefore, behaviour involves **choice in the context of constraints.** The degree of choice is limited by the availability of facilities and, more particularly, by financial constraints and the sites which a person can reach in the available time. The latter is defined by a **space-time prism** (Hagerstrand, 1970) which delimits the area within which the individual's opportunity set lies.

From an activity perspective, the observed daily travel pattern is a sub-set of an activity pattern (i.e. the sequence of activities undertaken during the day) which results from a process of **activity scheduling,** subject to their timing and sequencing requirements, the availability of facilities in space and time and to any constraints imposed by others. In scheduling their day, the person has to recognise that it is not usually possible to undertake two major activities at once, nor to be in two places at once, and also has to allow sufficient time to travel between sites (taking account of public transport schedules and reliability, or the need for a margin for delays if travelling by private transport).

Most people also live in multi-person households and interact socially with family and friends and so have to take account of additional constraints imposed through **inter-personal linkages.** These affect which activities are undertaken as well as when and where they are to be carried out.

The formation of multi-person households leads to the creation of different organisational structures, as individuals modify their personal activity patterns to take account of three factors:

1) **Greater role specialisation:** when two or more adults share a dwelling unit, this enables duplication of effort to be avoided and some activity consolidation among the group (e.g. with regard to meal preparation or dwelling maintenance) which, **ceteris paribus,** reduces the amount and range of servicing activities which each person has to undertake. Conversely, when dependent children form part of the household the extent of, and commitment to, servicing activities may increase substantially, leading to a considerable

decrease in uncommitted time and increase in space-time constraints on adult members - although, here again, tasks can be shared where there is more than one adult present.

2) **Competition for resources:** Although larger households will tend to have more resources in total than single person households (e.g. more living space, higher incomes), many resources are still relatively scarce and have to be allocated (e.g. money) or scheduled (e.g. space, at different times) between members who often have competing claims. The necessity of **bargaining for resources** is an important element in family life and may be a source of uncertainty and tension. 'Classic' examples include decisions about who has priority in the use of the household's car under different circumstances, and the tendency for larger families to evolve a time-table to cover the use of the bathroom in the morning.

3) **Joint activity participation:** The sharing of servicing tasks within a household tends to reduce the amount of time that each individual has to set aside for such activities, but the associated **increase in inter-dependence** between members results in a higher level of **spatio-temporal constraint** that offsets the scheduling benefits of this reduction. Where activities are carried out jointly, participants have to agree on the precise nature of the activity and the time and place in which it will be carried out, taking account of the other individual commitments and levels of mobility.

Given these basic concepts, it is possible to represent a household's daily organisation and activity travel pattern in the form shown in Figure 3.1. Here time of day is represented along the horizontal axis (from 06.00 to 24.00) and a crude measure of space (i.e. home and non-home) on the vertical, with separate time-space traces for each member of a three-person household. The day's events are read from left to right, taking one individual at a time. Each person begins the day at home and continues there until a solid line (representing travel) shifts the person to the next activity at another point along the vertical axis. Linkages between the activities of household members are shown as vertical lines joining specific events (dotted lines indicate supervision rather than joint activities per se).

The example depicts a three person household: a husband (H) and wife (W) in their late twenties / early thirties, and a six year old son (S). The husband has a fairly typical working day: from 8.45 to 17.15 with an hour for lunch and a three quarter hour commute to and from work, giving him an effective working day from 8.00 to 18.00. Their son has to be at school between 09.00-12.30 and 14.00-15.30; he comes home for lunch and has a quarter hour

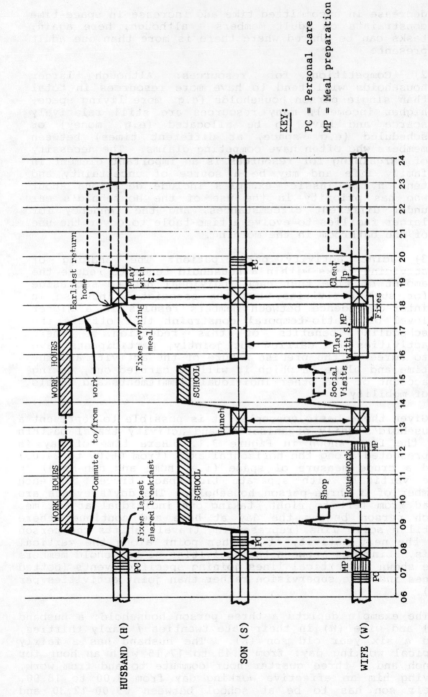

Figure 3.1. The organisation of household behaviour

KEY:

PC = Personal care

MP = Meal preparation

walk to and from the school. Superficially, the **wife's day may appear to be the least constrained** in the family because of the lack of institutional constraints on her activities, but once account is taken of her roles inside the household, as housewife and mother, and her resulting commitments to its other members, then, in many ways she turns out to be the **most restricted person in the household.**

Much of her daily behaviour is linked to or indirectly constrained by the other two household members. Key factors in this process involve:

a) Meal times: breakfast and evening meals are dictated by H; lunch is constrained by S's free period.

b) Bathroom arrangements: the morning routine hinges around H; W goes in before H and S follows, after having breakfast with his parents.

c) Meal preparation: this is mainly done immediately prior to the meal, so W prepares breakfast while H is in the bathroom and S is asleep; she prepares lunch before meetin S (it's easier) and also spends an hour before dinner in meal preparation.

d) Travel: her basic travel pattern is based on escorting S to and from school; H leaves too early and gets back too late to share this task. It is most efficient for W to fit in other non-home activities around this routine; shopping is done in the morning, after dropping off S - it's easier without him around- with a second 'chance' on the way home from school in the afternoon. Social visits are made between 14.00 and 15.30 en route to the school when friends with children at school are also free to chat and relax.

e) Child care: W has primary responsibility for looking after S from 8.00 to 18.00, while H is away (except when S is in school); at other times, it is a joint responsibility.

f) Housework: W gets most of it out of the way in the morning (two and one half hours net) leaving one and a half hours in the afternoon for a break before collecting S from school and having to devote time to him.

g) Leisure: W has a restricted opportunity for leisure participation during a 'window' of free time in the early afternoon. There are also opportunities for leisure activity in the evening after S has gone to bed, although these can only be pursued away from home if she goes alone, or the couple are able to arrange a babysitter.

Inter-personal linkages can have complex and varied impacts on daily activity patterns and, hence, travel in ways that have not been given detailed consideration in the travel or activity literature. The typical family comprising parents and one or two children are most affected by this kind of scheduling factor, because of the wide range of roles which its members have to perform and because of the high level of dependency of the young on adults.

3. Empirical analysis of household structures and travel behaviour

The examples used in this chapter are either taken from an activity diary survey undertaken in Banbury, Oxfordshire (Jones et al., 1983) or a similar survey carried out in Adelaide, South Australia (see Bernard, 1981). In both cases data is analysed for household groups defined in terms of life cycle stage. The definitions used are reproduced in Table 3.1 and are based primarily on the composition and age structure of the members (especially the youngest child).

a) Aggregate measures of behaviour

Looking first at broad time allocations to activities (Figure 3.2), we see clearly the differential impact which change in life cycle stage has on **wives compared with husbands.** Men show remarkably stable time budgets until retirement (Group H), whereas women, on average, are much more strongly affected by the transitions associated with parenthood.

Time spent by women in the Banbury sample on paid work drops sharply to be replaced by an equivalent increase in household chores and child care activities; the distribution of time shows a partial reversion to the Group A pattern once all children are at school (Groups D-F)- though it is important to recognise that we are dealing with cohort effects (e.g some of the older women in the later life cycle groups belong to generations where they never entered the paid labour force).

If the time budgets are divided into in-home and out-of-home time, wives are found to spend more time in the home than do husbands, with large significant differences in Groups B, C and D when young children are present. Stage C wives spend only 15% of their time away from the home, compared with 38% in Stage A; the corresponding figures for men are 41% and 44% respectively.

Differences in time allocation among husbands and wives in the eight groups are largely mirrored by the corresponding trip rates (Figure 3.3).

Table 3.1. Descriptions and definitions of life cycle groups

Descriptions of group	Definitive features
A Younger (married) adults without children	Youngest person under 35 and no children
B Families with pre-school children	All children under 5
C Families with pre-school children _and_ young school children	Youngest child under 5 and another child 5 or over
D Families with young school children	Youngest child 5 or over but under 12
E Families with older school children	Youngest child 12 or over but under 16
F Families of adults, all of working age	Youngest 'child' 16 or over
G Older adults, no children in household	Youngest person 35 or over _unless_ in Group H
H Retired persons	All persons 65 or over, or at least one 65 or over and none with full-time job

Figure 3.2. Differences in time allocation by life cycle stage

TIME BUDGETS FOR:

(i) Husbands

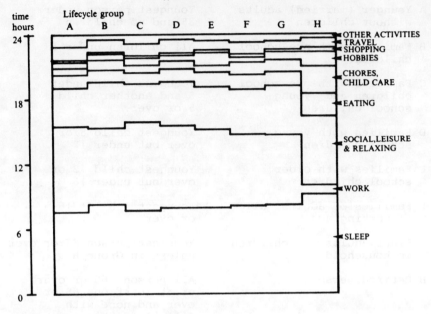

(ii) Wives

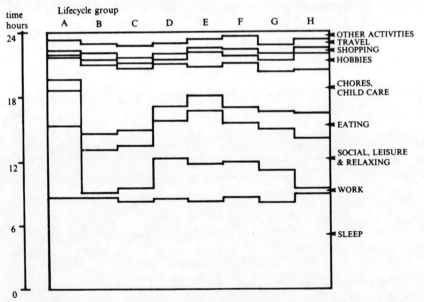

Figure 3.3.   Mean trip rates by life cycle group

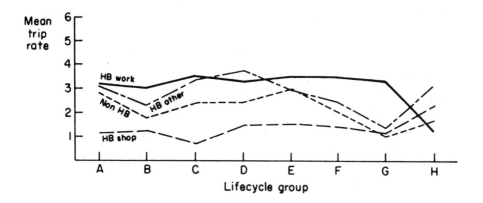

Mean trip rates per person, by trip purpose, for husbands

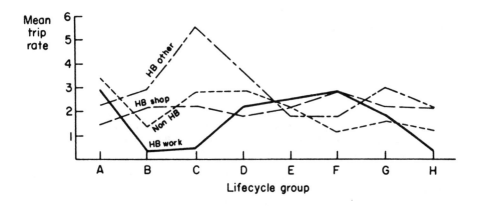

Mean trip rates: wives

Note the relative stability of male trip rates until retirement with only a slight dip in travel with the arrival of a baby in the household, and a gradual decline in discretionary travel with increasing age. Women, on the other hand, show much greater variation on average.

Shopping trips remain relatively stable, but work journeys decline sharply until all children are at school when (from the recovery in trip rates compared with time budgets), it is evident that many women are in part-time work; home based 'other' trips are predominantly 'serve passenger' trips which reflect the amount of effort put into taking children to/ from school, playgroup, etc. Note that for husbands the equivalent peak is in Group D, when children are increasingly chauffeured for evening and weekend activities, being too young to travel safely on their own.

The broad impacts of differences in the behaviour of adult household members by life cycle stage can be seen in other ways too. Jones and Clarke (1988), using the Adelaide time budget data, develop various measures of day to day variability in behaviour by comparing daily activity patterns. They find that women in life cycle groups B and C show much more **day to day variation** in their behaviour than do men in the same households; this is entirely **role-related**, however, since in retired households or single person households no such gender differences are found.

b)   Detailed analysis of household organisation

In order to consider the factors which lie behind the differences in aggregate measures of behaviour, it is necessary to examine more closely household organisation among members in terms of patterns of behaviour. For illustrative purposes, two of the life cycle groups have been selected to provide a contrast: Group A (young single persons and married couples without children) and Group C (households with pre-school and school aged children). Figure 3.4 shows how the time allocations in Figure 3.3 translate into differences in activity patterns between stage A and C for individual household members. The diagrams show 'prototypical' activity patterns, based on what people described as their usual week-day routines during unstructured in depth interviews.

Figure 3.4a shows the prototypical activity patterns for households in stage A, where both adults are usually employed. At this stage, most activities tend to be **synchronised** and carried out jointly. A study of car owning households (Dix et al., 1983) found that where there were two car owning individuals who formed a joint household, it was quite common for one of the cars to be given up in the process of household formation (or some time afterwards, as a lagged response), both in order to save money at a time when first house purchase may be

Figure 3.4.   Prototypical activity patterns for two life cycle groups

(a) Life Cycle Stage A:

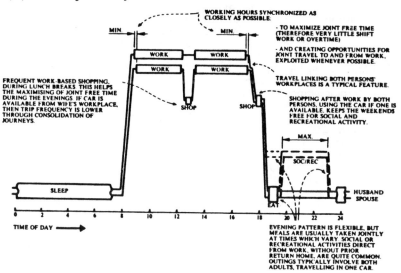

(b) Life Cycle Stage C:

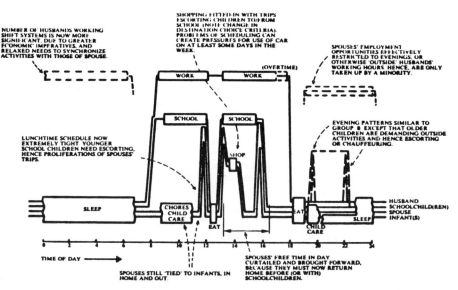

underway and because of the redundancy involved when many activities are carried out jointly. Work hours tend to be synchronised wherever possible and partners often shared a car to travel to/ from work. Shopping either tended to be carried out near the workplace (more commonly by the female in her lunch hour) or jointly by both adults en route from work to home. Such couples go out frequently together socially in the evening, either straight from work or after having a meal at home; using National Travel Survey data, Knapp (1983) found that the Group A members in his population sample spent most time out of home in the evening, with an average of about 30% of them being out between 9 p.m. and 10.30pm.

By stage C, however, the activity-travel pattern of the husband and wife in our Banbury sample have become highly differentiated (see Figure 3.4), with very little joint activity participation outside of the home. The structure of the husband's day has changed little, although he now spends less time outside of the home in the evening and joins in some activities with his children. Evening outings from home are often without the wife and involve chauffeuring or escorting older children to clubs or school activities, or going out alone to play squash, visit the pub, etc. while the wife looks after the children.

Conversely, the wife is now very home centred, in her roles as mother and wife, spending little time away from the residence, although generating a large number trips. These are associated mainly with escorting the elder child(ren) to/ from school(s) - up to four return trips each day - and fitting in shopping and social/leisure activities within this very constrained schedule. Shopping is now undertaken close to home and school, rather than near the work place, and performs an important social as well as domestic function. The elder child(ren)'s day is based around educational activities (e.g. school and associated after school activities), with most evenings spent at home or (in the summer) playing in the immediate neighbourhood. The younger, pre-school child(ren) tends to be home centred, like her/his mother, and mirrors her activities except in rare cases (in our sample) where a wife has a part-time job. Given the complexity of the wife's travel patterns, pressure for her to have access to a car increases through stages B and C, which may result in:

i) The husband switching to public transport for his work journey or car sharing so that the household car is available for the wife to use on at least some days of the week.

ii) The purchase of a second car (though this is often delayed until the wife returns to the labour force to obtain the income and gain the independent status to have one).

iii) A non-licence holding wife learning to drive.

In our surburban Adelaide sample, the car was the dominant mode of travel among Group C wives. Walking was seen only as a leisure activity, something to be done with the children when there was plenty of time; given the activities which our sample of women did pack into the day, it is clear that if each trip were to take four or five times longer (as it would on foot, instead of by car), then it would have been impracticable to maintain the same living pattern in most cases. As one mother explained:

"The reason I use a car is because it's so quick - I seem to be in a hurry all the time."

Public transport use was rarely mentioned by wives, except for an occasional visit to the city or to the beach by bus or tram during the school holidays, as a treat for the children - "they think it's great fun".

The dependence on the car was illustrated in one Adelaide interview, where the wife had cut her hand and was unable to drive the car during the survey day. No thought was given to using public transport, which was not seen as practicable for the type of intra-suburban journeys she makes, and instead she relied on lifts from friends and relatives. Her daughter got a lift to/ from school in a neighbour's car, the respondent's mother took her to/ from play group and shopping, and another friend took her to/ from a pre-arranged hairdresser's appointment. In the evening, she went out with her husband who drove the car. The only suppressed trip was between lunch at home and the hairdresser when the mother might otherwise have driven her younger daughter to a nearby park to play.

The aggregate effects of these various factors on the activity patterns of Banbury households in stage C are shown in a quantified way in Figure 3.5. Five person types are distinguished (i.e. head, spouse and three age groups for the children): for each is shown the percentage taking part in one of six non-travel activities at different time periods during the day (horizontal axis), with band widths summing to 100 per cent. Note in particular the following features:

* most household heads have a basic home-work-home pattern from morning to evening, but in a significant number of cases this is reversed, because of night shift work (mainly at Alcan and General Foods).

* few wives work, and where they do, it is either during the day (when children are at school) or in the evening once husbands have returned home and are able to mind the children.

Figure 3.5.   Aggregate activity patterns for sampled households in life cycle stage c

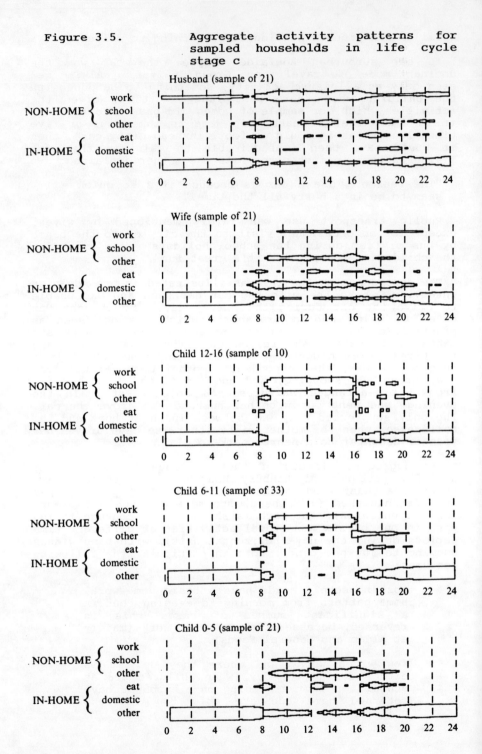

*   for school-aged children, there is a very
    clear pattern of home-school-home, with the
    addition of some later afternoon and early
    evening activities, extending later into the
    evening for older children.

*   husbands are much more likely to go out in
    the evening than wives, and are mainly
    responsible for fetching and collecting
    children from evening activities.

*   the activity patterns of pre-school children
    mirror very closely those of their mothers;
    in cases where the latter are in paid work
    during the day, the former are at play school
    or with a child minder.

It is thus evident that activity needs (particularly
those associated with role fulfilment), coupled with
related space-time and inter-personal constraints, have a
strong influence on the content and overall structure of
people's activity patterns, to the extent that distinctive
patterns - in these examples, associated with life cycle
stage - can be observed at an aggregate level.

Some of the implications of these household
organisational structures for patterns of travel (rather
than individual trips) are shown in Table 3.2, which looks
at the composition of **trip circuits** or **chains**.   It
tabulates the percentage of trip circuits from home during
which the traveller takes part in the activities or
combinations of activities that are listed.   There are a
number of features of interest here, which relate to the
earlier discussion about roles and constraints; in
particular:

a)   **Specific activities.** For husbands, work
     retains its relative importance in the daily
     travel pattern from Stages A to C, but note
     the relative decline in shopping and 'other'
     activities, and the sharp increase in serve
     passenger events, related particularly to
     chauffeuring children to/ from evening
     activities and, in some cases, dropping them
     off at school on the way to work. For wives,
     the level of trip making is higher in stage C
     than stage A.   In percentage terms, the
     largest changes are associated with the
     switch in roles, with work and serve
     passenger activities exchanging positions as
     the most and least frequent activity in a
     circuit.

b)   **Activity combinations.** The percentage of
     simple, one-stop circuits stays approximately
     the same for husbands in stages A and C, at
     around 70%. For this group, the pattern of

participation in combinations of non-home activities is largely unchanged, with the exception of 'work and shop'. In Group A, shopping is often done jointly, by husband and wife, during a shared journey home from wor; in Group C, however, shopping is either done by the wife alone, or if the husband is involved, it is carried out on a separate circuit from home.

In the case of the wife, most activity combinations change significantly in relative importance; in general, those involving a work activity decline sharply between A and C (except 'work and serve passenger', which relates to the use of play school activities) and those involving serve passenger increase markedly in relative importance, for the reasons already discussed. Note, in particular, the importance of 'shop and serve passenger' in stage C, where shopping is fitted in during escorting trips to/ from school. Table 3.2 also confirms the more home-oriented nature of wives' travel, with an increase in simple circuits from 58% to 67%.

4.   Adaptations to changing conditions

The importance of household organisational structure, and the nature of linkages and role commitment becomes particularly evident when households seek to adapt their behaviour in response to some change, and so break free from their habitual routines which dominate much of daily life. The stimulus for change may arise from three main sources:

a) **Changes in role.** Thi is most commonly associated with moves between stages in the family life cycle, or perhaps the death of a spouse. In present circumstances, redundancy and unemployment can also have a large impact on a household's behaviour, because of role re-assignments and:

b) **Changes in resources.** Household activity patterns are adapted to the resources available (e.g. income level, number of cars owned, size of house) and so an increase or decrease in the resource level - usually brought about (directly or indirectly) by financial circumstances - will lead to a revised pattern of behaviour.

c) **Changes in the external environment.** The stimulus for action may lie outside the home.

Table 3.2. Weekly trip circuits by life cycle group

Life cycle group	Household head		Spouses	
	A	C	A	C
Percentage of circuits which include:				
a) Specific activities:				
work	56	55	53	12
shopping	26	17	46	40
serve passenger	15	31	7	52
other	39	27	50	40
b) Activity combinations:*				
work and shop	14	4	31	6
work and serve passenger	12	12	2	7
work and other	9	9	18	5
shop and serve passenger	5	5	0	18
shop and other	5	4	13	12
serve passenger and other	5	6	4	13

% of simple circuits (1 stop)

* No sequence implied

Often it is associated with an improvement (e.g. new shopping centre) or a deterioration (e.g. reduction in bus service) in the quality or number of activity and travel facilities available. Sometimes it may be a more general factor such as a growing fear of going out at night on foot.

Figure 3.6 is taken from a detailed survey of household organisation and travel behaviour in the Reading area (Jones and Dix, 1978) and shows how one family coped with fairly extreme shifts worked by the husband at Heathrow airport. The household is in the life cycle group D (see Table 3.1) and comprises a husband, wife and daughter attending primary school. The husband works an alternating shift system, with two weeks on early shift (06.00-14.00), followed by two weeks on late shift (1400-22.00). There is one car in the household which the husband uses for work.

When the husband is on early shift (Figure 3.6a), he leaves home before the rest of the family get up, and returns by early afternoon. The wife has breakfast with her daughter and escorts her to school (on foot) and then catches a bus to work. The daughter has lunch at school and in the afternoon returns home to be looked after by her father; this means that the wife does not have to rush home to meet her daughter, so is able to spend time after work in shopping or social activities, on her way home by bus. The family have dinner together, and the husband remains home in the evening; this gives the wife a chance to make social visits using the household car. The change from early to late shift not only affects the husband's activity pattern in a major way, but also those of the daughter and the wife. When the husband is on a late shift, (Figure 3.6b), the family have breakfast together, and the husband drives his daughter and wife to school and work respectively. He then takes part in shopping, service or social activities before returning home to cook lunch for himself and his daughter; he then leaves for work. The daughter now comes home from school during the day, and on her return home from school in the afternoon is met by her mother. For the wife, this means having to rush home by bus from work after a hurried shop, to be there in time for her daughter's return; after which she has to remain at home for the rest of the day in order to look after the child (and partly because of lack of transport which would enable them both to go visiting together).

The timing of the husband's work activity thus has a major impact on the whole family, in part because of the role switching at different times of day (relating to who is available to look after the daughter), but mainly because of his wish to spend as much time as possible with his daughter, and the parent's wish to make full use of the car. In travel terms, the minimum household trip rates (i.e. excluding optional leisure journeys) are 7 trips with the husband on early shift compared with 11 trips when he

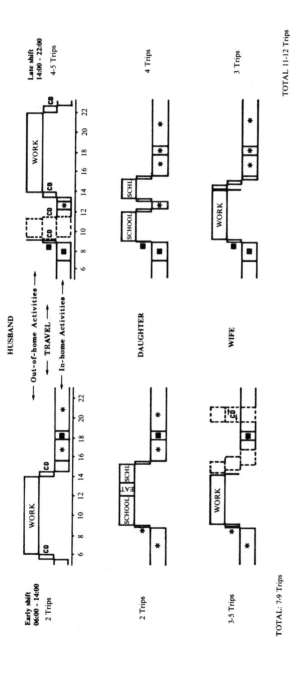

Figure 3.6. Effects of husband's alternate shifts on household activity-travel pattern

.is working late - yet the content of the activity patterns are substantially the same.

5.   Simulating organisational re-structuring

Although opportunities arise to study the effects of changing institutional constraints or other factors on household behaviour, more can be learnt about the processes of adaptation by using gaming simulation techniques to explore the re-structuring process (including the nature of role re-definition, bargaining, etc.). One such technique is HATS (Jones, 1979)- Household Activity Travel Simulator. This uses display boards on which household members simulate their reactions to policy changes by first building and then manipulating a representation of their daily behaviour patterns; these are built up using coloured blocks of different size along time lines for in-home, out-of-home and travel activities (in the format shown in Figure 3.6) with a map showing the location of facilities and the travel modes used and routes taken between locations.

HATS interviews are designed to explore three aspects of household organisational adaptation:

a)   The decision **context**: the nature of the existing organisational and behavioural structures and the constraints which limit the response options.

b)   The decision **process**: the procedures by which the preferred response is selected, relating to trade-offs, bargaining power, etc.

c)   The decision **outcome**: the direct and secondary adjustments to household activity, travel problems and role re-definitions considered necessary to cope with the new situations.

The interview has both qualitative and quantative dimensions: changes in household activity patterns can be measured in some detail and tape recordings of the discussion provide a rich source of information about power structures, etc. within the household - the simulation exercise appears to be realistic and reveals information of which respondents themselves are not consciously aware.

HATS studies have been carried out in several countries and contexts (including impacts of car restraint and the problems of families containing a wheel chair bound member). The examples given here are taken from two studies looking at the effects of school hour changes on household organisation; this is a particularly interesting stimulus since a change directly affecting one child in the household for a limited period of the day can have knock-on effects at other times and on other people.

Figure 3.7 shows the simulated effects on household's of a proposal to advance school hours at a school in West Oxfordshire by half an hour, in order to enable school transport facilities to be provided more efficiently. The figure depicts changes in activity patterns by recording the number of respondents who altered the type or location of their activity as a result of the school hour change, for each 15 minute time period through the day. The figure distinguishes between changes entirely within the home (e.g. now eating over the period 07.45-08.00 instead of washing) and those which affect the use of out-of-home facilities (e.g. now travelling at time period t instead of waiting at school, or visiting a youth club instead of watching television at home).

The pupils at the school were forced to modify their behaviour in the periods when school hours changed (i.e. 08.30-09.00 and 15.30-16.00), as well as a varying additional amount due to the local school bus service revisions, but the figure shows that there were significant secondary effects at other times of day and involving other household members. It is apparent that household activity patterns were affected up to two hours either side of the school hour changes, and that about 20% of pupils were affected well into the evening. Note that the impacts on other household members were relatively small in this instance because in the rural area surveyed most pupils were provided with free school transport - in an urban context, the effects would be much greater. Further details are provided in Jones (1978).

A similar exercise was carried out in Adelaide but looking at a wider range of policy options, including earlier and later school hours, as well as changes in work hours; the objective was to see whether changes in institutional hours would reduce peak hour traffic congestion and be acceptable to the public. The full results are available in Jones, Clarke and Dix (1986). Again, using the earlier school day as an example, this time a proposed advance of 90 minutes, the main advantages and disadvantages are summarised in Figure 3.8. The balance of opinion varied both according to overall household structure (especially the number of employed people) and the role which individuals perform within families. In terms of parent-child contact, for example, the earlier school day was of benefit to non-working wives but had disadvantages for husbands in full-time employment.

The effects on morning travel arrangements would be complex and variable. Where parents went to work early in the morning, the earlier school start would avoid children being left unattended at home and would enable some parents to drop children off on their way to work. For those with a later job start, however, the linkage would be broken and

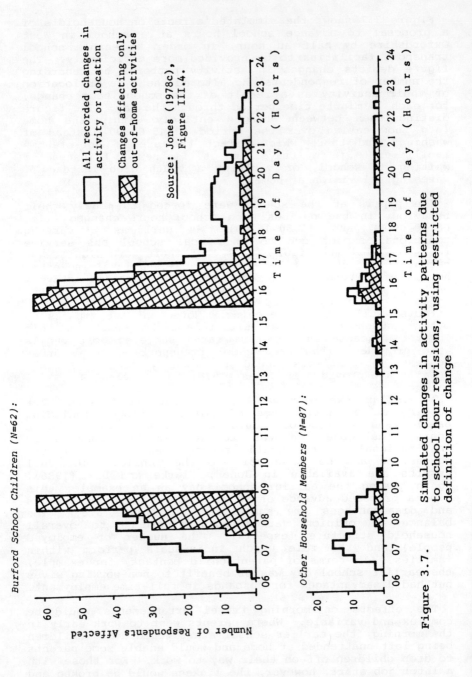

Figure 3.7. Simulated changes in activity patterns due to school hour revisions, using restricted definition of change

Burford School Children (N=62):

Other Household Members (N=87):

All recorded changes in activity or location

Changes affecting only out-of-home activities

Source: Jones (1978c), Figure III.4.

Number of Respondents Affected

Time of Day (Hours)

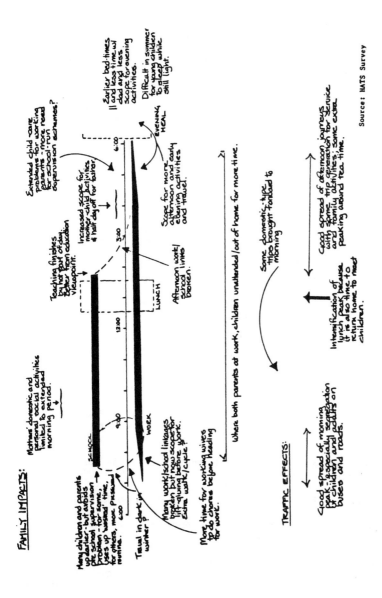

FAMILY IMPACTS:

Mothers domestic and personal social activities limited to extended morning period.

Many children and parents up earlier - but avoids the school supervision problem - for some, eases up "wasted" time, for others, more pressured routine.

Teaching finishes but last part of day: better from education viewpoint.

Increased scope for mother - child activities & half day off for tutor.

Extended child-care problems for working parents - more need for school-run supervision schemes?

Earlier bed-times ll less time w/ dad and less scope for evening activities.

Difficult in summer for young children to sleep while still light.

Many work/school linkages broken but now scope for lift-giving before work.

Scope for more afternoon and early evening activities and travel.

Travel in dark in winter?

More time for working wives to do chores before work.

Afternoon work/school links broken.

Where both parents at work, children unattended/out of home for more time.

TRAFFIC EFFECTS:

Good spread of morning peak, especially segregation of children and adults on buses and roads.

Some domestic-type trips brought forward to morning.

Intensification of lunch peak because it is also time to return home to meet children.

Good spread of afternoon journeys with some trip generation for service and family activities; some extra peaking around tea time.

Source: HATS Survey

Figure 3.8. Some consequences of earlier school hours

either a special chauffeuring journey would have to be made to / from school, or the children would have to make their own way there on foot or by cycle or bus; given traffic would be lighter at those times, this would probably be more acceptable, although there are worries about children being allowed to make their own way to school in winter in the dark.

It was in the afternoon, however, that the major consequences of an earlier school day would be felt. All recognised the educational benefits of finishing teaching before the heat of the day in the summer, but there were strong pros and cons as regards how the rest of the afternoon would be spent. For working parents, there were worries about how children would cope being left unattended for an extended period in the afternoon, and, indeed, whether, it would still be feasible for some mothers to have a part-time job. Some schools already have after school recreation programmes to 6.00p.m. to cover for working parents, and it was hoped that such programmes would be implemented more widely by the community as part of a general move towards an earlier school day. If this happened, it would actually help reduce the problem of 'latch key' children.

Non-working mothers would experience more of a polarisation in their day, with a longer period in the morning free for domestic type activities and a larger block of time for joint social/ recreational activities with children after school. Two possibilities were recognised here:

a) Extra activities in the afternoon:

"A whole load of things could get done. We can never (at present) find the shopping hours to get children's clothes; you can't get them to the dentist's or doctor's because you can't get them there before school, and after school that one and a half hours just isn't enough - we've got music, gymnasium, tennis - there's always something filling it up."

b) Rearrangement of activities to provide more free time in the evening:

"Probably they would get their homework done earlier and we'd perhaps go out to visit people, and we'd still be home early enough for them to go to bed."

Among husbands who worked flexi-time, there were also suggestions that a substantially earlier school day might encourage them to take off extra blocks of time during the week:

"A half day now is really pretty pointless, because if I come home from work, say at one o'clock, then there is no point other than to come home and do something that I had to do on my own. If we wanted to do something as a family, then we'd be stuck until the kids come out of school; so bringing that forward and having them finish at half one or two might entice me to take a half day off every so often."

Otherwise, they would have less time to spend with their children during the school week:

"The children would have to go to bed earlier, so they could wake up to go to school next day, so their sleeping time would have to change to cope with that."

There were worries about whether this would be feasible for younger children in summer, who would be unlikely to settle before it got dark and would then be half asleep the next morning.

In traffic terms, the earlier school day was seen as the 'best' solution in respect of first order effects, since both the morning and afternoon peaks would become much more spread, although there are dangers of the earlier afternoon school peak impinging on late lunchtime peaks in traffic. Many parents thoght that these benefits could be realised by a slightly later 8.00 a.m. start to the school day which they felt would be much less disruptive to family routines. When taking account of second order effects, however, the benefits were likely to be significantly reduced, since:

a) The early school start would lead to fewer school-work linked trips, but many of these might be replaced by pre-work two-way serve passenger trips, so increasing traffic volumes and energy consumption (especially in winter, when parents may be unhappy about their children walking or cycling to school in the half light).

b) The long period of uncommitted time in the afternoon, between school and the evening meal, may encourage parents and children to take part in extra non-home activities, thereby still creating a child-generated traffic peak around tea-time.

Only through an understanding of household organisation and adaptation is it possible to anticipate these complex response patterns and assess the attitudes of different groups towards proposals such as school hour changes.

Table 3.3 shows how one Adelaide household assessed the pros and cons of different institutional re-timing policies and the preference order in which they ranked them. As part of this project, a computer based survey technique

Table 3.3. Trade-offs among timing options in one household

(Lifecycle Group C: wife has part-time job.)

POLICY OPTIONS. In final order of preference.

1)   **Earlier school day for child:**
Child: net benefit. Home earlier, so more time with mother and better educationally
Mother: net benefit. Has to take child to school earlier, but has more time to tidy up before going out to work, and more time with child in the afternoon
Father;   net disbenefit. Less time with child after work (because of earlier bedtime) and may lose joint evening meal; may also be asked to take child to school in the morning.

2)   **Later working day for husband:**
Child: net disbenefit. Loses playtime with father in evening and would either have a very late dinner or lose this linkage with father
Mother: net disbenefit. Husband in way in morning; either has very late evening meal, or has to prepare meals separately for her plus child and husband
Father: net benefit. Prefers starting and finishing work later - suits personal bio-rhythm. More time to shop, etc. before work, though less time with family in the evening.

3)   **Later school day for child:**
Child: net disbenefit. Worse educationally, less time with mother during week
Mother: net disbenefit. Worst option: no time to tidy up in the morning; wasted time, yet rush to get to work after taking child to school, and little time with child in afternoon
Father: net benefit. More time with child in evening before bedtime.

4)   **Earlier working day for husband:**
Child: net benefit. More time with father in afternoon/ evening and earlier evening meal
Mother: net disbenefit. No help with child in morning, more of a rush to prepare earlier evening meal, so less time with child
Father: net disbenefit. Would lose opportunity to shop, etc. before work in morning, and would have to work less agreeable hours - also some danger of working on to existing time.Some gain from having more time with family in afternoon / evening.

using a colour monitor has been developed to obtain information on re-organisational strategies and re-structuring preferences in a more structured way. Called ATAQ (Adelaide Travel and Activity Questioner), the programme asks respondents to devise optimum household activity travel patterns for different types of policy or other change and then select between them on the basis of changes in travel costs, journey times, etc. Although developed primarily to assess household responses to major policy initiatives, the technique could also be used to look more directly at the patterns and processes of household formation and organisation. The ATAQ technique is described in Jones, Bradley and Ampt (1987).

6.   Conclusion

Travel behaviour can be a very complex phenomenon but this chapter has sought to demonstrate that through the study of household organisation in terms of a **linked set of activity travel patterns** using appropriate qualitative and quantative techniques, it is possible to measure and understand the phenomenon and assess the likely consequences for future changes. Although much of the work reported here has an explicit policy orientation, it is evident, that the approach could also be used to investigate fundamental issues such as the process of household formation, the inter-personal linkages and power relationships and the dynamics of adaptation.

The activity approach also has the advantage that it brings together many aspects of human behaviour within a common framework enabling complex interactions to be examined and knock-on effects on behaviour to be assessed. In a transport context, it becomes possible to study the effects on travel behaviour of changing social roles, institutional organisation and technological developments that may have nothing directly to do with travel; conversely, the implications of change in transport supply for household organisation can also be investigated.

Seen from this perspective, it is possible to consider questions that cannot be answered within a more conventional, trip-based paradigm and evaluate non-transport solutions to travel problems. Burns (1979), for example, used Hagerstrand's concept of the time-space prism (section 2) to explore the accessibility implications of different Transportation Systems Management schemes. He was able to show that policies designed to increase travel velocities (higher speeds or reduced public transport headways) were less effective at increasing personal accessibility than policies which reduced individuals' timing constraints (e.g. flexible work hours) or the amount of committed time (e.g. labour saving devices in the home).

In a small study of single and two parent families with workers and young children, Kam (1982) was able to substantiate this finding using HATS, in conjunction with activity diaries and attitudinal questionnaires. He found that the introduction of flexi-time "...not only releases more uncoupled time to individuals, but also redresses the 'imbalances' in family role sharing" - which, he concluded, were as much caused by time-space constraints as by sociological factors. He also found that:

'...a flexible work starting time can introduce a relaxed feeling in individuals. Although the real increase in discretionary time during the morning hours is only marginal in most instances, the removal of a perceived constraint which leads to the feeling that individuals can schedule their activities at their own pace is a significant contribution to feelings of well being.'

An indication of the feelings of people affected by policy measures often forms an important component of the output of such exploratory studies.

Finally, the activity approach offers a very fruitful framework for inter-disciplinary study; this is essential if a proper understanding of household organisation and travel behaviour is to be obtained and in particular if the important influences of gender and role are to be correctly identified.

4 Trip chaining behaviour: a comparative and cross cultural analysis of the travel patterns of working mothers

SANDRA ROSENBLOOM

1.   Introduction

There have been substantial changes in the structure and activities of the 'typical' family in a number of Western countries in the last two decades.   One of the most profound changes is the largely unanticipated growth (Smith, 1976) in the **salaried employment of mothers** in both intact and single parent households.

France and the U.S., like most O.E.C.D. countries, currently have female labour force participation rates in excess of 50%; the Netherlands, 38%.   The **fastest** growing component of the female labour force in **all three** countries is mothers with children under six, over 80% of whom are in full-time employment (Rosenbloom, 1984).

These demographic changes have important implications for transportation planning because families with two workers and single parent households will behave differently than the traditional family on which we currently base planning methods (Rosenbloom, 1984; Wachs, 1982; Meyer and Miller, 1984).   More specifically, Rosenbloom (1988), Hanson and Hanson (1980), and others have suggested that **women** in such households may have different transportation patterns than comparably situated men because, in addition to their employment responsibilities, they will continue to assume disproportionate **domestic responsibilities**.

This paper explores differences in the transportation patterns of men and women by focusing on one indicator of the **complexity** of individual travel behaviour; **trip-chaining**, or linking trips to or from work with trips to carry out personal or household responsibilities. The paper analyses descriptive data from in-depth interviews with parents in two-worker families, and with single parents, in three industrial countries: France, the Netherlands and the United States.

In the following sections, the paper first explores differences between full-time salaried men and women with children of different ages in **each** country individually. The paper next compares trip-chaining behaviour in all three countries, and then contrasts the travel patterns of married women, single mothers and married men in these three countries. Finally, the paper focuses on how the travel behaviour of Dutch and American women varies considerably more when the 'age of children' variable is further disaggregated.

While comparisons between countries with very different social and economic environments should be made cautiously, the data analysed in this paper show several clear patterns. First, in all countries married women had more complicated travel patterns than comparably situated men; they were generally more likely to link trips to and from work than men. Secondly, the age of the youngest child in the household seemed to impact travel behaviour; most adults were **less** likely to link trips when their children were older, but the drop in trip-linking was generally most pronounced for men.

There were important differences as well. Single women in the European countries were far more like married women than such parents in the United States. American single parents generally made fewer linked trips to or from work than either married parent and these linked trips tended to decline more rapidly as their children grew up.

The following section describes the background of the study and the organisation of the paper.

2.   Study background

The analyses presented here are part of a larger study of the transportation implications of the increasing involvement of mothers in the paid labour force in France, the Netherlands and the United States. The study is or has been funded by the German Marshall Fund of the United States, the U.S. National Science Foundation, the Centre National Recherche Scientifique and the Rockefeller Foundation. Small scale attitudinal surveys were undertaken between 1982 and 1985 in all three countries; respondents were married and single workers with children of various ages living at home. Both full-time and part-time female workers were interviewed although this paper addresses only those working **35 hours per week or more.** Households were selected for interview on a random quota basis; all parents in intact households were asked a variety of descriptive, attitudinal and hypothetical questions about their travel patterns and needs.

The French survey was undertaken in Lyon; 101 intact and 49 single parent families were interviewed. The Dutch study in Rotterdam interviewed 150 intact families and 50 single parent families. 100 intact and 50 single parent families were interviewed in Austin, Texas. The cities are not particularly alike; they were chosen to meet internal research and financial constraints. This obviously makes meaningful comparisons **between countries** problematic.

The small scale of the study makes it difficult to draw statistically significant conclusions, particularly when focusing on sub-groups within the overall study population. However, the data, while descriptive, can be indicative of larger patterns. The following section describes data on the home-to-work trip-linking behaviour of salaried adults in households with children under and over six years of age. Note that all married men described here are married to full-time working women.

3.   Intra-country comparisons

Tables 4.1 and 4.2 display data on the trip-linking behaviour of salaried adults with children in three countries; Table 4.1 describes trip-linking behaviour to work while Table 2 describes trip-linking behaviour from work. In all three countries women had different trip-linking patterns to men, and single mothers were often very different to both genders of married parents. In the following sections, these three kinds of working parents will be compared within each country.

Table 4.1. Percentage of full-time working parents combining trips to work by age of youngest child

	French		U.S.		Dutch	
	<6	>6	<6	>6	<6	>6
Married women:	38	23	65	40	28	23
Married men:	39	23	42	50	12	15
Single women:	86	38	20	18	43	15

77

Table 4.2   Percentage   of   full-time   working   parents
             combining trips from work by age of youngest
             child

| | French | | U.S. | | Dutch | |
	<6	>6	<6	>6	<6	>6
Married women:	65	62	81	96	52	68
Married men:	43	31	67	75	24	12
Single women:	91	65	78	62	50	32

a)   France

In France, married men and women had similar trip-linking
behaviour on the way to work; slightly less than 40% of
married parents with children under six and not quite 1/4
of those with children over six linked trips to work.
However, on the way home from work both married and single
women were far more likely to link trips than men; over 60%
of women but only 31% of men with children over six linked
trips from work.

Differences between married parents and single parents
are striking, single women being far more likely to link
trips both to and from work, regardless of the age of the
youngest child. Approximately 90% of single mothers with
children under six linked trips in both directions.

Single women were less likely to link trips if they had
older children but they were still more likely to engage in
such behaviour than married parents - 65% of single mothers
with children over six but only 62% of comparable married
women and 31% of married men linked trips home from work.

All adults were less likely to link trips to work than
from work and were more likely to link trips when they had
younger children.

b)   The United States

American married men and women had travel patterns
different form one another and markedly different from
single mothers. Married men were less likely than married
women to link trips either to or from work when they had
young children but slightly more likely to link trips home
from work when their children were older. Only 42% of
married fathers with younger children linked trips to work
compared to 65% of comparable married women; 67% of married
men with older children linked trips home from work

compared to 81% of married women. Married men were more likely to link trips to work when they had children older than six; half of all such men but only 40% of comparable women linked trips to work.

Single American women had sometimes remarkably different travel patterns than married adults of either sex. Only roughly 1/5 of such mothers linked trips to work regardless of the age of their youngest child. While, as with married parents, more single parents linked trips home from work, single women only linked trips more often than married men when they had children under six. Single mothers never linked trips more than married mothers, to or from work, regardless of the age of their youngest child.

c)   The Netherlands

Dutch women in general, but particularly married women, were almost twice as likely to link trips to or from work than men, regardless of the age of their youngest child. Dutch single women were both less and more likely to link trips than married women, their behaviour varying with their children's age and the direction of the trip.

At the maximum, less than 1/4 of all Dutch men linked trips to or from work; only 12% of Dutch men with children under six linked trips to work. Maximum trip-linking was among married men with children under six on the way home from work; 24% of these men linked trips. In contrast, 52% of married women linked trips from work when their youngest children were under six; almost 70% of married women with children over six linked trips on the way home from work.

There is no consistent pattern among single women. They were most likely to link trips home from work when they had young children; they were least likely to link trips home from work when they had older children. In most cases, they were far more likely to link trips than married men; they equalled men on linked trips to work when both had older children - 15% of both these groups linked trips.

Single parents generally linked trips less than married women except for trips to work when they had younger children; 43% of such single women linked trips to work compared to 28% of comparable married women. Single women with younger children, however, were roughly as likely to link trips from work; 50% of single women and 52% of such married women linked trips.

4.   Inter-country comparisons

Trip-linking behaviour in the three countries differs with the sex and marital status of the adult, with the age of the youngest child, and with the direction of the work trip. Table 4.3 summarises the propensity of adults in the three countries to link trips as their youngest child grows up; Table 4.4 compares trip-linking behaviour to and from work.

Table 4.3 shows that all groups in France were less likely to link trips to and from work as children grew up. Neither U.S. or Dutch patterns were so consistent; Americans in all three groups were less likely to link trips to work as their children aged but both married parents were more likely to link trips from work. Dutch married men were more likely to link trips to and from work as their children grew up but Dutch married women were less likely to do so. Dutch single women were similar to married women.

Table 4.3. Parent's work trip-linking propensity as youngest child grows up

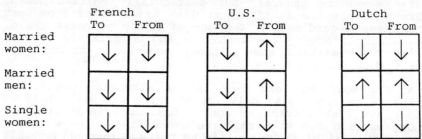

	French To	From	U.S. To	From	Dutch To	From
Married women:	↓	↓	↓	↑	↓	↓
Married men:	↓	↓	↓	↑	↑	↑
Single women:	↓	↓	↓	↓	↓	↓

Table 4.4 summarises patterns that might be evident in the discussion in the previous section. All parents in three countries were more likely to link trips from work than to work; these data are supported by other research in the three countries.

Table 4.4. Comparing trip-linking behaviour to and from work

	French To	From	U.S. To	From	Dutch To	From
Married women:	−	+	−	+	−	+
Married men:	−	+	−	+	−	+
Single women:	−	+	−	+	−	+

Greater % linking trips +

Lower % linking trips −

a)   Comparing individual parents

There are great differences and great similarities between comparable parents in the three countries. Figures 4.1 and 4.2 compare each set of parents to one another for trips to and from work. European respondents were more like one another than they were like American respondents; in general, they were less likely to trip-link than Americans. Part of this is due, no doubt, to greater dependence on public transit, whose lack of flexibility reduces trip-linking but whose greater coverage may make trips to chauffeur children, etc, unnecessary.

Figure 4.1 shows that married men in all three countries are more alike than other salaried parents; they tend to make fewer linked trips to work than either single or married mothers. When their children are young, French and U.S. fathers are not very different while the Dutch are less likely to link trips. As their children age, all fathers, except the Dutch, make fewer linked trips; with children older than six fathers are the most similar in travel behaviour.

U.S. married women are more likely to link trips to work than their counterparts in Europe, U.S. single women, who often depend on transit and carpools, have limited ability to deviate from the direct trip to work.

Figure 4.2 describes trip-linking home from work; here U.S. men and women are more similar to one another and different from their European counterparts. U.S. married parents are more likely to link than others by sizeable margins; 70% of men and 90% of married women with older children link trips home from work.

American single mothers link trips from work less than French single women but more often than both the Dutch and than they do on the way to work.

b)   Disaggregating children's age

The data above suggests that travel behaviour changes when children reach 6 - school age in the U.S. (many European children start full-day school at 3 or 4). However, additional analyses suggest that there are at least two natural breaks - one when a child turns 5 and one when a child turns 12.

Figures 4.3 through 4.6 show the trip-linking behaviour of American and Dutch women in three groups; those with the youngest child under 6, those whose youngest child is 6-12, and those whose youngest child is 13-17 (and living at home). (Comparable data are unavailable for men or for French respondents).

Figure 4.1.   A comparison of full time working parents in three countries: % who link trips to work by age of youngest child

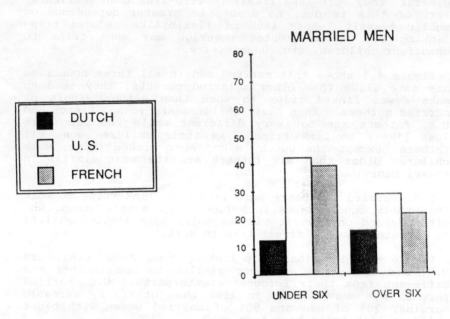

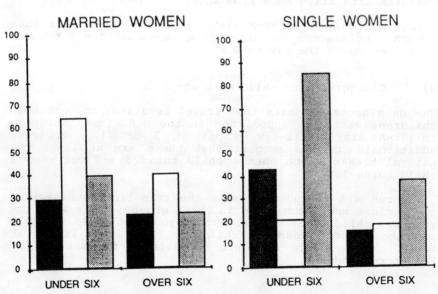

Figure 4.2.   A comparison of full-time working parents
               in three countries: % who link trips from
               work by age of youngest child

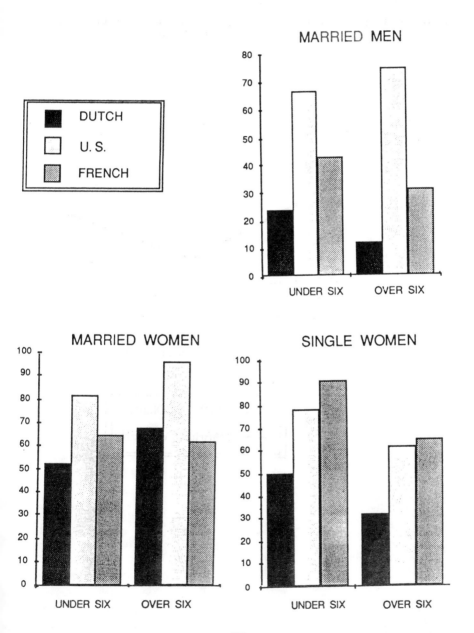

Figures 4.3 and 4.4 display the travel patterns of American women to and from work; married women display a U-shaped curve. They are most likely to trip-link when they have young children or teenagers, although slightly more with younger children. Single women, who generally make fewer linked trips, display the same U-shaped curve on the way to work, but show a steadily declining pattern on the trip home.

Figure 4.3. Percentage of U.S. mothers who link trips to work by age of youngest child

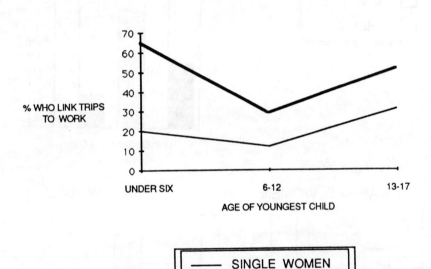

84

Figure 4.4. Percentage of U.S. mothers who link trips from work by age of youngest child

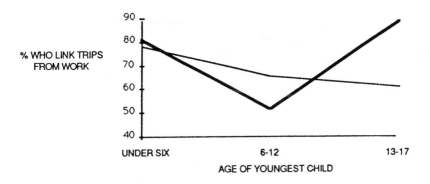

Figures 4.5 and 4.6 show similar analyses for Dutch women; as with most comparative data analysed in this paper, there are important differences as well as similarities. On the way to work, Dutch women also display a U-shaped curve although the contrast between the three groups is not as great for married women and markedly more so for single women. Both female marital groups are more likely to link trips for their young children and their teenagers than for their children 6-12.

Figure 4.5.   Percentage of Dutch mothers who link trips to work by age of youngest child

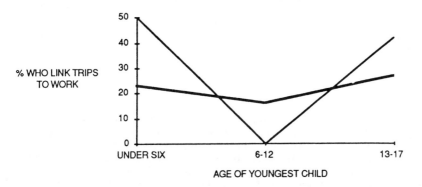

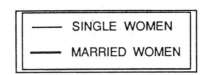

85

Figure 4.6.   Percentage of Dutch mothers who link trips
                      from work by age of youngest child

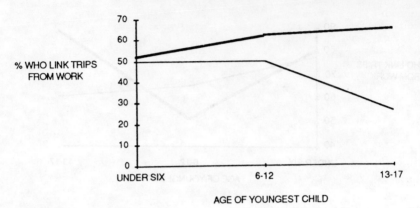

Figure 4.6 shows that Dutch women have different patterns on the way home from work. Here Dutch married women are likely to increase trip-linking as their children grow up, while single women are less likely to link trips as their youngest child grows up.

These analyses suggest, but of course do not prove, that some part of the trip-linking behaviour of women in both countries is a response to their children's varied needs at different stages of their lives. In other work, Rosenbloom (1988) has argued that women have markedly different travel patterns than comparable men because embedded in all their travel needs are the travel needs of their children; European children in general have more options available so trip-linking behaviour is less required by parents of older children.

5.   Conclusions

In all three countries, women have more complicated activity patterns than comparably situated men, as measured by trip-linking behaviour. The data analysed here are not sufficient to indicate the cause of such behavioural differences but other work by Rosenbloom has concluded that most of the differences in trip-linking behaviour are created when women accept both salaried employment and major domestic responsibilies (Rosenbloom, 1988). Moreover, other examinations of these data (Rosenbloom, 1987), and the work of other researchers (Pas and Koppelman, 1987), suggest that women's linked trips are not constant over a week; the household and child-chauffeuring determinants of trip-linking appear to create day by day trip variations.

Whether or not Rosenbloom's explanation of such variations is correct, the observed differences in the travel patterns of full-time working parents in all three countries suggest that both transportation policy makers and planners must **consider alternative ways** of **delivering transport services** now and in the future. Conventional **fixed route** transit services are not responsive to the needs of working parents whose day-to-day travel patterns differ markedly. Nor are current transportation planning methodologies likely to accurately capture or project these complicated travel patterns.

5 Fostering as employment: the mobility component

PENNY RHODES

1. Introduction: 'fostering is women's work'

Traditionally, the 'appropriate' role for women has been one of domesticity and child care within the confines of the 'family', in other words, **immobile** and tied to the home. Fostering was regarded as little more than an extension of this motherhood role and, as such, was devalued as a form of legitimate employment. Recent developments, however, in particular the drive to recruit more foster parents and to return child care to the 'community', have led to a re-evaluation of the conventional model of 'family life', and women's role within it, as a basis on which to assess the suitability of potential foster parents. Secondly, new demands and expectations made on foster parents have resulted in an increasing 'professionalisation' of foster care and this has challenged the traditional image of fostering as a vocation or charitable service as opposed to a 'proper job' with payment and conditions on a par with other forms of legitimate employment. Not only has the fostering role thus changed but the pool from which foster parents are now recruited has changed and these two factors have considerable implications for **the degree of mobility** possessed by would-be foster parents.

2.   The concept of family and women's role within it

The principal aim of foster care is to provide children who, for whatever reason, cannot live with their natural parents, with a home which conforms as nearly as possible with some notion of 'normal family life' (ABSWAP, 1983).

The notion of family is one of the most potent ideological concepts of our time (Barrett and McIntosh, 1982:26). The conventional image is that of employed husband and his dependent wife and children. It prescribes the relations between husband and wife, parents and children and the division of labour between the husband's 'work' outside the home in his role as breadwinner and the wife's domestic duties as wife, mother and home-maker. The woman's role within the family is traditionally conceived as one of nurturance and subordination. The model is essentially functionalist (e.g. Parsons, 1949) and derives from the biological concept of Darwinian fitness (Rapoport et al, 1977) and, because it embodies assumptions about 'how families ought to be' (Robertson Elliot, 1986:4) is both morally coercive and avoids important and empirical issues (Lambert and Streather, 1980).

The family is portrayed as a grass roots institution (e.g. European Parliament Committee on Social Affairs and Employment), the fundamental institution of the people and main bastion against state interference in people's lives. The 'working class', according to Ferdinand Mount, 'is the true defender of liberty and privacy' within the family (1982:7,175). Certain Marxists and feminists have made similar claims, although for different reasons: Morgan (1979), for example, sees the working class family as a repository for revolutionary values and Humphries (1977) as the basis of cohesion and solidarity necessary to class struggle. In a different vein, Betty Friedan (1982) has defended the family as a source of protection for women allowing them to express their individuality in the face of state intervention and pressure to conform to socially defined roles (Robertson Elliot, 1986:204). Other strands of 'conservative pro-family feminism' promote the family as the seed bed of the nurturant values of motherhood as opposed to patriarchal values (Thorne, 1982). An attack upon the family thus becomes an attack upon the people (Mrs Thatcher, The Guardian, 6.6.1986, 'Our policy starts with the family').

The class based (Burgoyne, 1987), sexist (Oakley, 1987) and ethnocentric (Satow and Homans, 1981) character of much of this political rhetoric is disguised amid claims about the conventional family as the 'natural' and 'fundamental unit of society'. The coercive elements of the dominant ideology are turned, by a political sleight of hand, into the defence of 'ordinary people' and what is rightfully theirs, in other words, the right to enjoy a 'normal family life'.

The 'ethic of the sentimental nuclear family' (Oakley, 1987) and especially that of the mother-child bond is enshrined in religion, biology, sociology, media imagery (Barrett and McIntosh, 1982:32) and government policy (Zaretsky, 1982: 195; David, 1986: 41, 47-49; Nissel, 1980). It is justified as 'the will of God', and as a biological and/ or sociological given. Its existence is predicated on the needs of society (usually men in society) and the needs of children and, although it is portrayed as woman-centred (e.g. Mount, 1982:239), women are not regarded as having capabilities, needs or desires independent of their caring/ nurturing role.

"The era of enforced conformity of women to happy housewife and mother stereotypes is still with us." (Oakley, 1987)

"(All) the evidence suggests that the housewife-mother role continues to be defined as women's primary role and to dominate their lives." (Robertson Elliot, 1986:89)

In contrast with men's paid employment, the role of wife/mother is sentimentally revered as a vocation which demands women's 'exclusive personal loyalty' (Wainwright, 1978). Compared with this, women's other possible achievements or spheres of interest are devalued or dismissed. In Ann Oakley's words, there is

"an implicit definition of women as wives and mothers to the virtual exclusion of any other life area". (Oakley, 1974:17)

Until recently, women and women's work in the home were more or less invisible in sociology. In 1974, in a chapter headed, 'The Invisible Woman: Sexism in Sociology', Ann Oakley wrote

"The concealment of women runs right through sociology. It extends from the classification of subject areas and the definition of concepts through the topics and methods of empirical research to the construction of models and theories generally."

A conceptual distinction is drawn between the **public** world of male employment and social life outside the family and the **private** domestic world of family life. And it is within the family that women have been firmly confined. In fact, housework and child care were not regarded as 'real work' at all but as the natural duties of women which it is their biological destiny to fulfil.

"The old ideals of marriage ...assume a biological ethic - a series of duties of nest-gathering, nursing, feeding, protecting and teaching, all involving the sacrifice of self". (Mount, 1982: 241)

Feminism, by this argument, is doomed to fail because

"'it runs up against biology..against the biological ethic, against self sacrifice for husband and children". (Mount, 1982: 242)

The proportion of a woman's **time budget** which she spends in the home i.e. sedentary, becomes taken, therefore, as a measure of her worth not only as a wife, mother and home-maker but as a woman.

Several writers have traced the rise of the model of the sentimental nuclear family and of the 'cult of Motherhood' as a relatively modern phenomena (Oakley, 1976; Burgoyne, 1987) yet, despite this, societal ills continue to be interpreted in terms of a socio-biological imperative and concern about the family and more specifically about women's role within the family. Women, for example, who have transgressed the public/ private divide by engaging in paid employment, 'working women', 'working wives', 'working mothers' have been defined as a social problem (Oakley, 1974: 17-18).

"Quite frankly, I don't think that mothers have the same right to work as fathers do. If the Good Lord had intended us to have equal rights to go out to work, he wouldn't have created man and woman." (Patrick Jenkin speaking in a television interview on Man Alive when Secretary of State for Social Services, 1979).

As Ann Oakley comments,

"Any move towards greater independence for women is....likely to evoke a reaffirmation of family values." (1987)

Mrs Thatcher's speech to the Conservative Women's Conference, 1986, was a strident example. The importance of family life and, central to the concept of family life, motherhood within the context of marriage is being vigorously reasserted as the ideal and as a full-time vocation , whereas non-motherhood is increasingly being frowned upon (David, 1986: 43).

3.   Women and employment

Where women venture into the public sphere of employment outside the home, they seem to have readiest access to occupations which are, in some sense, an extension of their familial roles or the feminine areas of more traditional, 'masculine' occupations (Robertson Elliot, 1986:91; Podmore and Spencer, 1987).

'Gender', as Game and Pringle (1984:14) point out, "is fundamental to the way work is organised; and work is central to the social construction of gender". In other words, women are caught in a tautological trap: on the one hand, certain types of work are defined as 'women's work' on the basis of the stereotypical female characteristics which they are thought to display and, on the other, the ways in which women are characterised are based, in part, on the types of work they do.

'Women's work' is not generally regarded as 'real work' and, therefore, tends to be relegated to the unskilled category (Hosking, Ch.6). But as Janet Harvey (1987) argues, notions of skill are, in part, political constructs and are gender-related. Gender, she concludes, is a power relationship (1987: 74).

The majority of men continue to regard domestic labour either as exclusively or predominantly female responsibility (Harvey, 1987; Oakley, 1987) and, despite the fact that a large proportion of women are in paid employment and that the money they earn often makes a significant contribution to the family income (1), the position of women on the labour market, compared with men, is one of low pay, low status, low skill attribution and relative powerlessness (Hakim, 1979; Harvey, 1987; Robertson Elliot, 1986: 90).

4.   Foster care

Fostering straddles uneasily the division between public and private, economic and domestic, society and family. Traditionally, it has been considered as an extension of the motherhood role and, as such, has been devalued as a form of **legitimate employment**. Virtually the only skills required to become a foster parent were the 'female' virtues of being a wife and mother, **with their implicit ties to the domestic space**, and there was no formal training provided. It was generally regarded as a domestic vocation rather than as a proper job and its payment, status and conditions placed it on a par with charitable service rather than as an acceptable form of employment.

Foster parents' image of themselves, like that of the social workers who recruit them, has been one of people who are providing a charitable service 'for the love of children' and from 'the goodness of the heart' rather than one of people who are engaged in a form of **skilled** and paid employment. There is still a widespread suspicion of people whose motives may be in part financial.

The rates paid to foster families are usually regarded as **tokens**, both by the recruitment agencies and by the foster parents themselves. Some attempt is made to cover expenses, although this is rarely adequate as the many letters on the subject to 'Foster Care', the journal of the National Foster Care Association, reveal. Until recently, there was no inclusion in the payments of any components based on the skills required or on the amount or quality of the work which the fostering task involved (Patterns of Foster Care, NCB, 20.10.1978).

"Extraordinarily, one local authority had reduced expenses to its foster parents on the basis that they should be 'doing it for love'!" (Report on London Working Party on Teenage Fostering, 30.5.1986, Friends Meeting House, Euston in 'Foster Care' Sept. 1986)

Some 'professional' fostering schemes, however, are beginning to take these factors into account and higher rates are sometimes paid to foster parents who take in difficult teenagers or childrent with mental and/ or physical handicaps (LBCRPC, 2.12.1982). Traditionally, single women were not accepted as foster parents and the money married women earned was regarded as 'pin money' rather than as a significant contribution to the family income.

Through fostering, the conventional ideal of family life was preserved. (In fact, the wife's employment outside the home, even if only part-time, is still a disqualification for fostering in many cases).

Children's social and moral welfare were protected by removing them from 'broken' and 'inadequate' homes (usually the homes of poor people whose family arrangements differed from those of the conventional norm) and by placing them in homes which, in the eyes of those making the placements, most closely conformed to the bourgeois ideal (George, 1970; ABSWAP, 1983).

Recruitment posters encouraging people to apply to become foster parents usually feature photographs of a happy two-parent family smiling down from their comfortable haven of domestic bliss. Newspaper features on fostering concentrate on foster mothers rather than foster fathers and emphasise the foster mother's warm, nurturant qualities rather than the organisational and 'professional' skills which the fostering task increasingly entails. In other words, it is the foster mother's qualities as a mother which are invoked rather than her 'professional' skills as a person engaged in an often difficult and demanding task.

The conflict is most apparent when it comes to parting with a foster child who has spent some time in the foster mother's care where ties of love and affection which are deemed so fundamental to the motherhood role are broken. Here the traditional mothering image proves inadequate. The 'good' foster parent is, paradoxically, one who does not form bonds with the foster child which can not easily be broken . There is an implicit recognition that fostering is not merely an extension of the motherhood role and that it often requires a 'professional' attitude towards the foster children which does not necessarily mirror the popular conception of a mother's relationship to her children.

93

That fostering is still regarded as essentially 'women's work' is made conspicuous in a recent article in Foster Care ('Men can play an active caring role', March, 1987) which begins

"In the beginning there were foster mothers..."

and where the argument is made for the greater involvement of foster fathers in the care of foster children. According to the writer,

"Many fathers seem reluctant to change, and the ability of being able to drop into a full caring role without losing any of their masculinity in the process is a very real threat indeed, not only to themselves as people, husbands, fathers/ males, but also to their traditional roles in life...."

"Throughout history", he explains, "the traditional role of the husband/ father has been one of provider, decision maker, boundary and discipline keeper, not only within the home but also within the community.....Many men have in the past been reluctant to take on the caring role, even with their own children, such as bathing, feeding or dressing, often waiting until the children have grown older before allowing themselves to take a real interest."

As a consequence

"the acceptance of foster fathers as part of the caring team has left many foster fathers uncertain as to their true role in the family."

In searching for a niche in which the foster father can sit comfortably without danger of losing his masculine identity, the writer resorts to popular male stereotypes.

"Males", he tells us, "are portrayed as the less emotional of the species and although foster fathers can, and do, become emotionally involved with the foster children in their care, we (foster fathers) should be able to look objectively a their placement and be practical as well as emotional in the decision making, such as reviews, and not be reticent about putting our own views forward."

He advocates involvement "in a wider sphere - involvement in th reviews, case conferences, group meetings and, of course, foster associations". The implication in his words, although not always made explicit, is that women are more emotional, less practical and less able to make objective judgements than men and are therefore less competent to take part in important decision making. In other words, the foster father arrogates to himself the more 'professional' managerial and, certainly in the writer's eyes, the more prestigious role. He talks, for example, of 'compensation for any lack of status (the foster father) may feel' and advocates 'a supportive but not servile' role in relation to his wife. The foster father is encouraged to take on the dominant role in interactions with the public world - in reviews, case conferences and so on - in an attempt to preserve intact the boundary with the private domestic world of the family and the woman's role within it.

To the foster mother fall the mundane tasks of day-to-day child care and the emotional involvement which is believed to be both woman's strength and her weakness. As the writer correctly perceives, recognition of the potential contribution of foster fathers is a fairly new development. Hence the concern with the demarcation of male/ female roles within the foster family and with the maintenance of conventional boundaries.

Previous lack of involvement of foster fathers has, perhaps, contributed to the often cavalier and patronising stance of many social workers towards foster parents and their automatic assumption of superiority. Foster parents complain that they are not consulted and often not even informed about decisions affecting the children in their care. The relationship of social worker to foster parent was one of professional and expert in child care to well meaning but unqualified helper. The foster parent's skills and experience were devalued and unrecognised compared with the professional knowledge and expertise of the qualified social worker (Letter to Foster Care, March, 1986).

In other words, the social worker adopted the male role of decision maker and often also of provider and disciplinarian. The social worker was often the main link with the public sphere outside the family, taking decisions about the child's schooling, medical care and so on, whereas the foster mother's role was not considered to extend beyond the motherly duties of providing physical care, warmth and affection in the domestic space.

5.   Recent developments in foster care

Fostering has taken on a new prominence within child care policy as a whole. There are a number of reasons as to why this is the case.

1) The widespread closure of residential children's homes (e.g. the **decentralisation** of state child care facilities), conveniently justified on theoretical grounds of good child care practice as well as on economic grounds (boarding out is by far the cheaper alternative - see DHSS, Feb. 1981), has meant that energy and resources have been diverted into fostering as an alternative form of care.

2) Secondly, there has been a reassertion of the idea that every child has a 'right' to a 'normal family life' amd fostering and adoption placements have been sought as the nearest approximation to the ideal of life in a nuclear family composed of husband and wife and their natural children.

3) Children brought up in residential homes are denied the experience of 'ordinary family life' and suffer from the stigma of institutional care. For black and ethnic minority children, it is argued (ABSWAP, 1983) the problem of identity is intensified because they are not only deprived of normal family life but of any knowledge of or contacts with the culture of their natural parents. Unlike their white counterparts, they lack **role models** of similar skin colour, cultural and ethnic background and find themselves discriminated against on grounds of skin colour and association with cultural groups of which they have no personal knowledge. Black children in these situations have come to think of themselves as white and to deny their own blackness. Such considerations underpin the slogan 'Black homes for black children (ABSWAP, 1983) and the increasing drive to recruit more foster families from amongst black and minority ethnic groups.

4) Renewed interest in preventative measures designed to avoid permanent separation from the child's family of origin has meant that foster placements are increasingly being used as short-term temporary measures with work directed towards eventual rehabilitation of the child with his/ her natural family (Stevenson, 1980).

5) A fifth factor is the principle of permanence where the main thrust of work is towards finding a permanent placement for the child, preferably in an adoptive or long term foster placement (Morris, 1984).

6) Another important factor is the moral panic provoked by the recent spate of highly publicised cases of child abuse. It has been claimed that social workers have become so cowed by the hostility of recent media reports that many are now operating a policy of minimal risks whereby children 'at risk' are received into care at the slightest hint of trouble (Stevenson, 1986).

7) There has been a change in attitudes towards the nature of the population of childrent in care who are considered suitable to be fostered. Since Rowe and Lambert's 1973 study, 'Children who wait', which identified a large group of children within the care population who were either left to drift in residential care or who were considered 'hard to place', successful efforts have been made to find family placements for many children who would previously have been considered unplaceable. These moves have, in part, been a response to Rowe and Lambert's depressing findings and, in part, a

response to the changing dynamics of supply and demand. As the supply of healthy white babies dwindled prospective adoptive and foster parents expressed increasing interest in children from the 'hard to place' groups.

The new emphasis on fostering and resultant changes in the dynamic of supply and demand have had two important effects.

1) They have stimulated efforts to recruit more foster families and this, together with the changing nature of the care population, in particular, the wider range of children now requiring foster care (Jordan, 1985; Parton, 1986), has prompted a reassessment of ideas about the type of families able to provide suitable placements.

2) In line with these developments, the demands and expectations now made of foster parents have changed in the direction of providing a more professional and more professionalised service.

Both these developments have considerable implications for the degree of mobility now required of foster parents.

In order to enlarge the pool of potential recruits the standard middle class criteria of acceptability have had to become more flexible. Current moves to recruit foster parents from amongst the less affluent sections of the population and, in particular, from black and minority ethnic groups have forced social workers to reappraise the image of family life upon which past recruitment practice has been based - in other words, to challenge the conventional nuclear or conjugal family of popular ideology, the happily married couple and their children, which has become 'crystallised in television advertisements which (have) promoted as 'family products' everything form holidays and cars to beefburgers and disinfectants' (Burgoyne, 1987).

During the 1960s, the optimistic belief that society in general was becoming not only more affluent but more egalitarian was reflected in a sentimentally rosy portrait of ordinary family life. The family on the back of the cornflakes packet and in the T.V. advertisement became a symbol of national well being, the heart and focal point of the new consumer society. This sentimental ideal, however, is based on the conceptual separation of emotional from material considerations. Thus real happiness is thought to lie within the close personal rlationships formed within the nuclear family. Love, affection, loyalty, self-sacrifice, are the qualities of family life within which the individual is cherished and protected from the vicissitudes of life outside the family (Mount, 1982). Economic and material considerations are not only regarded as secondary but as potentially damaging to this portrait of emotional well being. In the spirit of the well known addage, 'Money can't buy happiness'.

"......'materialistic' becomes a dirty word and we all join hands in agreement that riches do not necessarily lead to happiness." (Burgoyne, 1987)

The importance of the economic and material side to family life has recently been exposed in a study of stepfamilies in Sheffield by Jacqueline Burgoyne and David Clarke (1984).

"the connections between access to material resources and emotional well being affect families of all kinds" (Burgoyne, 1987)

For the families studies, divorce meant not only the break up of a family but financial insecurity and a lower standard of living.

"The emotional significance of this reduction in resources become apparent when (the families) began to talk about meeting a new partner and beginning to 'build a new family life together'".

Financial and material considerations were

"inextricably interwoven with their testimony to their growing sense of closeness as a couple and security as a family unit."

The artificial separation of the emotional and affective aspects of family life from economic and financial considerations, Burgoyne argues, has encouraged

"the widespread belief... that family life is, in some senses at least, the same for everyone; a universal experience and thus a kind of lowest common denominator and potential source of national unity."

"It is all too easy for politicians, policy makers and others to believe that the persistent and deepening social divisions within our society have little effect on the essentials of family life because they seem to have very little to do with economic inequalities."

According to Burgoyne,

"(The) meanings (attached) to home, family and domestic life are created and maintained against a blackcloth of contradictory images and values. On the one hand, our assumptions about the structure and content of ordinary or normal family life are largely the product of postwar affluence with is unparalleled rise in domestic standards of living and services. On the other, those families whose standard of living lies well below the norm are expected to believe that access to the kinds of standard enjoyed by the average family is unimportant, that what really matter are the relationships themselves."

One of the most potent symbols of family life is that of the family home and Burgoyne has shown how greater inequalities in families' ability to buy their own homes, coupled with growing normative pressure to buy rather than rent, has left those who still do not own their homes with the feeling that 'they may be depriving themselves and thir children of one of the most basic buidling blocks of family life'. An equally important element in the image of normal family life is, as I shall argue later, the family car.

In their role as public servants, social workers are expected to serve as guardians of social mores and social morals and, as such, find themselves in the unenviable position of being caught between, on the one hand, the power of mainstream public opinion and commitment to the nuclear family ethic and, on the other, the need to adopt a more flexible approach in order to recruit more foster parents. From the conceptual separation of the emotional from the material and economic aspects of family life, it is a small step to believing that the emotional and relationship problems of poorer families derive, in some way, from flaws in their make-up or in the personalities of their members and are unrelated to financial or material considerations. Moreover, since the image of normal family life promoted in the media, by politicians and by academics is considered to be universal, deviations have come to be regarded as, at best, inadequate and, at worst, pathological.

For years, social workers placing children for fostering and adoption have recruited families predominantly from the middle classes, working on the implicit assumption that emotional and material well being go hand-in-hand. Recent research on trans-racially adopted children emphasised the material advantages of their middle class upbringing and television and journal interviews with young adults who were trans-racially adopted or fostered in their childhoods reveal the importance placed on the material circumstances as well as the emotional and affective ties with their adoptive or foster families. The emphasis is on the opportunities provided by their middle class upbringing compared with the lack of opportunities which they believed they would have experienced had they not been fostered or adopted into middle class homes (Laurance, 1983; Daily Mail, 1984).

Whereas previously social workers placing young children for fostering or adoption have recruited families predominantly from the middle classes, today, however, foster parents are more and more being recruited from amongst the poorer sections of the population. Emphasis on measures to prevent permanent reception into care and on rehabilitation with natural parents has meant that greater use is being made of short-term respite foster care (NCB,

Oct. 1978). Placements are being sought in the child's local area to enable the child to maintain links with family and friends and to attend the same school and, thereby, to lessen the impact of reception into care and work more effectively towards rehabilitation. This often means seeking foster placements amongst families from the economically disadvantaged communities from whence the children are drawn. These are also the communities where many of the black and minority ethnic group families are to be found. Families in these communities have little access to many of the resources available to the rest of the population: these are the families on low incomes, living in rented accommodation and **totally reliant on public transport for all their travel needs.** Current moves to recruit foster and adoptive parents from amongst black and minority ethnic groups have inevitably run up against the fact that these groups are significantly under-represented amongst the more affluent sectors of the working and middle classes.

Social workers, typically, seem to have attempted to resolve the dilemma by resorting to the dichotomy between emotional and material life. A number of agencies, however, are now beginning to make strenuous efforts to dispel the 'myths' of past practice (but as my own research in one London borough reveals, such myths are proving very persistent and social workers are finding it difficult enough to change their own ideas and practices, let alone to persuade others that they have changed). Recent recruitment posters and advertisements emphasise that the traditional middle class attributes of home ownership, the husband's steady job, financial security and the domestic goods and standard of living which go with it are not necessarily conducive to a happy family life.

Secondly, drawing on the arguments of **cultural pluralism,** it is stressed that culturally different patterns are not necessarily culturally inferior and that different approaches to family organisation and domestic life should be treated with equal respect.

Where these efforts represent a challenge to the prevailing view, they are to be applauded but, where they merely avoid confrontation with the fact that many families are **materially disadvantaged** in their efforts to build a happy family life, they ought to be exposed. Uncritical acceptance of culturally different patterns without reference to the financial and material circumstances in which they may be grounded ignores the stresses and strains which inadequate resources may engender or intensify. As Jacqueline Burgoyne points out,

"although access to the kinds of resources enjoyed by the majority of the population is not necessarily any guarantee of happiness, those without it have fewer choices."

The normal family life of popular conception is not simply a middle class myth which can be conveniently swept aside. What is needed is a re-evaluation of the impact of fostering not only on the social life of a family but on its economic base. The model of the sentimental nuclear faimly (Oakley, 1987) needs to be reassessed not simply as a template for social organisation but as a consumerist unit. Bill Jordan (1985) underlines the dilemma nicely when he points out that

"social workers are increasingly involved in the business of trying to keep people going under massive economic and environmental stress. As the poverty and disadvantage of social work's clientele increase an almost infinite amount of material resources could be devoted to helping parents bring up children. Conversely, a large and growing number of children could be made better off just by removing them from unemployed, depressed, ill-housed and impoverished parents, and placing them with comfortably off middle class foster parents or adopters."

It is not enough for social workers to adopt more flexible criteria of assessment in order to recruit from groups previously underrepresented in the foster parent pool, if they are not also prepared to recognise that, for these groups, financial and material considerations are likely to be very important. And, of these material considerations, **adequate access to transport** is not the least important.

6.   Fostering as a proper job or profession

Not only is the population pool from which foster parents are recruited changing and, in consequence, ideas about what makes a good foster family, but so too are the expectations and demands made on foster parents.

The changing care population, in particular the boarding out of children previously considered 'hard to place', has meant that many foster parents are now asked to care for children with a multitude of different problems and handicaps. Few children arrive without a history of disrupted family life, problems at school or with the police and/ or some form of emotional or behavioural problem, physical or mental disability (NCB, Oct. 1978). Caring for such children is often a highly skilled, time consuming, physically or emotionally demanding job. In recognition of this, a number of recruitment agencies are running training courses for foster parents directed at the fostering of specific ages or groups of children. Many organisations now divide their pool of foster families into groups, each of which is specifically concerned with the fostering of a particular type of foster child. Recruitment campaigns are designed to attract foster parents for specific groups of children and specialist workers are employed with responsibility for the recruitment of families and placement of specific groups of children. Specialist agencies have been set up with the aims of placing specific groups of children. In some agencies, attending a training course is now a condition of acceptance as a foster parent (LBCRPC, 2.12.1982; Hardy, 1986). Thus, paradoxically, spending time outside the home, i.e. **mobility**, becomes an important requirement within the acceptance process.

A number of agencies have set up so called professional fostering schemes which cater for children with specific needs and within specific age ranges (Shaw and Hipgrave, 1982; Hardy, 1986). Most pay an additional fee in addition to the regular boarding-out allowance and require the foster parents enrolled on the schemes to undergo compulsory training. Barnado's North West Professional Fostering Project for severely mentally handicapped children, for example, states that

Financial reward is considered an important part of the scheme and a professional fee of £62.50 per week is paid in addition to the regular boarding-out allowance. This fee is paid in recognition of the agency's high expectations of professional foster parents. As well as offering the secure, loving home that a parent would provide, Barnado's foster parents are also expected to :

a) implement an agreed developmental plan
b) keep a diary of the child's progress
c) contribute to a six-monthly review
d) liase with other professionals who may be concerned with their child.

The expectations and Barnado's commitment to offer support services are laid down in a written contract which is signed by the foster parents and the agency.

Such moves are essentially pragmatic in recognition of the fact that fostering today involves far more than a mere extension of the motherhood role. In order to provide an adequate standard of care, placement agencies are finding it necessary to train their foster parents not only in the skills required in the care of difficult, disturbed, physically or mentally handicapped children but in the management and organisational skills necessary for report writing, liasing with social workers, attending meetings, case conferences and reviews, dealing with teachers, educational officials, health workers and the police, making court appearances and so on.

Another important development has been the promotion of **shared care** where foster parents are expected to work with the child's natural parents with the aim of eventual rehabilitation (Parton, 1986). Note that this practice of itself places increased **mobility and co-ordination responsibilities** upon the foster parents.

These developments have led foster parents to call for the recognition of fostering as a proper job and the introduction of payment and conditions in accordance with other forms of paid employment.

"The future of foster care lies in obligatory training and education for all those involved in foster care. Future courses should be designed to merit a qualification on completion. Such a qualification would, as in any other sphere, merit a salary plus a boarding-out allowance." (correspondent to Foster Care, March, 1983).

Staff in residential homes are required to undertake a residential care course. "Why", the Foster Care correspondent asks, "are foster parents not given similar training, since they are doing the same job and, it is admitted, getting more satisfactory results?"

The foster parents' demands have been fuelled by an awareness of the fact that fostering is a 'cheap option' and that, by closing down residential homes and moving children 'out into the community', local authorities are making considerable financial savings (LBCRPC, 1.12.1982).

This increasing professionalisation of foster care (Turner and McFarlane, 1985, 1986) has intensified the debate not only about fostering as a form of employment but about the relative status of foster parents vis-a-vis social workers. Many foster parents are no longer content to assume a subordinate role in relation to the social workers with whom they work but think of themselves as co-workers working in partnership or as part of a team with skills complementary and of equal worth to those of social workers.

"(The) system tends to look down on foster parents as tools, not as equal workers.....(They) should be valued a lot higher with their wealth of experience in the field which is much more than most social workers." (letter to Foster CAre, March 1986).

A further factor which has, perhaps, contributed to the professionalisation of foster care is the desire on the part of social workers to be seen to be providing a professional service and, thereby, go some way towards satisfying public opinion as well as their own view of themselves as professionals. The professionalisation of foster care is also a means of ensuring a more standardised quality of care and of providing a framework within which social workers are able to keep a tighter control.

There is widespread belief that the new more professional approach to fostering has contributed to greater fostering success measured in terms of fewer breakdowns compared with the traditional approach (LBCRPC, 1982), although the evidence from research is patchy (Shaw and Hipgrave, 1982).

Appreciation of the professional skills and qualities now demanded of foster parents, and recognition that the new role they are expected to play is no longer consistent with the traditional conception of fostering as a mere extension of the motherhood role, must go hand-in-hand with a re-evaluation of fostering as a form of employment and recognition that financial considerations are important for many applicants who look on fostering as an alternative to paid employment.

Recent efforts to recruit foster families from amongst black and ethnic minority groups expose these **conflicting images of female competence** at their sharpest. Many agencies have been confronted with patterns of family arrangement and domestic organisations which do not conform with the conventional model - with applications, for example, from single mothers, working women, older women whose families have grown up and families where both partners are unemployed.

a)   Single parents

Fostering is one of the few options open to single mothers as a source of income which is compatible with caring for one's own children. In line with popular thinking and their experience of working with clients, social workers have traditionally perceived single parent families as incomplete and as potential problem families. In order for social workers to overcome their own prejudices and those of other people in the acceptance of single applicants as suitable foster parents, a major exercise in re-thinking on the purpose and nature of fostering is required.

b)   Working women

There is a strong tradition within the Afro-Caribbean community of women taking on paid employment both within and outside the home (see Hiranthe, 1984) and the woman's financial contribution is often vital to the family income and to the maintenance of an acceptable standard of living. Combining paid employment with bringing up a family is common as is caring for the children of friends and relatives either on a voluntary or a paid basis. It is, therefore, not anything unusual for an Afro-Caribbean woman to consider taking on fostering in addition another job or to consider fostering as an alternative to other forms of paid employment.

To social workers, however, it presents a considerable dilemma. In accordance with popular opinion (3), their prejudice and training have taught them that the good mother is the mother who stays at home to look after house and family and that, like motherhood, fostering is a vocation and not a job. Applicants who look on fostering as a job and for whom the financial incentive is clearly important are regarded with extreme suspicion.

Here, black applicants, unaware of the tacit rules of the game, are at a disadvantage compared with their white counterparts for whom the financial motive may be equally important but who know that to admit it would be culturally unacceptable. The white applicants know how to manage their presentation of themselves in ways which are acceptable to the social workers assessing them. Each side knows the rules of the game and how to play them. The emphasis during interviews is thus on the foster parent's motherly qualities and motives and on the impact which taking in a foster child will have on the family as a social rather than an economic unit. Financial considerations are, by tacit agreement, played down or even denied and charitable and motherly motives stressed. The fiction of fostering as an approximation to normal family life, as something independent of and uncontaminated by material and financial considerations, is thus preserved. For many black and working class families, however, the fiction is becoming increasingly difficult to maintain.

c)   Unemployment

The need to recruit more black foster families has meant that some boroughs are now beginning to recruit from amongst the unemployed. This, in turn, has meant that social workers are having to reassess the popular assumption that families where the husband/ father is unemployed and which do not therefore conform with the stereotype of normal family life are in some way inadequate and prone to problems. In large part, such assumptions are based on conventional views about men and women's proper roles in family life. Through unemployment, the husband is thought to be deprived of a major source of his male identity as breadwinner and head-of-household and this is viewed as setting up stresses and tensions within the marriage.

This emphasis on the negative consequences of unemployment, however, ignores the positive qualities which many unemployed families could bring to the fostering task, notably the full-time care of two adults. Unemployment also gives the man scope to take on a more active and meaningful role as a foster father than is traditionally the case.

The main obstacle to the recruitment of the unemployed is probably not the possible emotional consequences of unemployment nor its likely impact on the relationship between husband and wife but financial considerations. Given society's material expectations of normal family life, the low rates which most agencies pay and the poverty trap into which families on Supplementary Benefits fall, many unemployed families are financially unable to offer an additional child a home.

Yet fostering is likely to be the only form of employment open to many families and increased recruitment of foster families from amongst the unemployed is inevitably going to lead to a questionning of the status of fostering as a charitable service rather than a form of employment and as something that a woman does for pin money, something peripheral or auxiliary to her husband's income and therefore not a challenge to his status as primary breadwinner (Morris, 1987).

7. The transport implications of changing foster practice

Any discussion about the transport needs of foster families thus involves three important considerations.

Firstly, the fact that, in view of their increasing professionalism and the additional demands now made of them, the degree of mobility required of foster parents is no longer compatible with the conventional view of fostering as merely an extension of the motherhood role and of the foster mother as static and tied to the home.

Secondly, since foster parents are increasingly being recruited from amongst the poorer sections of the population, the additional travel requirements are borne by families with least access to resources and most reliant on public transport. Within these families, the bulk of the burden is borne by the women and usually by women with young children at home since fostering is one of the few forms of employment compatable with bringing up a family.

Thirdly, social workers have traditionally conceived of the nature of the fostering role and have assessed foster parents on the basis of what middle class foster parents are able to offer and part of this image revolves arounf the family car. Foster parents who do not own or have access to a car are handicapped in their ability to provide the standard of family life which they feel is appropriate and which both social workers and foster children have come to expect.

The **increased travel component in fostering** is explained by two principal developments:

1) the adoption of group methods of counselling and training (Davis et al. 1981; Carroll, 1980) and

2) the increased travel entailed in the day to day job of fostering.

a)   The increased use of groups

The increased use of group methods of recruitment, assessment, training, post-placement support and so on stems from :

Economic considerations. It is far more economic in terms of social workers' time and resources to run group sessions in which it is possible to train and pass on information to relatively large numbers of people than it is to visit each applicant or foster parent individually. **Practical considerations concerning quality of practice.** It is believed that group methods are not only a more efficient but a more effective means of transmitting information. **Image considerations concerning the status of fostering.** The use of groups is important in enhancing the status of fostering and bringing it close to the professional status called for by an increasing number of foster parents and social workers. This is especially true of compulsory training courses which then become a necessary qualification for the job. **Issues connected with post-placement support and solidarity.** The establishment of support groups of foster parents who meet together at regular intervals to discuss mutual problems and concerns not only frees social workers from having to make as many routine visits to individual foster parents as they did previously but is supported by the belief that foster parents can often gain as much from each other as they can from social workers. Groups are a means of bringing together foster parents who, previously, often worked in relative isolation from each other. Foster parents are thus able to reassess their individual circumstances in the light of common experience and to organise as a group in order to campaign, for example, for higher status, improved training, payments and conditions.

Attendance at group meetings and training sessions often means travelling at night and involves the woman travelling alone on public transport. The need to arrange babysitters often means that the husband, older child, friend or relative who might otherwise have accompanied her has to stay at home (although social services departments will sometimes pay for babysitters). Shift-work similarly prevents many men from accompanying their wives. Meetings usually start at 7.00p.m. or 7.30p.m. which is incovenient for men who return home late from work and are reluctant to turn out without first having an evening meal.

These were problems for several of the women interviewed as part of a research project on the recruitment of foster parents (4) who had attended information meetings or training courses. Many expressed a dislike of travelling alone at night, especially when their journey involved a walk to and from the bus stop or tube station (see also Atkins, Ch.9). The location of the venue - proximity to bus and tube stops, how well the streets were lit and so on - was, therefore, a significant factor in people's decisions whether or not to attend. Not surprisingly attendance was down when the weather was bad. One or two women lived on estates where they were afraid to walk out alone at night and several had come to meetings with their husbands, a friend or older daughter specifically to **avoid travelling alone.** Travel at night is a particularly serious matter for single women who cannot call on a husband either to babysit or to accompany them.

"I don't go out at night so it was a bit difficult, you see, for me to go to the first meeting so I waited until my daughter could come with me."

"I don't like travelling on the buses at night. I am lucky because the bus stop is just down the road so I don't have to walk very far. But some of them (other applicants) probably wouldn't go because of that. I know one lady who didn't go."

"There's two of us come together, you know. We come on the same bus. I wouldn't go on my own. It's too dangerous at night. Even in the day things happen. No, I wouldn't go on my own at night."

"I don't like walking out at night on my own. It's not safe on the estate (where I live). So, you see, my husband he comes with me."

"I'm alright because my son he picks me up from the bus stop. I wouldn't go if he didn't do that. It's too dangerous on your own at night."

"I didn't go to that first meeting because my husband couldn't come with me and I don't like going on the buses on my own at night. So I didn't go to that one so I waited until they called us for the next one."

"My husband has to stay at home to look after the kids."

"My husband don't come because he works nights, you know. It's the same for a lot of men what work shifts, I think. That's why you don't see so many husbands at the meetings."

"It's all very well, the social workers saying husbands have got to come but what if they is working shifts? They can't get the time off for that."

These problems are exacerbated in the deprived inner city areas where many of the poorer applicants are increasingly being recruited. Very few of the applicants whom I interviewed were car owners and none of the women had access to a car. One **transport solution** might be for social services departments to provide their own **minibus** transport or to arrange lifts for foster parents attending evening meetings.

For foster parents recruited from outside the recruiting borough or local authority area, there are clearly additional difficulties and this raises a number of questions. Is the authority going to insist, for example, on the attendance at meetings and training sessions of foster parents living outside the area or is it going to make exceptions for people living, say, beyond a certain distance? A possible solution might be greater co-operation between local agencies and the provision of opportunities for foster parents to attend sessions run in their local area while offering their services in another. An alternative and more likely outcome is that agencies will **restrict recruitment to their local area.** Transport difficulties are, thus, likely to impact upon the size of the pool of foster parent applicants. This, in its turn, by reducing the number of selection options, may have consequences for the quality of foster care offered.

b) New and increased travel needs in fostering practice

The second factor of importance in assessing the travel needs of foster parents in relation to the changing nature of the fostering task is the day to day on the job requirements. The changing nature of the foster care population together with changing attitudes towards the placement of children in care have meant that a far higher proportion of children who are now being fostered have special needs. Many foster parents who are caring for children with often severe physical and mental handicaps are required to make frequent visits to their local GP, medical specialist, clinic or hospital. Many of the children also attend centres or schools for children with special needs. Others have emotional or behavioural difficulties which require psychotherapy sessions and/ or attendance at special schools or they may have learning difficulties and need to attend classes or schools for the educationally sub-normal. Many foster children come with a history of unhappy or disrupted family life, abuse and / or neglect and are emotionally and/ or behaviourally damaged in some way. They may be truanting from school or in trouble with the police and it is the foster parent's job to go and talk with teachers or to pick the child up from the police station. Many local authorities provide transport for foster children who need to attend special schools or educational units on a daily basis but **there is little or no provision for other types of journeys.**

Foster parents are more and more expected to take a more active role in the total care of the children in their care. They are now expected, for example, to make court appearances, to give evidence, for example, in adoption proceedings, proceedings to obtain court orders to remove children from the care of their natural parents, cases where the foster children in their care have been in trouble with the police. All this entails a much larger travelling component in the fostering role than was previously required, a factor which seems rarely to have been stressed by social workers when recruiting new foster parents but which active foster parents soon find out to their cost.

This burden is increasingly falling on the shoulders of foster families (or, more accurately, on the shoulders of the women within those families) who are recruited from amongst the poorer sections of the community and for many of whom fostering is one of the very few, if not the only, source of employment open to them which is compatable with bringing up their own families. For many of these women, often with several young children at home, the task of timetabling their day and of arranging alternative care so as to fit in these **extra journeys** is not at all easy. In fact, the difficulty of budgeting their time so as to fit in all the additional demands now made on foster parents was one of the aspects of fostering which the foster parent whom I interviewed found most burdensome.

Social workers have tended to assess foster parents on the basis of what middle class families are able to offer and, in view of the increased demands now made of foster parents, to assume access to a level of resources denied to many poorer applicants. Foster parents who do not own or have access to a car may not be able to taket their children on trips to the countryside or on educational outings, trips to museums or the zoo, or be able to ferry them to and from clubs, meetings, sporting activities and other leisure pursuits. The tendency on the part of local authorities and child care agencies to try, in this way, to compensate the children in their care for the loss of a normal family life, may mean that many children from residential care arrive in foster families with unrealistic expectations and are likely to be disappointed. Such considerations are likely to be taken into account when a family's application is first considered and, once accepted as foster parents, are likely to influence they type of placement which is eventually offered.

c)   The family car: a barrier to low income and ethnic
        fostering

A central component of the popular conception of the normal family life is, I have argued, the idea of the family home. Another important element is the idea of the family car. Applicants who do not own a car are handicapped not only in their ability to fulfil the more professional role now demanded of them but also in their ability to attain the sort of middle class life style which has come to be portrayed as normal family life. And these considerations may well affect their initial chances of being accepted as suitable foster parents. Evidence that the idea of the family car is important in many people's image of conventional family life came from comments made by applicants several of whom had not pursued their interest in fostering beyond an initial enquiry.

"Well, they wouldn't look at us. How you going to take the kids out without you have a car and all them things? No, they wouldn't look at us"

"No, they're not interested in black people. They want the person with the big house and the car. There's no way a black person will get in. Or, if they do, it's the one with the car like the white, with the big house and the garden for the kids to play and a car to take them out. They're not really interested in black people."

"I think I saw it (an advertisement for black foster parents) on the T.V but I didn't notice it much because I think, Oh, well, it's for people who have a home of their own and a car and things like that. So I didn't give it much thought......"

"If the fostering department send an interviewer to see anyone... and when they go and see that the person they come to see have a four and five apartment house, a car at the gate, they would think , "Ah, here is someone!" Tell me what you think. There would not be any trouble for a black person getting the fostering, you know. That's the way I see it."

"I went to the meeting and, when I went, there were a lot of black people there, you know. And I was talking to one or two that live around here. And white people may think that black people aren't interested in fostering but it isn't true. I can tell you a lot of black people is interested. It is just that when they get to it they won't get through. They (white social workers) just isn't prepared to put the effort to let them through. I know thee is some black people doing fostering, one or two here and there, but that is just to have a few black faces. And the idea that social workers have, the ones with the big house and the car and the money in the bank. But not most black people, they won't get through."

This evidence suggests that potential recruits may have been discouraged from applying to foster because they did not own or have access to a car.

A further consideration, of course, is the fact that, where families do possess a car, this is usually reserved for the exclusive or predominant use of the husband. More often than not the husband uses it for work which means that it is unavailable to the wife during the day. Since fostering is predominantly a female task, this means that, except in a two car family, access to a car as a resource is likely to be very limited.

7.   Summary

The philosophical shift away from residential care and towards family placement, together with the financial savings to be gained from the closure of children's homes, has meant that foster care has gained a new prominence within child care policy and practices as a whole. The increasing demands now made of foster parents, the need for new skills and the recognition of old together with the fact that foster parents themselves have become more articulate has meant that fostering is rapidly becoming both a more professional and a more professionalised service.

The traditional image of the foster mother (Fanshel, 1966) is clearly no longer consistent with the new professional image. The degree of mobility now expected of foster parents, in particular, conflicts with the notion of fostering as an entirely home-based activity and of the woman as static and tied to the home.

The changing nature of the foster care population, in particular the much wider range of children now considered suitable for family placement, plus changing ideas about the aims of foster placements and, especially, about the need to maintain local, family and cultural links, have stimulted efforts to find homes amongst groups previously under-represented in the foster parent pool. Homes are now being sought amongst black and minority ethnic groups and the poorer sections of the working class, including single parents and the unemployed.

The new professional service, underpinned as it is by the increasing articulateness of largely middle class foster parents and by the expectations of social workers accustomed to recruiting from a more affluent population, assumes a level of financial and material resources necessary to achieve a conventional middle class life style. Considerable disparity, however, currently exists between social workers' expectations of what the foster parent role involves and the ability of many new recruits to achieve them of which the degree of mobility now required to fulfil the foster parent role is an example.

What is needed is a reappraisal of fostering as an occupation as opposed to a vocation. The new professional fostering schemes which are being initiated in several social services departments and voluntary agencies go some way towards upturning the traditional approach. Some agencies are even offering help with housing and accommodation to families which are prepared to take in more than one foster child. Help with transport arrangements would be a further and, for many families, much needed incentive.

In 1978, Joan Cooper of the National Children's Bureau described fostering as

"a task, a skill, a job of work and a creative activity which can be described as a **home-based occupation**." (my emphasis)

For many foster parents and agencies this may be on the agenda but is, by no means, a reality and many agencies, as has been shown, still have a long way to go.

An additional challenge to the notion of fostering as women's work and, therefore, not a 'proper job' which is likely to become more important in the future is the involvement of men. This is especially so if efforts are made to recruit families from amongst the ranks of the unemployed. Some agencies are even considering applications from single men. The implications of this latter development for fostering as an extension of the motherhood role and as a home-based activity, in view of the differential mobility and access to transport between husbands and wives, have yet to be seen.

Notes

1. In the 1970s families increasingly required two wage earners to achieve a similar standard of living to that achieved by a single wage earner in the 1950s and the number of couples with an income below 140% Supplementary Benefit would have trebled were it not for the wife's earnings. For households as a whole, wives' income in 1983 constituted 16.1% of family income (Family Expenditure Survey).

   "the 1986 survey of women and employment showed that (leaving aside for the moment the vexed question of unemployment) very few women adopt the 'typical male pattern of lifetime employment'. Where husbands and wives are both employed full-time, 80% of the women earn less than the men. Two thirds of employed women work only with women doing the same kind of work as them. More than one in three women returning to employment after childbirth are taking a job at a lower occupational level than the one they had held before." (Oakley, 1987)

2. The National Foster Care Association takes the view that

   "all fostering is a professional task and looks forward to the day when all foster parents can receive a remuneration, if they so wish, from their fostering job." (Personal communication, 3rd June, 1987).

3. In a 1977 Sunday Times poll on family life one in two men said that children always suffer when their mothers go out to work (quoted in Oakley, 1987).

4. The interviews were conducted in 1985 in a London borough which has a significant black population and exhibits many of the characteristics of a deprived inner city area. They were carried out as part of a doctoral research project on the recruitment and assessment of foster parents for black children in care.

6 Organising the domestic portfolio: gender and skill

DIAN HOSKING

1.   Introduction

This book represents one of the first attempts in the United Kingdom to describe and seriously to discuss women's needs for, and experience of, different modes of transport, and the transport environment more generally.   Chapters have, for example, documented the temporal and locational patterns of women's activity, and the timing and methods by which they move from one place to another.

In this chapter, the innovative focus on women and transport is taken one step further; for perhaps the first time an attempt is made to develop a **skills perspective** on the area.   Just as the typical activity patterns and contacts of managers have been documented (e.g. Mintzberg, 1973), and consideration given to the ways these might reflect more or less skilful organising (e.g. Hosking, 1988), it is possible similarly to investigate the ways in which women might more or less skilfully organise their paid and unpaid activities, and the relationship between them.

A skills approach will here be illustrated through combining three kinds of description, two of which come from data presented elsewhere in this text.   Firstly, a psychological approach to skill is presented which is then developed in a very particular social psychological way. 'Skill' is defined, and the analysis grounded, not in relation to 'work' (see Hamilton and Jenkins, Ch.2) - but to organising. This is done by arguing that skills are employed and developed through 'moving around' so as better to build and mobilise **knowledge bases** and other resources. This model was developed out of a wide range of literatures describing the activities and interactions of organisers-not just managers - paid and unpaid, in formal and voluntary organisations (see Hosking and Morley, 1988); the model has been found to facilitate appreciation of the organising strategies of women's groups (Brown and Hosking, 1986) and extended family networks (Grieco and Hosking, 1987).

The skills perspective is here described through two types of empirical material presented elsewhere in the test. The account employs, as a first data set, the behavioural description of women's activities and the actual and potential **linkages** between activities, persons, times and places. A second set of data are also drawn on, that is, those that identify women's usage of different **modes of transport**, the transport environment and their evaluations of each; data which provide a picture of how women move around to perform activities, and move from one activity to another. These two data bases are combined with the skills model to provide the beginnings of a skills analysis and show how further work of this kind might be attempted.

2. The meaning of skill

Serious attention to the analysis of skill has focussed on certain areas of **work** - work typically being considered as paid employment (see Hamilton and Jenkins, Ch.2). Further, the areas of paid employment explicitly labelled as skilful -skilled manual - are not the areas in which women are typically employed (Roberts, 1988; Rhodes, see Ch.5). At the same time, unpaid activities - in which women, more than men, are engaged - have seldom been considered for the skills they might embrace and develop (but see Brown and Hosking, 1987; Rosser and Davies, 1986). In sum, skill is largely defined as a **male province** (see also Davidson, 1987; Rhodes, Ch.5).

Among the many issues raised by the above, there is the question of whether skill does, in fact, characterise the areas of paid and/ or unpaid activity in which women regularly engage. To answer this question requires the definition and analysis of skill. To analyse a performance in terms of skill requires investigation of activities which are **intentional**, that is, for which an actor can usually provide reasons. More than this, for the concept of skill to be useful, it must be restricted to actions for which the actor could show evidence of **organising** and **control** through the acquisition and implementation of **practical knowledge**, that is, understanding. To understand better what this means, a sharp contrast is found with reflexive actions such as an eye blink or a knee jerk: they are not intentional, not organised and not controlled through the use of informational feedback and other resources. More will be said about the meaning of skill a little later. For the moment, what is important is that when skill is analytically defined, it becomes clear that there are many activities which are, in this sense, skilful but which are seldom recognised in this way. Many of these activities are performed by women (see Davidson, 1987; Rhodes, Ch.5).

Skills can be investigated only in relation to a defined activity, role or task, or some set (portfolio) of these. To define them, it is necessary to place some, more or less arbitrary, boundary which identifies their termination. This set can then be described in terms of: the complexity of the components, the number and complexity of their linkages, and the ways in which these may constitute, or be constituted as **choices** and **constraints**. This is the arena in which skills may be exercised. Skill is found in the organising and control of, for example: the content of the portfolio, that is, in the **selection of activities**; in the potential **sequences** by which activities are learned and/ or performed (shopping after child goes to, or is collected from, school); in the potential **timing** of either separate trips for separate activities or trip-chaining (Rosenbloom, Ch.4); in the potential **location** of their performance (local, adjacent, distant or scattered); the potential **resources** (knowledge bases, social networks, transport modes) that might be harnessed, or created and mobilised in the performance of these activities (Whipp and Grieco, Ch.1).

3.   **Organising skills and the domestic portfolio: an overview**

a)   The domestic portfolio and transport

The chapters in this volume provide a picture of the portfolio of activities (paid and unpaid) performed by women in the United Kingdom, along with their patterns of transport use, and their evaluations of the transport environment. Variations are reported in relation, for example, to ethnic group, the woman's age group and the lifecycle stage of the household (Focas, Ch.8; Jones, Ch.3). What we observe is a more or less extensive bundle or portfolio of activities. These are often described as evidence of **multiple roles** (Hamilton and Jenkins, Ch.2). They include: social visiting (e.g. to elderly relatives), escorting (e.g. young children), caring for family who are ill; child raising, shopping and so on (Focas, Ch.8).

Adult women are shown to be likely to have a portfolio of activities which include both paid and unpaid employment. They are likely to abandon the former on the birth of their first child, returning to part-time, paid employment after having children (e.g. Davidson, 1987). The return to paid employment is likely to constitute an **additional set of activities** as women are found to continue to be active, for example, in housework, shopping and child rearing; 'women's roles are simultaneously' (Gutek, Larwood and Stromberg, 1986).

A woman's paid employment is likely to receive low pay, low status, and be in an area constrained by her male partner's work location, that is, in a local labour market (Focas, Ch.8). For a woman to have paid employment outside of the home involves demands for transport which are **in addition** to those arising from her unpaid employment.

What then are the facilities that women may draw upon to resource these demands for transport - demands arising from their portfolio of paid and unpaid activities. Perhaps most important is the finding that they are unlikely to have a driving licence, and even less likely to have substantial access to a car (e.g. Hamilton and Jenkins, Ch.2; Pickup, Ch.11); as a result, their resources for travel are poor (Pickup, Ch.11) - they must use public transport or walk. It appears they are most likely to walk or use the bus and least likely to use the underground (where available) or British Rail (Focas, Ch.8; Pickup, Ch.11). Their choice of transport mode seems partly to reflect their perceptions of its safety and, in particular, its safety after dark. The GLC's survey showed that, if it was at all possible, women chose not to travel at night, and 30% reported that they never travel after dark (Atkins, Ch.9). Different modes of travel are differently associated with fears for **personal safety**, and the beginnings and ends of journeys - involving waiting and/ or passing through unmonitored areas - are seen as the most dangerous. Choices of preferred mode of transport, to some extent intertwined with perceptions of transport environment, is overwhelmingly for car or taxi: these are perceived to be the safest means of travel. They are also the scarcest resource, available to only a few.

It should further be appreciated that the above described activities result in women making a **similar number of journeys** to the number undertaken by men. The difference between them lies, not in trip rates, but in the length of their journeys: a greater proportion of women's trips are local (Finch, 1984; Hamilton and Jenkins, Ch.2). Further, women's trips are often between suburbs, rather than between city centre and suburb, and often during off-peak hours (Hamilton and Jenkins, Ch.2). Their journeys may be multi-purpose in order to service their 'simultaneous roles': they may practice trip-chaining (Rosenbloom, Ch.4) such, that, for example, their return from work may include escorting children from school and/ or a 'social visit' to a member of the family who needs **support**. In sum, women have need for a transport resource which: they perceive as safe; is available at off peak times; services geographically dispersed locations within a fairly local area; fits with their financial constraints. Women need a transport resource which permits a wide range of **choice** in relation to timing, frequency and route; and which is inexpensive. Such **flexibility** is not found in the present organisation of the British system of public transport - a system which is **highly constrained** or (to use Galbraith's terminology (1973)) tightly coupled, for instance, in terms of its off-peak service levels. As a result, and adopting a needs perspective (Atkins, Ch.9), either the system must be changed, or women must find other means to link their capacities and demands (see below). This is where organising skills come in.

b)   Organising as decision making

Each are of paid and unpaid **activities** can be characterised in terms of choices, constraints and resource implications. So, for example, to exercise control and organisation in performance of the domestic portfolio (and, therefore, to exercise skill) requires the effective implementation of decisions about activities and their linkages or interdependencies.

Actual and potential linkages/ relationships provide scope for organising and control. Choices and constraints are experienced in relation to time, locations and persons. In the case of the latter, for example, the male partner is likely to have a schedule of activities which differs from his partner's. Further, the female partner is likely to perceive his schedule as 'incompatible' with her own (Pleck, Staines and Lang, 1980). This is an important constraint arising form relationships, as it is typically the male who has use of the household car (Hamilton and Jenkins, Ch.2). Linkages between **facilities** arise, for example, in respect of their proximity, and the possibilities for travel between them. In the case of **time**, linkages follow, for example, from relationships between the times at which different facilities (locations) are available, plus the times at which the various transport options are available and required (e.g. child care facilities are / are not compatible with the hours of part-time working).

It is within the context of these activities, their linkages and the transport implications that the domestic portfolio can be understood as an arena of skilled performance; an arena for organising and control. From here on, the term domestic portfolio will be used to embrace both paid and unpaid employment, and the term 'organising' will be used in a way which includes control (see Hosking and Morley, 1987).

c)   Organising as complex, political decision making

Organising - wherever it is found - constitutes complex decision making. Some of the reasons why this is so will

119

be described in order to illustrate why skills are potentially involved. Complexity follows from the range of actual and potential activities, linkages and transport implications. As a result there are choices and constraints concerning the content of the portfolio and the total workload (Broadbent, 1987), or overload (Gutek et al, 1986).

Decisions are also complex because they are **political**: they implicate differing, and sometimes conflicting, values and the parties are likely to differ in the resources they can mobilise in their own support. Following Steinbruner (1974), decisions can be said to be complex when a given policy (e.g. to have only one car) has a variety of consequences, some of which have a positive value (financial savings), and some of which do not (second car not available as an additional resource for **disjunctive activities**). The complexity is increased by the number of interdependent persons and groups, who disagree about the 'values at stake, the weight to be given to them, (and) the resolution of major uncertainties' (Steinbruner, 1974:18).

In the context of our present interests, 'interdependent persons', and perhaps groups, are found within the household. Interdependencies are also found between each category of household member and the providers of facilities (shops, child care, employers); the providers of transport (local authority, private contractors, employers); and those who provide the transport environment.

The significance of interdependencies in relation to **values**, and therefore, decisional complexity, is illustrated by developing the earlier example of the use of the household car. The man and woman reach a more or less negotiated agreement (policy) to have one car, and to allocate the resource to meet the demands of the male's activities (Hamilton and Jenkins, Ch.2). The woman, without this transport resource, experiences an increase in the constraints on her domestic portfolio. In brief, she: loses flexibility in relation to her time and activity budgets; experiences an increase in workload, and stress (Davidson, 1987); feels varying degrees of personal risk in using public transport, and may restrict her activities as a result (Atkins, Ch.9). In a recent survey, personal security was found to be the predominant concern or source of anxiety for working women (Atkins, Ch.9); considerations of personal security mean that, in addition to a **dense time-task co-ordination load**, the working woman also has to invest energy in organising safe routes or paths between home and the workplace. Considerable skill is required to effectively handle constraints such as these.

4.   The organising skills model

As has been seen, the domestic portfolio of activities is performed not just in one location, with one other person, at one point in time, but in **multiple and variable locations** with different persons at different times. Further, particular dynamic have considerable significance for organising skills: the location of activities has become considerably more dispersed in recent years (Pickup, Ch.11), the percentage of women working outside of the home has shown a steady increase (Gutek et al, 1986) and transport planning continues to support private facilities, particularly the car.

a)   Networking

It is clear that to achieve skilled performance people must move around their decision making environments - not just for the reasons already described - but to build and deploy informational and other resources to handle the **core problems** that characterise their organising.   In an abstract, and therefore general sense, the core problems of organising consist of working out: what is going on; and why (identification of issues); what to do about it; and the translation of these understandings into action.   In this sense, organising is all about practical knowledge (Hosking, 1988).

It seems that a major way in which actors move around to build and implement practical knowledge is **networking**. Networking consists of **building and mobilising social relationships** - relationships which provide information and other resources.   The relationships important for organising are often strong - depending upon practical understandings about **reciprocity**.   Agreements are **negotiated**, often tacitly, to **exchange information** (e.g. about the availability of facilities, about bus timetables, transport routes, and other resources) and **exchange of activities** (e.g. child minding for another whilst the other shops for both).   In these ways, actors build and mobilise relationships to help each other out.

Women invest a great deal in developing more or less extensive patterns of social relationships (Gilligan, 1982; Whipp and Grieco, Ch.1).   As has been shown elsewhere, these relationships may provide a very considerable resource for organising.   For example, close relationships may be developed and maintained within extended families so as to organise employment for the network as a whole.   A family member will migrate to a new source of employment and then provide the resources necessary to support the migration of the rest of the network.   The resources will include food and housing during job search, sponsorship with an employer and off-the-job training.   The resources shared will also be **informational** concerning, for example, potential threats to current employment and the reputational standing of potential employers (Grieco and Hosking, 1987; Brown and Hosking, 1986). The importance of female networking in arranging non-local sources of employment is by now well documented. From the perspective of the skills analysis presented here, it is important to note that women are involved in **long distance travel behaviour**, both as active participant and as **brokers** (Whipp and Grieco, Ch.1).

Networking has elsewhere been argued to facilitate skilful organising by building and mobilising four areas of practical knowledge or resource. These are referred to as **threats and opportunities, capacities and demands, dilemmas and domain specific knowledge and resources** (Brown and Hosking, 1986).

b)   Threats and opportunities

To handle the core problems which characterise their portfolio of activities, actors must work at building a practical understanding of issues and how to handle them. Issues can be regarded as changes, actual and potential, in the political environment of the domestic portfolio. Actors have changes happen to them, but they are also **agents**, within constraints, able to **initiate change**. In the case of the former, a transport authority may suspend a service, change routes, move to one person operated buses, and so on. Women might interpret in varying ways the significance of such changes for their domestic portfolio, and they might do so more or less collectively. Equally, they might do so with some skill: they might move around effectively so as better to understand what is going on (change as a threat or opportunity), why and what to do about it; skilful organising is partly a matter of skilful social construction of reality (Hosking and Morley, 1988).

There are many examples of changes women have initiated and negotiated so as to create opportunities for the protection and promotion of their values. In the public arena, the Women's Committee of the GLC use a variety of methods to give women influence over their transport services and transport environment (Goodwin, Ch.7). Separate initiatives in both Lewisham and Lambeth involved negotiations by local women with local authorities to get a 'women only' bus service to service short trips with flexible collects and stops.

There is a need for more ethnographic material which described women's perceptions of transport changes which they believe have major implications for their domestic portfolio. A potentially interesting example is found in the recent deregulation of the bus industry. This change could usefully be investigated to find out how women engaged in information search and interpretation concerning this possible threat or opportunity. It would be useful to know: how they searched for information on changes in fares, routes and schedules; how they more or less collectively interpreted the possible implications of these changes for their own portfolios of activities. In certain areas in the wake of deregulation (Pickup, Ch.11), there was often no written information at bus stops; information was often held in the public library where, for many, access would be difficult (time budget, cost) and changes were frequently made in schedules, routes and prices simultaneously.

c)   Capacities and demands

Social relationships can be used to facilitate the organising of the domestic portfolio: to reduce demands and to increase capacities. So, for example, a woman may draw upon her social network to obtain **escorts** for particular trips (Rhodes, Ch.5); women may often try to **synchronise** their timetables in order to do this. With an escort, a woman changes the meaning of the transport facility and environment - it converts from **threatening** to **defensible space**; in so doing, she can make a journey which she would fear to make on her own and, therefore, frequently **suppress.** Similarly, relationships may, in effect, be used to create **slack resources** (Galbraith, 1973). So, for example, neighbours or friends may care for a child after school until their mother returns from work (Pickup, Ch.11). This may help to resolve otherwise incompatible schedules, by permitting alternative sequencing of activities and flexibility in the **duration** of particular linked activities.

There are yet other ways in which strategic decisions may reduce demands or increase capacities. **Trip-chaining** (Rosenbloom, Ch.40 has been mentioned as a strategic sequence, or parallel processing, of tasks so as to reduce transport needs - to save a journey - and, therefore, to save time (scarce resource) for other activities. There may also be room to effect choice over which trips to chain; some links will be more constraining than others (e.g. because of bus schedules and times of work); similarly, choice may be critical for the reason that some combinations of activities produce more demands than others (e.g. escorting children form school, combined with shopping).

Lastly, brief mention may be made of the ways skill may be reflected in the **time links** between activities, and in the links **between the facilities** in which activities are performed. On first sight, to shop oout of peak hours is likely to require less time i.e. smaller or no queues for service and payment, car parking easier to obtain. However, such timing may be constrained by other activities in the portfolio (e.g. the hours of paid employment). Organisation and control may be achieved by obtaining and implementing knowledge of alternative shopping facilities with more convenient opening times (Guy and Wrigley, 1987).

This alternative is likely to be weighed in relation to other sources of decisional complexity such as the **geographical proximity** of (linked) activities (shops close to work, at point of inter-change, etc.), the potential for exchange of activities with male partner (Jones, Ch.3), and so on.

d)   Dilemmas

Dilemmas are endemic to organising because decisions have to be made between courses of action which seem to imply costs **whichever policy is adopted.**   Brown and Hosking (1986) have identified four analytically separable dilemmas.   First, there are those that derive from difficulties in managing relationships.   Second, are dilemmas concerning resource limitations and trade offs (see Goodwin, Ch.7 on the role of such trade offs in the public acceptance of one person operation).   Third, there are those arising from activities: what to do, how, when, where, for how long.   Fourth, there are those that follow from potential links between values about means and values about ends.

Where organising the domestic portfolio is concerned, there is the well known dilemma of whether to abandon paid employment in favour of personal provision of child care (Wells, Ch.10).   This **choice between activities** may also be seen to be compounded, for example, with choices about resources (e.g. balancing the short and long term), and relationships (e.g. how to be assertive about career without damaging relationships with partner).

The materials presented in this book reveal a number of decisional conflicts in which transport issues are implicated.   For example, there are areas of paid employment, performed by women, which demand a good deal of travelling (Wells, Ch.10). Yet many of the resources which allow them effectively to organise their portfolio may be termed **location specific capital** (Davanzo and Morrison, 19780.   In other words, many of their resources may not easily be found or transferred elsewhere: this dilemma will be particularly acute if much reliance is placed on social relationships i.e. for child minding, - a resource not easily transferred.   A similar phenomenon exists where a woman, in deciding whether to give up employment in the short term interest of personal child care, has to take account of the long term prospect of obtaining a commensurate job, when she decides to recommence as a full-time wage earner (Oakley, 1987; Hamilton and Jenkins, Ch.2).

e)   Other kinds of knowledge and resource

Organising is performed in the context of choices and constraints.   Greater choice, and, therefore, scope for organising skills cna be achieved when the organiser has **detailed knowledge of their decision making environment** and other resources, whatever they are, to make that knowledge practical. The exact content of this knowledge, and the nature of the other resources will depend upon the particular portfolio of activities and the decisional environment in which they are carried out. So for example, general managers have been found to be exceptionally knowledgeable about certain technical aspects of their environment; such as customers, production technologies, suppliers, competitors and so on (Kotter, 1982).

Here, the particular interest has been in the woman's portfolio of activities and how this might relate to gender, and to transport issues. No attempt has been made to focus down on particular activities in that portfolio, or on choices and constraints in relation to particular modes of transport or particular transport environments. If more detailed analysis were conducted of particular activities, it would be found that some women, at least, have extensive knowledge bases - comparable with those of the general manager. These include, for example, knowledge of: possibilities for employment in the local labour market; transport services and their links with places of employment; child care facilities; financial benefits that might be claimed for travel e.g. for hospital visits (Pickup, 1988) and funerals, and so on.

5. Conclusions

Not all women are equally skilled in organising their domestic portfolio. For this reason, it is preferable to avoid describing jobs or activities as, in themselves, skilled. Rather, the person, part shaped by, and part shaping their context, may be said to engage in more or less skilled performances. Perhaps the most general way of describing differences between the more and less skilled is that the former know what it is they need to know: experts, as compared with novices, know what kind of core problems they face and, therefore, know what will be efficient strategies for handling them.

It has been argued that knowledge of this kind cannot be achieved without moving around the decisional environment to search for information, to test alternative interpretations, to influence and effect choice. Skilled actors appreciate the importance of moving around in this special sense: they understand its significance for the learning and implimentation of skilful practice. Consider, as a last example, the relationship between **perceived safety** and **travel frequency**. The meanings attached to particular modes of transport and travel environments differ depending on the frequency with which they are used. Those who travel more find travel less fearful (Focas, Ch.8; Atkins, Ch.9) and create a **positive feedback loop**; those who avoid travel create a negative feedback loop, with learning - essential for the acquisition and implimentation of skill - being avoided. Skill is achieved through understanding the choices that could and must be exercised for organisation and control. It is hoped that this chapter has gone some way towards showing how and why women's skills might better be appreciated.

7 Problems of women's mobility and employment in the one person operation of buses

PHIL GOODWIN

1.   The context: one person operation of buses in London

The traditional mode of operation of buses was to have a driver - usually a man - in the cab, and a conductor - often a woman - collecting fares and assisting passengers. In the 1960s, the decline in bus demand and the increasing costs of operation were causing increasing financial strain.   With Government encouragement, bus operators in most towns proceeded to convert to one person operation (OPO).

In London, however, problems of the extra delays and congestion caused by OPO buses dictated greater caution, with 47% of miles run being converted by 1979 and 53% by 1983.   In September 1983, London Transport submitted a proposal to the Greater London Council that one person operation should be increased to 65%, with a longer term plan to convert to 100%. The proposal was strongly opposed by the Chairman of the GLC Transport Committee and reservations were expressed by a wide range of institutions and organisations representing passengers, motorists, police and other interests.

At that stage the Greater London Council with the agreement of London Transport invited the author to carry out a detailed independent assessment of the proposal. This report was submitted to the GLC in March 1985 but the abolition of that authority, increased commercial pressures on London Regional Transport, and the prospect of deregulation of buses in London meant that this detailed assessment was almost immediately overtaken by events.

Most of the work conducted did not focus on questions of gender, but on narrower questions of transport efficiency and broader questions of employment and public expenditure. (A summary of these findings is included in the Appendix to this chapter). However, important gender issues did arise and these will now be described.

2.   **Gender issues involved in the conversion to one person operation**

Two broad groups of problems were evident. These were:

a) the impact of one person operation on passenger requirements and

b) the impact of one person operation on job opportunities.

In written evidence, the Women's Committee Support Unit of the GLC (which included women professionals and also activists) summarised their key concerns.

"Conductors on buses often do a good deal more than collect fares: they give advice and information to passengers; help to the less able-bodied, elderly or people travelling with children or heavy shopping; they can give a greater feeling of security for people travelling at night. On the Underground also passengers may feel more secure travelling in a carriage with a guard, particularly at night. While it is recognised that conductors themselves are often vulnerable to personal attack, their help to the travelling public is vital and should be continued."

"Reductions in two person operation are also likely to affect women's employment on London Transport. At present 20% of conductors are women but only 1% of drivers are women".

In both of these concerns, a very clear line of argument emerged, namely, that the conversion to one person operation of buses caused greater hardship or difficulty to women passengers than men, and, similarly, reduced the employment opportunities of women more than those of men. But with both these fields of argument, there were also quite complex counter arguments, especially where, for example, due to financial constraints, the alternatives to OPO were felt to be even worse.

3.   Requirements of passengers

A survey was carried out for the GLC in May 1983, which indicated a two to one majority for reducing the one person operation of buses.   On the other hand, a survey was carried out for London Transport in July 1983 which showed slightly more people in favour of OPO than against it.

It is necessary to consider this conflict of evidence in more detail in order to try and explain the differences and judge which is the more accurate.   Both surveys were carried out by the same market research agency (Harris Research Centre), approximately the same sample size (1047 and 996 respectively), and the same sort of methodology (an interviewer administered questionnaire, carried out in the home, with a statistically representative sample of adults).   There are no obvious major differences in the samples in terms of age, sex and other characteristics.

In most cases, questions were worded differently but one question was asked in nearly the same way in the two surveys, about general satisfaction with the buses as shown in Table 7.1.

Table 7.1.   Satisfaction with bus services

| | GLC survey | LT Survey | | |
		Total	Male	Female
Very satisfactory	5%	8%	11%	6%
Satisfactory	51%	55%	57%	53%
Unsatisfactory	33%	27%	24%	29%
Very unsatisfactory	10%	11%	8%	13%

(GLC question: "How satisfactory are the bus services provided by London Transport?"

LTE question: "How satisfactory are the bus services provided by London Transport in this area?)

It is noticeable that women gave a consistently lower rating than men, but the difference is not very great.   On the precise topic of one person operation, the questions take a more differentiated form, as shown in Tables 7.2 and 7.3.

Table 7.2.   GLC question on one person operation

Do you think that the use of one-man operated buses should be:

Withdrawn altogether from all routes:	24%
Restricted to suburban routes with a few passengers only:	40%
Extended to all suburban routes:	17%

Extended to all routes including those in Central
London: 17%

Table 7.3.   LT question on one person operation

Generally speaking, are you in favour of or against one man
operated buses in this area?

	Total	Male	Female
In favour	41%	40%	43%
Against	39%	43%	36%
Don't know/ no opinion	20%	18%	21%

Here there are again only very small differences in the
balance of opinion between men and women, and these appear
to give a slightly more pro-OPO view among women, a point
which conflicted with other expressions of opinion and is
further discussed below.

It is well established that different ways of asking
related questions have a big effect on the results. The LT
survey went on to consider two possible influences on views
about OPO: first, the sort of buses people were used to
and, secondly, the effect of having to choose between, say,
reduced fares and two person operation.

There was a much greater hostility to OPO in areas where
there is mainly crew operation. LT comment:

"Respondents tended to favour the type of operation that
they were most familiar with.....This implies that
conversion of a route to OPO is, after the event, likely
to give rise to less adverse public reaction than would
be anticipated."

Alternatively, it may be the case that the routes which
have already been converted to OPO are indeed those which
were most suitable to it, and recognised as such by
passengers.   If this is the explanation, then further
conversion would give rise to increasingly intense adverse
public reaction.

Thus the two different explanations of the survey results
have directly opposite implications for policy.   It is,
therefore, of great importance to further investigate the
question of adaptation to OPO, this issue receives further
discussion below.   Questions were asked in the LT survey
about relative preferences for fares and crew operations;
by contrast, the context of the GLC survey was the

130

examination of preferences on transport policy generally, with fares being weighed against GLC ir Government support. In both surveys there was an obvious reluctance by respondents to approve of fares increases.

To summarise, both surveys agree in suggesting that the opposition to OPO in certain suburban areas is less than for busier or more central areas, and also in emphasising the importance in acceptability of OPO of ticketing, queueing and speed. They appear to disagree in the overall balance of opinion, though there is some reason to argue that this is in part due to differences in the wording of the surveys.

The two most important unresolved questions are:

a) the suggestion that people's attitudes to OPO are substantially influenced by the context of the question, especially the choice between crew operation and fares, and

b) that there is a process of adaptation with people eventually learning to like the new services.

These issues were further investigated by means of a series of in-depth discussions and a further survey.

a)   In depth discussions

Six tape recorded group discussions were organised with members of the public in Romford, Thornton Heath, Brixton and East Ham.   Each lasted from 1.5 hours to 2 hours with encouragement to range much more widely over the issues than is possible when using a questionnaire.   The groups were defined as shown in Table 7.4.

Discussions of this sort are not intrended to provide statistically significant analyses of public opinion; rather, they are much more effective at going outside the constraints of a conventional questionnaire, giving an understanding of possible cause and effect processes, and providing an important safety net in case important questions have not been asked, or asked in the wrong way.

Table 7.4. Groups for in-depth interview

	Group	Men	Women
		Attendance	
1.	Women with young children	–	4
2.	Frequent bus users	–	9
3.	Young people aged 17-24	4	4
4.	Women without young children	–	5
5.	Elderly people aged 65-74	2	6
6.	Infrequent bus users	1	7

(Groups 2, 5 and 6 were intended to have a more equal balance of men and women, but it was found difficult to persuade enough men to attend the discussions.)

b)   General attitudes

Adopting this methodology, by far the most dominant reaction was one of dislike and this cut across all the different groups, with only secondary differences of emphasis. One person operation with new doored buses was seen by many of the discussants as characterised by only three advantages - namely

warmth

safety from falling off a bus

the likelihood that you will be able to push onto the bus

None of these advantages was agreed by everybody. But the disadvantages were much more extensive, including (not in order of importance):

slow journeys

having to queue too long

vandalism and a threatening environment upstairs

doors prevent you jumping on and off between stops - and also to avoid trouble if it starts

crushed travelling conditions, being boxed in, panic

no help with shopping, children, pushchairs

hassles about change

harassment to think about too many things at once, when getting on

can't get to the door in time

young children separated from parents (by doors or while paying)

very jerky rides, 'boneshakers'

insecure seats, easy to fall off

inadequate stanchions or straps while standing

danger of catching bags or arm in doors

dirty, graffiti

difficulties for fat people

useless failed self service ticket machine - 'that thing'

steep and awkward stairs

barriers in silly places

unfriendly and stressed drivers

can't wait on bus at terminus

c)   Security

Several women reported that they simply would not go
upstairs in one person operated buses at all, and treated
the upper derck as a no-go area characterised by noise,
smoke, violence and threats of violence.

"I'd rather stand downstairs than go upstairs".

"It's nerve wracking on a bus at night. No way I'd go
upstairs on a bus....I sit by the driver."

Additional points emerging were that the availability of,
and response to, bus radios is perceived as inadequate, and
that two person operation with a woman driver and a man
conductor is viewed as the best from the point of both
quality of driving and security - or perhaps, the second
best:

"The best form of security is being on a bus with a lot
of other people - a lot of them women."

Two particular issues were discussed in some depth.
First, it is emphasised that feelings of security must be
considered as important, quite apart form the actual rate
of attacks or harassment, since these feelings will
directly influence the amount of use people make of buses.

Secondly, it is clear that security is a wider question
than simply whether there are conductors; the location of
bus stops, the frequency of buses and the density of bus
routes all affect security, since they determine where and
how long the passenger has to walk and stand. When there
is a direct choice between one and another of these
aspects, there can, therefore, be competing claims on
resources.

Some suggestions were made that routes and bus stop
locations could be altered for the least secure times-
specifically after the evening peak from about 7 p.m.,
until after pubs have emptied and people got home by about

11.30 p.m.. In this case, it was suggested that these hours were when conductors were most needed.

Statistical data on matters affecting passenger security are weak. Fights and assaults on passengers reported to the LT Communications Centre in 1983 totalled 264 (compared with over 1,000 assaults on staff which, however, would tend to have a higher reporting rate). These would tend to be only the more serious incidents. Verbal threats, harassment not leading to physical assault and generally offensive behaviour would not be reported. There are about 90% more reported fights per bus mile on OPO than on crew buses (2.3 compared with 1.2 fights per bus mile). The differences are just statistically significant at the 5% level.

There was some tendency for women to mention problems of security more than men, though not exclusively. It was a man (an infrequent bus user), for example, who referred to what happens upstairs:

"schoolkids .... the language that comes out - a load of yobs swinging around and gobbing out the windows - I don't agree with that - I wouldn't take my baby on it."

c)   The convenience of the encumbered traveller

Women are, most frequently, the ones affected by travelling difficulties with shopping, pushchairs and young children, and also, because of the age structure of the population, there are a great number of elderly women. The conductor is seen as of central importance for such groups for two reasons. First, the conductor is able to offer help:

"Some of them pride themselves on how quickly they can whip a buggy off the bus."

and secondly the experience of getting on a bus with a conductor is less stressful:

"There's a chance to catch your breath before getting the money ready - it cuts down on the number of things to think about at once."

Contrast this with the description given by a bus driver of his own and colleagues' practice when driving without a conductor:

"You get a young wife with a pram and two children. The driver just says "Come on, love, we can't stay here all day" ".

There is also a particular sensitivity about the separation of children from parents with OPO - in getting on, because the child is sent off on its own to get a seat, to be out of the way while its mother is paying the fare, and also in getting off, where on a crowded bus the doors can close before everybody is off. An incident was described where a child and parent were separated in this way - the problem was solved by urgent shouts to the driver. Such an event does not happen often, but when it does it is a very disturbing experience for both parent and child. It should be noted that representatives of women's organisations do not feel that their suggestions on bus design - especially related to steps, luggage space, and stanchions - have been sympathetically received by LT.

It was not only mothers with young children who mentioned difficulties with children and pushchairs, and the question of the 'jerkiness' of bus travel came up with every group- so that even the youngest and the fittest noted

"those front seats, they're death traps, man".

These aspects, when they occur together, often add up to a general feeling of pressure and harrassment:

"with your shopping and a pushchair and a child of four ......they don't give you a chance to sit down."

In some cases, people actually said that they would let an OPO bus go by and wait for a conductor bus to arrive.

4.   Adaptation and modification of attitudes

Here we consider not the static picture - do people like OPO? - but the process of change and adaptation over time. There are two aspects of importance concerning the short term effect of widening the context of discussion (costs, fares, unemployment), and the adaptation of attitudes as people get used to OPO after its introduction.

a)   Costs, fares, unemployment

In each group, after about one to one and an half hours of largely unprompted discussion, the interviewer put for discussion a topic (based essentially on the LT survey question) about whether people would prefer lower fares or crew operation. By this point, the disadvantages of OPO, of doors, or both had been stressed more strongly than the advantages by participants in every group.

As had been suggested in the LT survey, such a question reduced the firmness with which OPO was rejected, and in every case, there was a degree of argument about the preferences shown in Table 7.5. (In group 5, there was a vote, but in all the other cases the balance of opinion shown would represent a fair chairman summing up a debated consensus).

Table 7.5. Group views on whether to choose lower fares or crew operation

Group

Balance of opinion

1.Women with young children	For two person operation
2.Frequent bus users	For lower fares
3.Young people	For two person operation
4.Women without young children	For two person operation
5.Elderly people	For two person operation with new buses
6.Infrequent bus users	For lower fares.

Note that Group 5 was the only one in which there was an explicit separation of 'new buses' (liked by this group, for the doors and the warmth) from OPO as such (disliked for the reasons stated above). An important aspect of these results, however, is the actual process of argument and discussion which led to them, which is not possible in a standardised questionnaire. Using this method, there were important differences emerging from among the groups.

Taking first the groups who maintained their opposition to one person operation, it was quite clear that the question was not easily answered - partly because its basic premises simply were not agreed. Thus:

If all buses were OPO "you wouldn't get a decrease in fares.......you would get a worse service." (Group 1)

"Is that the promise... if you make those men redundant we'll get a better service". (Group 1)

"How do you make out it's cheaper?" (Group 3)

"What are they going to do? Go down or stay the same as they are?" (Group 3)

"We're just being conned all the way...." (Group 3)

"The fares will go up anyway." (Group 3)

In other words, there is doubt about whether the choice is a real one, and certainly disbelief that fares would come down if OPO were extended. (A similar feature is often seen in surveys about, for example, 'rates or fares', because nobody believes that rates would come down anyway).

An additional aspect is the ease of coming to a choice, one way or the other. The group of 17-24 year olds was the most concerned about the fare levels in the earlier part of the discussion, yet also found it fairly easy to express a preference for higher fares once the question had been accepted; it was a group with very high unemployment, and they could not accept reductions in the number of jobs:

"that's more people on the dole, if you put it that way."

Group 1, the women with young children, found it more
difficult. Following acceptance of the question, there was
a long silence, broken by a doubtful:

"I don't think I'll pay for a conductor."

which was later followed by

"the only thing is, more men will lose their jobs...
they'll have to pay them more money if they lose their
jobs ....it's the same money."

The issue here is a more general one than simply the
exact wording of a question, important though that is.
Rather, it appears that the whole context within which the
question is put and discussed will influence people's
declared preferences. The attempt to put a two way choice
(fares or conductors) tended to be both resisted and
transformed by respondents into a three way choice (fares,
conductors, unemployment).

A further insight is suggested by comparing Groups 2 and
6, the frequent and infrequent bus users, both situated in
a mainly OPO area and similar in other respects.

The frequent bus users had the least difficulty in
accepting the choice as a real one

"I'd rather do without the conductors and keep the fares
down."

"People like myself, there's no need of a conductor. I
just want to get on the bus."

There was relatively little hesitation about opting for
the lower fares choice, quite quickly. It was only later
that the question of unemployment was raised by the
interviewer, and this caused some discomfort:

"You're saying x number of people have got to lose their
jobs so we can have lower fares - that's a terrible
responsibility."

But even so, the preference expressed was reasonably
clear. The infrequent users battled against the question
for a considerable period, trying to challenge its
assumptions, for example

"the fares used to be lower when we had a conductor"

"more people would use the buses if the fares came down"

and so on. When finally persuaded by the interviewer to
accept for discussion the proposition that OPO buses might
indeed be cheaper, the response was uncomfortable

"People like us ....we would have to be forced to pick the lower fare. It wouldn't be a choice really."

Thus while both groups opted for the lower fares, the interpretation is quite different.

b)   Adaptation to OPO

Extending the comparison of the frequent and infrequent bus users group, it was noticeable that some of the frequent bus users were the only ones who explicitly talked of "getting used to OPO" in terms similar to the LT hypothesis referred to above.

"We didn't like them at first. Nobody liked them at first. In retrospect when you look back and you know you're going to get on the next bus, it is for the better. Things couldn't stay the way they were."

"We've all got used to the one man buses."

(Even here, the preference was modified by an immediate return to talking about how nice and friendly the old buses used to be, and how much more reliable the buses were 10 or 15 years ago - though not 4-5 years ago.)

No similar process was noted amongst the infrequent users, who said

"It's got worse over the last year or so."

nor in the other groups, though one of the women with young children pointed out

"We've only got preferences now because there's a choice...before, nobody ever suggested that you did away with conductors ...it was just the service people wanted improved."

The group of young people also felt that things were getting worse - especially in relation to violence

"It's getting worse since 1983 - there's a lot of wickedness about now."

Before drawing conclusions from this about the process of adapting to OPO, we consider the specific issue of changing attitudes to, and behaviour of, bus staff.

5.   Attitudes to bus staff

With the exception of the young group (whose rather more complex attitudes are referred to below), there was a

138

surprising degree of unanimity about conductors and drivers. Three conclusions emerge strongly.

First, conductors are warmly appreciated.

"When there are conductors, they always help."

"You used to get to know the conductors ...it makes for a bit of feeling on the bus."

"The (conductors on) old buses used to help you on with the pushchair."

It may be that this warmth about a golden age in the past is sometimes exaggerated but, nevertheless, it was firmly and widely stated. In public relations terms, conductors are clearly a success.

Secondly, that warmth is not transferred to the driver-operator, about whom there are many negative feelings

"Staff are less polite now ...some of the drivers don't care about anything." (Group 1)

"The bus drivers used to wait for you - stop wherever they are. They see you running now, they put their foot down. It's a completely different attitude." (Group 2)

"Most of them don't want to know." (Group 6)

(when drivers go past)

"I don't think they want to see, a lot of the time." (Group 4)

It should be noted that sometimes these negative feelings take the form of suggestions that drivers deliberately adopt practices causing intense annoyance to passengers e.g. bunching, late running or "playing cards while passengers are waiting in the rain" at the end of the route. Such suggestions may be based on extremely small numbers of cases, since the aggravation caused tends to encourage exaggeration but this then contributes to a general mode of dissatisfaction with the quality of services offered.

Thirdly, there is even so some feeling of sympathy or understanding for the OPO driver

"You can't blame them, can you?"

"It's tiring.....frustrating...stressful...a lot of them suffer from backache." (Group 6)

"Let one man do one job ...it's too much of a strain, trying to do everything." (Group 4)

"Some seem to hate their job ...... I don't think a lot of them like those one man buses...."

"It's a very frustrating job, I wouldn't like to do it." (Group 2)

Putting these attitudes together, there is some support for the idea that the decline in service, friendliness and support to passengers is seen as being because of the greater strain put on the driver-operator of a one person bus. There would then be a vicious circle effect, with passengers and drivers getting increasingly unfriendly to each other. (A similar suggestion has been put strongly by drivers: see below).

Such features are seen in a particular strong form in the discussion of the young group, who tend to expect a certain amount of antagonism from both driver and conductor

"they think they can take liberties".

However, the driver seems to be seen most negatively - both in the case of the one person bus

"they show you up on the microphone, in front of everybody"

and the crew bus

"the driver comes round ready for a fight."

whereas the conductor is sometimes seen as more tactful. Paradoxically, there was some feeling that the driver of a crew bus should come round as a sort of independent arbitrator, rather than automatically taking the conductor's side.

6. Evidence from the third survey

Because of the conflict of evidence and interpretations, a third survey was organised in March 1984 specifically to investigate the questions of preferences in different areas and passenger adaptation. The questions were worded as far as possible in such a way as to assist comparisons between the differently worded GLC and LT surveys. However, for reasons of economy and speed the sample size was halved (to 501) and the interviews were carried out by telephone, so exact comparability was not achieved.

This survey produced further evidence on the possibility of adaptation and changes in reactions over time. The starting point was a clear finding as in the earlier surveys that the feeling in favour of OPO was mainly in OPO areas and the feeling against OPO was mainly in two person operation bus areas. This is consistent with two conflicting theories - the idea that people get used to

OPO and the alternative idea that OPO had until then only been introduced in areas for which it is relatively suitable.

To take this further, a question was asked about whether respondents in general were now using buses more or less than they used to. The exact time scale was not defined but they were asked to confine the comparison to the time since they were living in that area. (Of course the reasons for travelling more or less will include all sorts of changes in personal circumstances, which for any individual will generally be more important than whether this area has buses with conductors. These other factors will include reasons for increasing bus use approximately as often as for reductions). Table 7.6 shows these results.

Table 7.6. Change in bus use

Bus services in the area	More	Less	Same	Sample
Mainly OPO	23%	24%	56%	237
Mainly 2PO	30%	15%	55%	107
Mixed	25%	32%	42%	156
Attitude to OPO in the area				
In favour	26%	24%	51%	225
Against	21%	28%	51%	191

It is noted that in OPO areas (where opinion in favour of OPO is strongest), the larger proportion of passengers report a decline in their bus use (for whatever reasons). This decline is strongest amongst those who oppose OPO. While the sample sizes are small, and the problem complex, the table does lend some support to the suggestions that people have, over a period, been voting with their feet. This suggests that the theory that "people will get used to OPO" while comforting, should be treated with great reserve.

The survey also investigated the effect on preferences of introducing questions about the effects of OPO, especially fares reductions and unemployment. This is shown in Table 7.7.

Table 7.7. Attitude to extension of OPO

	If 10% fare reduction			If job losses at LT		
	Total	Male	Female	Total	Male	Female
Yes	67%	63%	70%	22%	28%	17%
No	30%	33%	27%	74%	67%	79%
Don't know	3%	3%	3%	5%	5%	4%

In spite of the small sample sizes, the effect here is quite clear. If OPO were to result in a 10% fare reduction then there is a 2 to 1 majority expressing views in favour. If it were to result in job losses at LT, there is a 3 to 1 majority expressing views against. In both cases, the majorities among women were greater than among men - i.e. women were more strongly against OPO if it caused unemployment and more strongly in favour of it if it resulted in fare reductions. This means that a greater proportion of women were forced with having to resolve a contradiction in choosing between two unsatisfactory alternatives. This may explain why in the earlier surveys women and men had rather similar views expressed statistically but not when judged by the degree of complaint and conviction.

Thus making these conditions explicit has a very large effect indeed on the balance of opinion. It follows that the implicit assumptions made about these factors by respondents in the earlier surveys may also have had an effect on their answers and this would be influenced by, for example, public awareness of problems of inflation or unemployment at the times of the surveys.

7.   The impact on employment opportunities

There was concern about employment on three levels. Firstly, it was felt that the disappearance of conductors jobs (and also other support jobs within London Transport) was reducing employment in all the types of jobs which have been relatively easy for women to obtain.

Secondly, it was felt that there were inadequate channels for women to become drivers in London Transport, either by transferring from conductors or from outside. The suggestion is that a higher standard was applied to women in training, together with generally unsympathetic attitudes.

Thirdly, there was a local effect. Many women were constrained only to seek local jobs and if conversion to OPO occurs on a garage by garage basis a whole set of local jobs will in effect be removed even if other garages elsewhere stay crew or remain mixed.

LT provided statistics on bus applicants and recruits by gender, and these are shown in Table 7.8.

Table 7.8.   Analysis of bus recruits by age and sex
1.1.83-1.11.83

	-24	25-29	30-34	35-39	40-44	45-49	50-54	55-59	60+	Tot
APPLICANTS:										
Drivers:										
Men:										
	2263	1736	1212	937	634	430	210	84	4	7510
Women:										
	50	27	13	12	8	3	0	1	0	114
Conductors:										
Men:										
	1653	512	281	168	146	92	37	19	0	2908
Women:										
	280	78	31	29	13	9	1	0	0	441
ACCEPTED FOR TRAINING:										
Driver:										
Men:										
	214	219	159	151	78	42	15	2	0	850
Women:										
	1	4	0	3	2	0	0	0	0	10
Conductors:										
Men:										
	136	55	27	21	21	9	1	2	0	272
Women:										
	39	7	6	4	2	2	0	0	0	60

It is clear that there was a higher proportion of younger workers, and women among those accepted for training as conductors than as drivers. A large part of the reason for this is simply that so many more men than women apply to be drivers - 66 men applicants to be a driver for every woman.   For conductors there were just under 7 men applicants to each woman. However, the success rates are also different, as shown in Table 9.

Table 7.9.   Success rates in acceptance of training

	Driver	Conductor
Men	12%	9%
Women	9%	14%

(This table does not indicate successful completion of training.)

It is also the case that pass rates for transfer from conductor to driver were very much better for men than for women.   Earlier work carried out by LT in 1982 indicated that pass rates are related to age, sex, whether a car licence is held, and citizenship; the age and sex elements of this are shown in Table 7.10.

Table 7.10. Conductor to driver pass rates (%)

Age	-20	21-24	25-29	30-34	35-39	40-44	45-49	50-54	55-59
Men:	64	53	36	23	14	9	5	4	4
Women:	46	38	28	20	13	7	3	1	0

These figures do not show whether there are practices within LT that discriminate against women or whether the barriers to application, acceptance and transfer are outside of LT's control. In any case, they do confirm that, under current conditions, progression to OPO would bear significantly on women's employment prospects within LT. Four times as many women apply to be a conductor as apply to be a driver, six times as many currently get accepted.

It might be added that the conductor's job has in no sense been earmarked for women. In absolute numbers, more men apply for and are accepted as conductors than women and it has been observed elsewhere that in times of recession women are sometimes displaced by men even in traditionally women's jobs.

Finally, we note that women drivers are popular - most groups had an anecdote about the high quality of their one or two local women drivers. There was more than one report that women drivers are not encouraged by LT, for example

"I do hear it's very hard for the women to be accepted by LT ...you have to battle... my friend (a conductor who applied to be a driver)... she came up against a lot."

If it is true that the small number of women drivers are indeed of noticeably high quality then the causes for this may include pressures which require a woman driver to be better than a man in order to succeed, but the evidence on this is not strong enough to reach a definite conclusion on the matter. In any event, one suggestion was that the ideal combination was a woman driver (for quality of driving) with a man conductor (in case of trouble), which is the exact opposite of the classic division of roles.

8.   Conclusion

There are four conclusions which may be drawn from this study. Firstly, one person operation does have some significant disadvantages for the passenger. These disadvantages include some which are more strongly felt by women passengers than by men, especially the absence of help with pushchairs, shopping, etc. from a conductor, and feelings of insecurity.

Secondly, reduction in the number of conductor jobs is likely to bear more heavily on women than would an equivalent reduction in the number of driver jobs.

Thirdly, interpretation of the evidence on public response is greatly influenced by how the choices are presented - for example, effects on fare levels and on unemployment create a dilemma whose constraints the private citizen feels unable to resolve and which increases the feeling of resentment without giving clear guidance to policy.

Fourthly, statistical differences in attitude between men and women about the conversion to OPO exist, but they are not very large. In general, concerns expressed by women were also expressed by men.

Finally it should be said that this exercise has in part been overtaken by events. The growth of mini-bus services, for example, raises questions of one person operation in rather a different form than when applied to conventional big buses. In addition, reduction in the amount of subsidy available and increasing reliance on deregulated market forces will certainly influence the extent and manner in which factors such as those discussed here will be considered by bus operators.

Appendix

Extracts from summary of **One person operation of buses in London**. P.B. Goodwin, Oxford University Transport Studies Unit, Report 287, March, 1985.

There were two main parts to the economic evaluation which LT carried out: a financial estimate of the cash costs and savings to London Transport and a social assessment which gives money value to the delays, accidents and some other costs and benefits to travellers.

London Transport estimated that conversion to 100% OPO would initially save £57.2m but 57% of this is taken up with increased cash costs and reduced revenue of operating OPO buses. A further 24% is offset by time losses to passengers and delays to other traffic. A small sum increases the benefit due to reduced accidents to bus passengers and a final £7.4 m worth of benefit is gained by passengers as a result of the knock on benefits of the fares reduction or other improvements that can be bought with the remaining financial saving. Overall LT estimated that conversion to 65% and then 100% OPO would be worthwhile.

Discussion of elements included in the LT evaluation

1. Effects on passengers

The evidence in the LT submissions confirms that other things being equal, conversion to OPO will offer a lower quality of service to passengers. This is broadly consistent with the results of various opinion surveys, which confirm that conductors provide much appreciated practical and public relations services. However, there are conflicts of evidence in these surveys about passenger attitudes to OPO, with a greater resistance to OPO in areas at present served by crew buses. Consideration of the surveys suggests that there is a complex process of adjustment and adaptation by passengers which is likely to have four main effects:

a) Attitudes to OPO are influenced by the general condition of public transport (fares, service levels, etc.). If these get worse, passenger resistance to OPO is likely to increase; if they get better, it is likely to reduce.

b) Over a period, at least some of those people who continue using public transport may reduce their initial opposition, as they become accustomed to new features of the service.

c) However, other passengers will not reduce their opposition, and there will be an increasing loss of passengers over a long period than is currently taken into account. This is likely to erode the financial advantage of OPO.

d) Passenger attitudes to OPO are influenced by what they perceive as being the main consequences. A majority would be in favour if it caused substantial fares reductions: however, a majority would be against if it caused increased unemployment.

2.   Benefits

The biggest estimated benefit of OPO in the LT evaluation is the reduction in fares which could be achieved with the cost savings. This figure is nearly 80% of the estimated traveller benefits. The benefit is assessed using the results of some studies which show that the social benefits of fares reductions are greater than their cost. However, if cost savings will in practice be 'clawed back' by the Government in reduced subsidy, then it would be correct to include this element in the calculation of traveller benefit. This would reduce the total estimated net benefit by about a third.

3.   Boarding times

The calculations for 100% OPO (unlike those for 65% OPO) assume a very substantial improvement in boarding times, to 2.5 seconds per passenger. This assumption must be treated with great caution, as operating conditions in Central London at present are likely to cause greater, rather than less boarding delay. The general view of interested parties who were consulted including those in favour of 65% was to view the possibility of successful OPO in Central London with great doubts, and then only if the improvements in boarding times were achieved. Otherwise, it is unlikely that 100% OPO would be operationally or financially advantageous and it would certainly cause serious problems of delay to bus passengers and other road users.

Discussion of elements not in the LT evaluation

1.   Employment and public expenditure

The LT framework does not take into account effects on the national and regional economy of which the most important are employment and public expenditure.
      Increased unemployment represents a cost to the Exchequer of the order of £5,000 per year per job lost. Considering conversion to 65% OPO a net loss of 1000 jobs would represent £5m per annum cost in public expenditure. About one third of this represents a transfer from taxpayer to unemployed, the rest being a reduction in

receipts from the unemployed, derived from the economic value of the output or services they would otherwise produce. For 100% OPO the costs would be broadly pro rata but there is the additional difficulty of forecasting the state of the economy in 5 or 10 years time.

When jobs are lost, there is a reduction in consumer expenditure and this has a further effect on shops, suppliers, etc. However, the effect is offset by some extra spending generated by higher OPO drivers' wages and employment in the bus supply industry. It is suggested that the net effect would be a loss of about 50% as many jobs again.

The additional public expenditure cost, using the same assumptions as above, is approximately £2.2m p.a. from 65% OPO.

There are additional effects on economic activity generally which are likely to lead to a reduction in national income over a period of three or four years. Current official thinking suggests that from about the fifth year the increased unemployment would lead to reduced wages, increased productivity, higher exports, and renewed growth which would after another three or four years more offset the earlier decline. However, current thinking is also that increased public expenditure would have the opposite effect by crowding out manufacturing investment. There is no consensus on the long term effects on the economy of simultaneous increases in unemployment and the public sector borrowing requirement.

2. Driver stress and assaults

The evidence is partial but what there is all points in the same direction i.e. that OPO driving is more stressful especially in those circumstances where passengers themselves dislike OPO operation. The stress has one of two effects. The first response is for drivers to reduce the stressful character of the job by reducing any source of conflict with the passengers (e.g. not challenging over riding) increasing mental ease at the expense of doing the job properly. The alternative response is to undertake both tasks conscientiously, sometimes at the expense of greater agitation and worse relations with passengers.

There is some indirect evidence that these responses are related to age and experience.

There is a conflict of view between LT and Unions about the relative risk of assaults to OPO drivers. The balance of evidence is that there are fewer assaults, and that this is partly a result of the 'avoid trouble' strategy of drivers.

Conclusion

London Transport have proposed to extend one person operation in a way that is intended to soften the blow as much as possible, by achieving very substantial improvements in boarding times, running more buses to compensate for slower speeds and unreliability and ploughing the remaining savings back into fare reductions.

It remains to be seen whether the improved boarding times can be achieved: without them the social and operational case for OPO in Central London falls and the financial case is in doubt. It is also possible that external constraints will put greater pressure on LT to convert to OPO without running the planned extra buses, or reducing fares. If this is the case, then OPO extension may well turn out to be financially worthwhile, but would not be justifiable by considerations of traffic and passenger costs and benefits.

If 20% of unemployment costs are included in the calculations and if all LT's other assumptions are correct, this would tip the balance so that conversion to OPO should be done in such a way that employment should be maintained and the staff used for service improvements. If all unemployment costs are included, it would not at present be worthwhile to proceed with further OPO conversion.

8 A survey of women's travel needs in London

CARALAMPO FOCAS

1.   Introduction

Women's main concerns regarding travel in London are that
the public transport system is not geared to satisfy the
types of journeys they make (or want to make) and that they
often feel unsafe while travelling.   This is a
simplification of the results that have emerged from a
survey of women's travel needs in London.   This research
was commissioned by the, now defunct, Greater London
Council (GLC), and conducted in separate stages between
1984 and 1986.   Called the 'Women on the Move' survey, its
results produced a wealth of subjective impressions of
women users of transport and, when analysed in conjunction
with the data of the Greater London Transportation Survey
of 1981 (GLTS) and the London Travel Survey, produce a very
detailed and sharp relief of women's transport needs in
London.

This chapter is essentially an outline of these survey
data sources.   Firstly, the methodology of these surveys is
described.   This is followed by a section which sets out in
detail the findings of these studies in respect of women's
work and shopping trips, mode choice and car availability
for making such journeys and women's fear for their
personal safety while travelling.   These findings are then
summarised in a short section.   A discussion of the policy
implications of this evidence forms the concluding section
of this chapter.

2.   Research methodology

There are three main data sources used in this chapter. The most important of these is the Women on the Move survey of the GLC. The other two are the Greater London Transportation Survey of 1981 and the London Travel Survey. In addition to this, the chapter also makes use of data drawn from the Family Expenditure Survey of 1984, the Census of Population of 1981, the 'Crime on the Underground' survey (1986) and the Islington Crime Survey of 1986.

a)   Women on the Move

The GLC's survey on the particular transport needs of women was a novel departure in the field of transport planning in Britain.   In May 1982, the newly elected Labour administration of the GLC set up a committee with the specific remit of promoting policies for the benefit of women in London.   The origins of the Women on Transport survey - better known as Women on the Move, a descriptor taken from the title of a series of booklets published by the GLC outlining the survey's results - were in informal discussions with women in London carried out by the GLC's Women's Committee during 1982 and 1983.   These showed that transport, and in particular, public transport, was of great concern to women who felt that transport services and policies were not well suited to their needs.

The first stage of the research on women's transport needs was a preliminary investigation of the issues that concern women in relation to their travel requirements. This stage involved ten group discussions (consisting of about ten women each) held in the summer of 1984.   It was carried out by the Harris Research Centre.

The main objectives of the preliminary research - the discussion groups - was to feed into the construction of a questionnaire.   The questionnaire was used for a household survey, 905 women were interviewed out of an original sample of 1,600.   The sampling method used was that of random selection from the electoral register, clustered in forty wards, chosen on the basis of a criteria of diverse patterns and levels of public transport usage.   The response rate of 57% was disappointingly low.   This part of the research project was, however, carried out by the GLC's Survey Services Group during the Winter of 1984-85 which was a particularly severe winter.

The main source of bias was due to the survey's low response rate.   In particular, a serious under-representation of women of Afro-Caribbean and Asian origin was observed when compared to projections made from the 'country of birth' question in the 1981 Census of Population.   To ameliorate the situation, a supplementary survey was carried out on a quota sampling basis in five wards with a high proportion of inhabitants of Afro-Caribbean and Asian origin. The women interviewed in this sub-survey were all of Asian or Afro-Caribbean origin. An extra 101 interviews were collected in this way. For the supplementary part of the survey, ethnic matching was used (i.e interviewers and interviewees were of the same ethnic group). The importance of ethnic matching is illustrated by the fact, for example, that a much higher level of attacks were reported by Asian women to Asian interviewers in the supplementary survey than to white interviewers by Asian women in the main part of the survey.

The last section of the Women on the Move research project was a separate qualitative survey on lesbians and their transport needs. Four discussion groups were held (with lesbians meeting already for social and other purposes) and five individual unstructured interviews conducted with other lesbians. These were held in 1986 and conducted by Social and Community Planning Research.

b)   GLTS 1981

The GLTS 1981 was a major survey conducted by the GLC as part of its information gathering on London's population. This was the third such exercise, previous surveys being carried out in 1962 and 1971. The GLTS 1981 had a number of diverse components, including traffic counts and passenger counts on modes of public transport. Of particular relevance for our purposes here is the major household questionnaire that was conducted, as part of this study, involving over 90,000 individuals. Questions were asked on transport behaviour (the interviewees also kept a weekly travel diary) as well as on general household information, such as income, car ownership, etc. The survey took place in 1981 and was conducted over an area slightly larger than that covered by the GLC.

c)   London Travel Survey

The London Travel Survey is the descendant of the GLC/LT (London Transport - now LRT, London Regional Transport) Diart Panel, which started in 1980. This was a bi-annual travel diary panel with people who dropped out being replaced by new panellists. There were about 2000 panel members who completed a diary detailing all journeys made during the sample week.

Because the people who dropped out were not distributed uniformly amongst all sections of the population, the sample became progressively more and more biased. It was, therefore, ended in 1985 and replaced by a 3,000 systematic sample survey based on household interviews detailing two days of travel. This is now called the London Travel Survey. It was last carried out by the Harris Research Centre on behalf of LRT in June 1986.

d)   Crime on the Underground

In 1986, London Underground Ltd set up a steering group to
investigate the level of crime on the Underground. The
group analysed existing police statistics and conducted two
small surveys; one on passengers' views on safety and the
other with London Underground staff on the same issue.

e)   Islington Crime Survey

In 1985, the London Borough of Islington commissioned the
Middlesex Polytechnic Centre for Criminology to undertake a
crime survey of the Borough. A random sample of 1722
individuals was carried out and a booster sample of 255
individuals from ethnic groups was also carried out. The
latter involved ethnic and gender matching.

3.   Results emerging from these studies

In this section of the chapter, the evidence from these
five sources is presented in the form of diagrams and
tables, with an appropriate sub-sectioning. The analysis
and consideration of this evidence takes place in the two
subsequent subsections of the chapter.

a)   Women's trips

As shown by the Women on the Move survey, journeys most
commonly made by women on a regular basis are those to paid
work. However, over half the sample of women interviewed
(52%) never travel to work. The dominant reason for women
to go out is for shopping purposes. 64% of women go out
shopping at least one day a week. The other important
reasons for women to go out are for journeys to escort
others (e.g. taking children to school) - some 14% of women
making such journeys at least five days a week; and
entertainment and social journeys, made by more than half
the women at least once a week.

Table 8.1 shows that shopping is a most prominent and
frequent activity in women's lives, with 88% of women
shopping for basic items at least once a week. No other
activity is so universally participated in by women.

Having examined the purpose of the journeys that women
make, we now turn to a consideration of the frequency at
which these trips are made. The low level of usage of the
Underground and British Rail services is striking. About
64% of women travel by Underground either less frequently
than once a month or never. The equivalent figure for
travel by British Rail is 81%. These low usage levels are
even more striking when women's dependence on methods of
travel, other than the private car, are taken into account

Table 8.1. Frequency of travel for each journey purpose by women

	5+ days a week	1-4 days a week	About once or twice a month	Less often	Never
Paid work:	38%	10%	–	–	52%
Unpaid work/ voluntary work:	1%	8%	3%	2%	86%
Basic shopping:	24%	64%	4%	1%	6%
Other shopping:	1%	19%	45%	29%	7%
Escorting others:	14%	8%	8%	4%	66%
Social/ entertainment:	7%	48%	24%	12%	9%
Other:	1%	5%	1%	1%	92%

Source: Women on the Move.

and suggest that rail services are not well suited to the sort of journeys women need to make.

Women clearly have very different travel patterns from men, and also have different requirements in respect of the transport system.

Table 8.2. Frequency of travel for each method of transport by women

	5+ days a week	1-4 days a week	About once or twice a month	Less often	Never
Bus:	19%	33%	18%	16%	14%
Underground:	8%	12%	16%	32%	32%
British Rail:	5%	3%	11%	39%	42%
Car driver:	19%	7%	2%	2%	70%
Car passenger:	13%	44%	17%	14%	12%
Motorcycle/ Moped:	–	–	1%	1%	98%
Walking all the way:	56%	31%	6%	3%	92%
Taxi/Minicab:	1%	8%	15%	31%	45%

Source: Women on the Move.

Table 8.3 shows for women and men the average number of journeys per head made each week by each mode of travel.

Table 8.3. Comparative use of each travel mode: trips per head per week

	Bus	Under-ground	British Rail	Car	Walk (10min+)	Total
Women:	3.2	1.3	0.7	6.2	4.5	14.4
Men:	2.4	1.8	0.9	8.1	3.0	15.4

Source: London Travel Survey.

Figure 8.1. Comparative use of each travel mode: trips per head per week

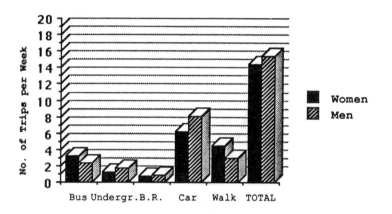

This shows that on average men make just over one more trip per week than women. The modes of travel used, however, differ markedly, with men using a car far more than women.

b)   Travel to work

According the GLTS 81, almost 40% of women travel to work at least five days a week, and a further 10% at least one day a week. On the other hand, voluntary work is an important reason for travel for about 10% of the sample. 20% of all trips women make are to and from work (GLTS 81).

According to the Women on the Move survey, for those who are in full-time or part-time paid work, the most commonly used method of travel to work is the car, as the driver (24%). About 21% of women with a job travel by bus, and 21\5 walk all the way. About 8% of women use British Rail to go to work and 13% the Underground (work journeys account for two thirds of women's travel by Underground and British Rail). 9% travel as a car passenger.

Of the women surveyed, 20% said that they worked where they did because it was close to their place of residence. This was more the case for women in the 20-59 age group,

and for women with young children. This reflects many
women's child care commitments. Lastly, the proximity of
the workplace to place of residence was also a very
important and determining factor for women of Asian origin
and women with a disability.

Table 8.4. Work trips per head per week

	Bus	Under-ground	British Rail	Car	Walk (10min+)	Total
Women:	1.4	0.9	0.5	1.7	1.0	5.5
Men:	1.3	1.2	0.7	3.6	1.0	7.8

Source: London Travel Survey.

The same information is provided in diagrammatic form in
Figure 8.2.

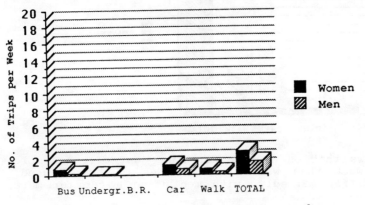

Figure 8.2.   Work trips per head per week

Half of the women in full-time employment find it a
problem to find the time to do their shopping; this
proportion decreases to 35% for part-time workers and to
20% for those not in paid work.   37% of women full-time
workers do their shopping from or on the way to work.

c)   Shopping

A quarter of women go out shopping for basic (grocery)
items at least five days a week and a further 64% go out at
least once a week. Only 6% of women never go out shopping
for basic items. Shopping for other items (e.g. clothes,
furniture) is also important for women, with 20% of women
going out at least once a week and nearly half of women
travelling at least once or twice a month.   23% of all
trips women make are for shopping compared to only 13% for
men (GLTS 81).

According to the Women on the Move survey, 42% of women walk all the way to the shops. 12% complained that the shopping was too heavy, 22% that the shops were too far and a further 22% that the local shops stocked a poor range of goods. 25% of women of Asian origin complained that the shopping was too heavy.

Table 8.5. Shopping trips per head per week

	Bus	Under- ground	British Rail	Car	Walk (10min+)	Total
Women:	0.7	0.1	–	1.3	0.8	2.9
Men:	0.3	0.1	–	0.8	0.4	1.6

Source: London Travel Survey.

The same information is provided in diagrammatic form in Figure 8.3.

Figure 8.3. Shopping trips per head per week

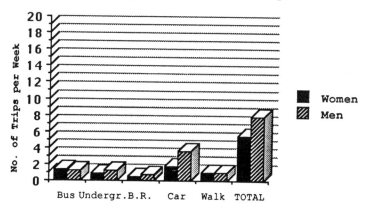

Of women under 20, 62% did their shopping on foot. The pattern for women with young children is quite different, with only 40% going by foot and 42% going by car.

d)   Car driving

The importance of walking is likely to be a reflection of women's lack of access to cars, as compared to men and the fact that many of their journeys are fairly short in length (particularly local shopping trips). However, this in itself is a reflection of the unsuitability of public transport for many of their needs.

Table 8.6. Car availability by age and gender

	17–24		25–64		65+		Total	
	Men	Women	Men	Women	Men	Women	Men	Women
Driver:	45%	28%	71%	39%	36%	7%	50%	26%
Passenger:	24%	36%	5%	31%	8%	23%	21%	38%
No car:	31%	36%	24%	30%	56%	70%	29%	36%

Source: GLTS 1981.

Women have a much lower driving rate compared to men and are far more likely to be non-drivers in car owning households and suffer considerable mobility and accessibility impediments as a consequence. These impediments can range from the quite mild, of having to depend on and fit in with someone else's (car driver's) routine, to the severe, such as an elderly housebound person being isolated in the home without being able to visit friends and relatives, or be visited by them (the friends and relatives often being non-drivers as well). These constraints are outlined in detail in Focas, 1987.

According to the Women on the Move survey (and the GLTS 81), only 34% of women in London have a licence to drive a car. Of these, two thirds (or 23% of all women) only have a car to drive part of the time, and 11% (4% of all women) do not have a car available at all. Thus, 70% of women are always dependent on public transport, walking or on other people to give them lifts in order to drive about in London.

Driving licence rates vary extensively by socio-economic group. While women managers, professionals and employers have a driving licence rate of 63%, only 12% of unskilled women workers have a driving licence. Women who had a driving licence were asked why they had learnt to drive. The most common reasons given were:

Table 8.7. Women's reasons for obtaining a driving licence

'Just wanted to/ Felt had to'	27%
'For independence/ Flexibility/ Less dependent on others'	29%
'For convenience and quickness'	21%
'To take children out'	8%
'Feel more safe to travel by car'	7%

Source: Women on the Move.

The same information is provided in diagrammatic form in Figure 8.4.

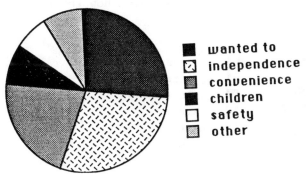

Figure 8.4.   Women's reasons for obtaining a driving
                licence

For women who are physically disabled, the demand to become a driver, if it is at all possible, can be very strong due to the great improvement in mobility and accessibility that car driving may offer. A woman with a physical disability described her reasons for becoming a driver:

> "I decided to get a car so I'm not trapped any more, not bashed around from pillar to post. I'm not standing in sub-zero temperatures in the middle of Oxford Street for three bloody hours waiting for a number 7, that then comes along, and because it's been raining, splashes me, and doesn't stop. I don't get hassled any more."

The need to be independent of others and the need for flexibility and convenience provide strong pressures on women to learn to drive. However, most women do not drive and they were asked why they had not learnt to drive a car. The major reasons were:

Table 8.8.   Women's reasons for not learning how to drive

'Too nervous/ Haven't got the confidence to cope with London's traffic'	23%
'Never felt the need/ Not interested in learning to drive'	17%
'Can't afford to learn to drive a car'	17%
'Already learning/ Waiting to take the test'	12%
'No particular reason'	8%

Source: Women on the Move.

The same information is presented in diagrammatic form in Figure 8.5.

Figure 8.5. Women's reasons for not learning how to drive

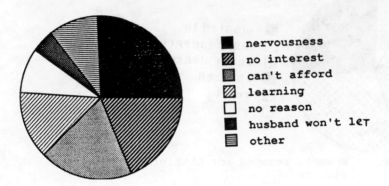

■ nervousness
▨ no interest
▩ can't afford
▨ learning
☐ no reason
■ husband won't let
▤ other

In addition, some 5% of women gave reasons associated with their husbands or families - "My husband / family drives me around" or "My husband won't let me" - as their main reasons. Thus, husbands and families are a factor in inhibiting nearly 10% of women without a licence from learning to drive.

In looking at levels of car driving for women of ethnic groups, we notice that they are below the aggregate average for all women. For example, while 34% of all women have a driving licence, only 25% of Asian women have one and the figure for Afro-Caribbean women is only 15%. There is, however, a change occurring regarding these figures, especially for Asian women, who are now learning to drive in large numbers. A third of all Asian women had learnt to drive within the past five years.

Driving rates have recently increased very rapidly for women who are in full-time employment. The level recorded by Women on the Move was 54%.

Finally, one parent families in London of which 96% have a woman as head of household (Census of Population, 1981) have very low car ownership levels. The Family Expenditure Survey of 1984 found car ownership for one parent families was 30% while for two parent families it was 80% (national figures).

e)   Safety

Women's views on their safety, whilst travelling or walking around London, vary according to the method of travel, time of day, as well as by how often women use that particular

mode, age and ethnic group. Tables 8.9-8.12 show the
proportion of women who feel safe using each mode of travel
during the day and night according to how often they use
that mode. It is clear that women who do not use a
particular mode of travel are much more likely to think it
unsafe, particularly at night. For instance, over a
quarter of women who travel by Underground at least once a
month think it unsafe to travel by night, whereas only 10%
of women who rarely use the Underground think it safe at
night. In 1985 there were 15,300 crimes reported to the
police on the Underground, of which 1,600 involved violence
(Crime on the Underground). In that year 725 million
journeys were made, making the incidence of crime quite
rare. It is probable that many women who think it unsafe
to travel by any mode also seek to avoid using public
transport, but equally safety may be perceived to be worse
than it is by those who never travel by that mode.

Table 8.9. Proportion of women feeling safe travelling by
bus, by frequency of use

Frequency of bus travel	In daytime	At night-time
At least once a week	94%	41%
Once or twice a month	96%	40%
Less often/ never	74%	27%
All women	88%	37%

Source: Women on the Move.

Table 8.10. Proportion of women feeling safe travelling by
Underground, by frequency of use

Frequency of Underground travel	In daytime	At night-time
At least once a week	73%	25%
Once or twice a month	71%	29%
Less often/ never	51%	11%
All women	59%	17%

Source: Women on the Move.

Table 8.11. Proportion of women feeling safe travelling by
British Rail, by frequency of use

Frequency of British Rail travel	In daytime	At night-time
At least once a week	70%	19%
Once or twice a month	71%	24%
Less often/ never	58%	14%
All women	60%	16%

Source: Women on the Move.

Table 8.12. Proportion of women feeling safe whilst walking, by frequency

Frequency of walking	In daytime	At night-time
At least once a week	85%	15%
Once or twice a month	76%	12%
Less often/ never	58%	9%
All women	83%	15%

Source: Women on the Move.

Women's perceptions of safety also vary by age, as shown in Tables 8.13 and 8.14. In general, women aged over 60 and those aged between 16 and 19 feel less safe than women aged between 20 and 60.

Table 8.13. Proportion of women feeling safe travelling during the day by age group

	By bus	By Underground	By British Rail	Whilst walking
16-19 years	83%	54%	54%	78%
20-54 years	91%	67%	69%	87%
55-60 years	86%	54%	50%	80%
Over 60 years	83%	42%	45%	74%
All women	88%	59%	60%	83%

Source: Women on the Move.

Table 8.14. Proportion of women feeling safe travelling at night, by age group

	By bus	By Underground	By British Rail	Whilst walking
16-19 years	48%	9%	11%	11%
20-34 years	41%	19%	16%	12%
35-54 years	45%	21%	21%	21%
55-60 years	36%	13%	16%	17%
Over 60 years	21%	12%	10%	15%
All women	37%	17%	16%	15%

Source: Women on the Move.

Tables 8.13 and 8.14 show that women in all age groups feel safer travelling by bus during the day than walking around. Underground and British Rail are considered to be similar to one another in terms of their perceived safety. They are seen as being much less safe than walking around

162

even during the day. Less than half of the women over 60
feel safe travelling by Underground or by British Rail,
even during the day. The survey also showed that women
with a disability were less likely to feel safe travelling
by any method than able bodied women.

A slightly different picture emerges at night. Within
the age group 20 to 54 years, there is some variation, with
women aged between 35 and 54 feeling considerably safer
than women aged 20 to 34, particularly in relation to
walking. Women over 60 and between 16 and 19 feel
considerably less safe than women in other age groups.
With the exception of bus travel, attitudes of older women
are similar to those of women aged 16 to 19.

Many women avoid going out on their own at night, mainly
for reasons of safety but also for other reasons. Overall,
about 30% of the women strongly agreed with the statement
"I don't go out on my own after dark". This proportion
rises with age, from about 15% of women aged 16 to 39, to
20% of those aged 40 to 44, to 35% of women aged 45 to 60
and 60% of women over 60.

f)   Ethnicity

During the daytime, there is little variation by ethnic
group on feelings of safety by each mode of travel, using
the Women on the Move evidence, Asian women are more likely
to say that they feel less safe than Afro-Caribbean or
white women.

According to the Women on the Move survey, Asian women
feel less safe than either Afro-Caribbean or white women by
all modes considered. These results run contrary to the
findings of the Islington Crime Survey. The latter
indicates, as shown in Table 8.16, that white women are the
ones who feel most threatened when travelling outdoors.
This disparity may be explained by the fact that the women
who live in Islington have different social characteristics
to the ones living in the London Boroughs e.g. the
proportion of Asian women within the population in
Islington is far smaller than that of Greater London.

**Table 8.15. Proportion of women feeling safe travelling at
night, by ethnic group**

	By bus	By Underground	By British Rail	Whilst walking
Afro-Caribbean	38%	8%	8%	17%
Asian	14%	–	12%	8%
White	45%	21%	19%	17%
All women (16-60)	43%	19%	18%	17%

Source: Women on the Move.

163

Figure 8.6. Proportion of women feeling safe travelling at night, by ethnic group

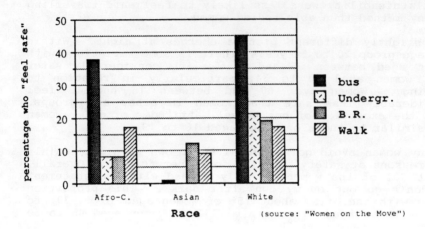

(source: "Women on the Move")

Table 8.16. Proportion of men and women feeling unsafe in Islington

	Feeling unsafe travelling after dark		Feeling unsafe at home	
	Men	Women	Men	Women
White	27%	73%	17%	35%
Black	24%	69%	23%	50%
Asian	33%	67%	24%	35%

Source: Islington Crime Survey.

g)   Victims of crime

In the Women on the Move survey, the interviewees were asked whether they themselves had been attacked, threatened or harassed whilst out in London. Overall, about 10% of women said that they themselves had been attacked, threatened or harassed in the last year. A higher than average proportion of women who said that they had been attacked were aged between 20 and 39, and a lower than average proportion aged 55 or more. Unfortunately, the sample of the Women on the Move survey is too small to show any variation by ethnic group. A quarter of the women who said that they had been attacked had been attacked more than once; they were more likely to be in the age range 20 to 35.

In interpreting these figures, it must be borne in mind that the women interviewed talked of attacks they had been involved in only if they wanted to, and that some women were prepared to talk more than others about this experience. Only 40% of the attacks recorded in this survey were reported to the police at the time of the occurrence and these were more likely to be thefts or attempted thefts, than any other type of attack. None of the Asian or Afro-Caribbean women who had been attacked had reported the incident to the authorities, whereas half of the white women had done so.

Of the attacks on the respondents, just over half occurred in the street, 13.5% on trains, 8% at bus stops, 8% in parks and open spaces. A third were between 12.00 and 16.00 hours, a third between 16.00 and 19.00 hours and a third between 19.00 and 1.00 hours. Since the survey showed that women are far more likely to be out during the afternoon than later on in the evening, the risk of attack is far greater the later it gets in the evening/ night. Equally, since women spend more time walking in the street than travelling by train, the risk of being attacked at a station or on a train are by far greater than walking on the street. The Islington Crime Survey also found that women's greatest fear was to travel alone at night. It also found that most women had a much exaggerated perception of the magnitude and extent of the threat of violence (as gauged by the level and type of crime reported to the Islington Crime survey).

The most common crime women were victims of, as reported by the sample, was attempted theft (accounting for 33% of all crimes - two thirds of which involved no assault or injury). The second most common was theft (accounting for 30% of all attacks - half of which did not result in assault or injury). Sexual attacks accounted for 8% of all attacks reported in the Women on the Move survey.

The Crime on the Underground survey shows that in 1985 of all reported crimes on the Underground, 46% involved pickpocketing where no violence was used. 75% of the victims of such crimes were adult women. Theft with violence accounted for only 5% of all crime and only 25% of the victims were women. According to the survey, data involving sexual assault was significantly under-reported. The Islington Crime Survey showed that 11% of all sexual assaults were committed on public transport, and 66% of them in the street.

Just over 10% of women said that they had been harassed or threatened in the last year. Asian women were more likely to record this than white or Afro-Caribbean women. The highest proportion of women who said that they had been harassed were those of the youngest age group (30% of women aged 16 to 20). This proportion falls steadily with age to only 3% of women aged over 60. Almost half the incidents were in the street, 20% on trains, 10% at stations and nearly 15% at bus stops or on buses. The most common from of harassment was verbal abuse (45%), threats (25%), being followed (15%) and indecent exposure.

h) **Knowing another woman who has been a victim of a crime**

Almost a third of the women interviewed said that they knew another woman who had been attacked or threatened in the last year. Young women were more likely to know of another woman who had been attacked than were older women (40% of women aged 20 to 30, while only 20% of women aged 60 or more did so).

Knowing of another woman who has been attacked or harassed, or having experienced it for herself, affects a woman's attitude to going out, particularly at night. About half of such women consider that their attitude to going out has changed; this is particularly the case for Asian women. The commonest reaction of those affected are to be more alert to what is going on around them (about 60%), and not to go out alone (about 25%). 7% of the women who could drive gave as the reason for learning, being able to go out without the fear of being attacked.

i) **Lesbians**

For lesbians, the fear of harassment and assault is likely to be more acute. The Women on the Move research shows that safety is an over-riding concern for lesbians. A quote from the survey exemplifies the problem:

"I've been thrown off the bus for like holding hands with a woman but blokes never get thrown off the bus for hassling us, ever. It's good on you mate, you know, go for it. But we were just like minding our own business and we got thrown off the bus."

Lesbians feel more vulnerable on public transport to harassment and attack if they display their sexual orientation. This means that many lesbians are having to modify their behaviour to disguise the fact that they are lesbians and thus become more 'publicly acceptable'.

4. **Conclusions**

One of the main results of this research has been its demonstration of present deficiencies in the collection of transport planning data with respect to gender. Although this data set enables an initial identification of women's transport and travel needs, further data is required in order to provide a more accurate and current assessment of the problems in women's accessibility to services and employment. The benefits of continuous monitoring of changes in women's travel circumstances are evident. All too often, women's specific needs are ignored and disguised under the cloak of household data, ignoring the great disparities that may exist in mobility, accessibility and wealth within the household itself.

The results of the Women on the Move survey, in particular, and the other surveys discussed, when taken together, clearly indicate that the public transport system is not presently geared to meeting women's travel needs. Women themselves have pointed out that they require a frequent and reliable public transport system, especially at off-peak times when journeys to shops are usually made or when part-time work often starts or ends.

Many women feel unsafe travelling alone during the day, and a majority feel so during the hours of darkness. The public transport system can be a hostile and intimidating place that inhibits travel after dark. Women need a public transport system which is safe, and seen to be safe.

Owing to the fact that the public transport system does not meet many of women's needs, women's mobility and especially accessibility is curtailed. This is further accentuated by the fact that cars are far less available to women than to men. In one car households, it is nearly always a man who is in control of the car - very often the women does not even have a driving licence to be able to drive the vehicle even if it were to become available to her.

5.   Policy implications

The results presented in this paper provide only general indications of the types of problems that women face in relation to personal mobility and accessibility. What is needed is a systematic analysis of particular problems in specific areas. One such attempt - albeit currently suffering from under-funding - has been made in the London Borough of Southwark (Campaign to Improve London's Transport Research Unit, 1987).

Two types of transport policy recommendations for meeting women's travel needs arise out of this research. The first is concerned with the public transport service provisions available to women and the second with the quality and perception of the service.

Women require an adequate off-peak public transport service to meet their shopping and part-time employment needs. It is an important requirement that the transport service on offer is safe for women and is perceived as safe by potential female users. This means having a train service which is adequately staffed; it also means improved lighting, cleanliness and high quality information services for both buses and trains. Furthermore, sexist advertising, especially the type that may incite sexual violence, should be banned. Local authorities can also play a role in increasing women's safety by funding women's minibus systems, run by women, where those are demanded by local women.

The staffing and design of buses and trains should take into account the fact that many of the women wanting to use these services may be encumbered with push chairs or prams, and many women are likely to be carrying heavy and bulky shopping.

A national policy of encouraging women to take driving lessons and to utilise cars available to them would alleviate problems of constrained accessibility suffered by many women who are non-drivers in car-owning households.

9 Women, travel and personal security

STEPHEN ATKINS

1. Introduction

Despite considerable media attention, both to detailed reporting of specific cases of violence and to 'Law and order' as a political issue, personal security has rarely been seen as a transport issue. Yet for women, apprehension about personal security, the fear of assault, attack, harassment and verbal abuse, is one of the major influences on travel decisions, particularly at night.

It is recognised that focusing on the issue of violence and intimidation against women entirely in the context of travel is only a partial assessment of a wider problem (1). Many women suffer greater physical threats in their private lives than in the public domain of travel and transport on which this chapter concentrates. However, many women are inhibited from undertaking journeys they would like to make, and hence are being constrained in their daily lives. Transport is a key facilitator in providing access to jobs, to facilities, to social and recreational opportunities. Restraint of travel limits effective participation in society and adversely affects women's quality of life. This intimidation is now at such a level as to warrant particular attention in any study of travel patterns. It is particularly relevant for this book where gender based analysis is the prime focus.

This chapter first presents some recent empirical evidence on women's perceptions of personal security risks when travelling. It then reviews those factors affecting women's perceptions and fears when travelling, considering both personal and environmental factors. This is followed by a discussion of the extent to which such fears are 'justified', given the relatively small number of recorded incidents.

A second section then considers a series of alternative means by which this problem could be remedied. These include not just design and operational changes, either already introduced or proposed by local authorities or transport operators, but more importantly suggestions made by women survey respondents. This section includes some discussions concerning the effectiveness of such solutions, particularly those comprising the 'situational crime prevention' approach.

A brief conclusion endorses the advantages of adopting a **needs-based** approach to transport planning, considering the particular needs of certain groups within society, rather than designing transport services to cater for the nominal average (male) traveller.

2.   **Empirical evidence**

Over the past few years, several surveys have examined the influence that personal security plays in women's travel decisions, and hence on their participation in all kinds of social activities.

The largest of these surveys were the British Crime Surveys (BCS) undertaken in 1981 and 1983, both of which had samples of close to 11,000 respondents (Hough and Mayhew, 1985). These victimological studies aimed principally to determine the 'true' level of crime, in contrast to that reported to, or recorded by, the police. Additional questions concerning the fear of crime and behavioural responses to that fear were also asked. BCS asked the question: "How safe do you feel walking alone in this area after dark?", offering response categories of very safe, fairly safe, a bit unsafe and very unsafe. In the 1983 survey, 48% of female respondents reported feeling either a bit or very unsafe, compared to 13% of men. Responses also varied by age and area of residence with 28% of all respondents (both sexes) feeling very unsafe in inner cities and 40% of women and 12% of men aged over 70 feeling very unsafe regardless of area.

The 1983 BCS probed more deeply into the reasons for anxiety. While many of the fears were non-specific, thirty per cent of women said they were 'very worried' about being raped, rising to 41% for younger women and up to 64% for young women in certain areas.

BCS also asked about responses to perceived risks. There were obvious reductions in night time activity by those feeling more insecure. Table 9.1, to be read vertically, shows the very different patterns of activity associated with different levels of perceived insecurity.

Table 9.1. Avoidance behaviour, by fear for personal safety (both sexes)

	Fear for personal safety			
	Very safe	Fairly safe	Bit unsafe	Very unsafe
% Avoid going out on foot at night because of crime	2	9	36	68
Average no. of nights out alone in past week	1.65	1.20	0.81	0.31
% Never go out alone at night on foot*	46	52	64	81
% Never go out because of crime only **	0.3	2	8	27
% Never go out because of crime and other reasons **	0.1	1	4	8

*   Asked only of respondents who had not been out alone in the last week.
**   Asked only of respondents who said that they never went out alone on foot after dark.
Per centages based on total sample.

Source: Maxfield, 1984. Table 5.1.

Although age related, age was not a sole explanation; feeling unsafe reduced night time activity for all age groups. In response to these statistics, Maxfield (1984) states:

"These figures suggest that fear for personal safety is a major factor in limiting personal mobility, and that it affects large numbers of individuals, particularly in inner city areas."

Another major victim-based study was the Islington Crime Survey (ICS), carried out in the London Borough of Islingtion in 1985 (Jones, Maclean and Young, 1986). This survey of over 1,700 people specifically included a number of more detailed questions on women, crime and policing. The question: "Do you yourself ever feel worried about going out on your own in this area after dark?" found affirmative responses from 73% of women and 27% of men. When asked: "Do you think there are risks for women who go out on their own in this area after dark?" about 60% of both sexes responded 'yes', and that the risks were serious. In common with BCS and many other surveys, ICS found a relationship between activity levels, here measured as frequency of absence from the home in the evening, and fear for personal safety (see Table 9.2).

Table 9.2. Percentage of women feeling worried about self after dark by absence from home

Absence from home in evenings per week	Percentage feeling worried for self
None	80
1-2	75
3 plus	62

Source: Jones, Maclean and Young, 1986. Table 4.6. p.165

Some discussion on the relationship between activity levels and perceived fears is given later in this section.

ICS also asked about avoidance behaviour. Purely in response to fear of crime, 37% of all women never went out after dark compared to 7% of men. Considering this, and other behavioural changes such as avoidance of certain streets or areas, ensuring company when going out, avoiding use of trains or bus and using a car rather than walking, the ICS authors conclude that:

"...women generally, and particularly older and black women, feel it is necessary to restrict their behaviour and avoid certain situations as a precaution against crime. In this sense, the ICS helps to illustrate that a 'curfew on women' appears to be implicitly operative." (Jones, Maclean and Young, 1986:167).

Further revealing statistics from ICS concern what is described as 'non-criminal street violence'. These incidents such as being stared at, being followed, being shouted at or called after are sometimes regarded as relatively minor, even trivial in nature. Although, ICS describes these as 'non-criminal', certain incidents, like being touched or held could indeed be crimes, but are seldom reported to the police. Including sexual offences and sexual pestering in a wider definition of harassment, ICS produces rates of reporting during the previous twelve months as shown in Table 9.3.

Table 9.3. Harassment by age, race and gender

	16-24		25-44		45+	
	Males	Females	Males	Females	Males	Females
White	21.8	60.9	24.0	40.8	7.3	8.9
Black	43.3	72.0	24.3	43.4	12.8	18.6
Asian	33.3	42.4	35.4	47.6	19.6	14.3
Other	44.4	64.7	37.1	33.3	15.2	30.0

Percentages indicate those respondents experiencing one or more incidents in the previous twelve months.

Source: Jones, Maclean and Young, 1986, Table 4.21, p.180.

Furthermore, most victims of harassment experienced several such incidents in one year. The effect of these so called 'minor' incidents, including the cumulative influence, is certain to exacerbate fear, apprehension and avoidance behaviour. The suspicion that today's harasser may be tomorrow's mugger or rapist certainly promotes feelings of insecurity (3).

A survey of more specific reference to transport was that conducted by the Greater London Council (GLC) on women's travel needs. Between November 1984 and January 1985 over 900 women resident in London were interviewed in depth about their travel needs and movement patterns. The results of the survey are reported in a series of nine booklets entitled 'Women on the Move' (GLC, 1985-1986 and LSPU, 1987).

The principal findings with respect to the issue of personal security are set out in Tables 9.4 and 9.5.

Table 9.4. Feelings of safety by mode of travel during the day

	Very safe	Fairly safe	Neither safe nor unsafe	Not very safe	Very unsafe	Don't know
Buses	50%	39%	2%	2%	1%	6%
Underground	22%	36%	5%	12%	3%	22%
British Rail	21%	39%	6%	12%	5%	17%
Walking	34%	48%	5%	8%	2%	3%

Source: GLC, Women on the Move, 1984-1986, Booklet 2.

Table 9.5. Feelings of safety by mode of travel at night, after dark

	Very safe	Fairly safe	Neither safe nor unsafe	Not very safe	Very unsafe	Don't know	Never travel after dark
Buses	9%	28%	5%	21%	14%	3%	20%
Underground	2%	14%	5%	25%	20%	10%	24%
British Rail	2%	14%	4%	28%	23%	6%	22%
Walking	2%	13%	5%	27%	29%	1%	22%

Source: GLC, Women on the Move, 1984-1986, Booklet 2.

The majority of women felt reasonably safe when travelling by day, although a significant minority did not feel safe using rail modes. After dark a very different situation prevails. Most women avoid going out on their own at night (63%), and many never travel after dark at all (30%). Only about 15% of women felt safe walking or using rail modes on their own at night. Buses were considered safer, perhaps because of the less enclosed feeling and the use of two person operation on several London bus routes. However, 70% of women did not think it safe to wait at a bus stop at night.

Two surveys on women's perceptions of safety in public places were carried out in Southampton in 1986. The first was undertaken as a student project (Lynch and Atkins, 1987), the second by the local authority (Southampton City Council, 1987). Neither involved a fully representative sample, being based around self completion questionnaires. Women with greater sensitivity to the issue were more likely to have completed and returned the survey forms. The student project questionnaire was distributed mainly through workplaces and voluntary groups. The local authority made copies available at civic offices and libraries, to trade unions and voluntary groups, at a women's open day at the Civic Centre and through a local free newspaper. While the student survey focussed on the security aspects of different modes of travel in a similar fashion to the GLC survey, the local authority questionnaire was targetted towards identifying specific locations for remedial actions. Both surveys achieved sample sizes of about 250 respondents.

The principal results from the student survey are summarised in Table 9.6. It was found that the greatest apprehension was felt about the beginning and end of journeys, rather than the in-vehicle component. Thus although car journeys were perceived as very safe, car parks and particularly multi-storey car parks were disliked with 13% being fearful by day and 30% by night. Similarly, waiting at bus stops and deserted railway stations caused anxieties. When walking, parks and subways were most often mentioned as places to avoid, particularly at night.

Table 9.6. Percentage of women feeling unsafe by mode
(Southampton 1986)

	Daylight	Darkness
Walking	34%	59%
Bus	1%	22%
Train	15%	25%
Car	1%	6%

Source: Lynch and Atkins, 1987

The report by Southampton City Council concentrates on identifying the areas in the city where women felt unsafe. While several respondents said they felt unsafe or avoided using all streets, or at least all quiet areas, side streets and back streets, 90 specific streets or general areas were identified by one or more respondent, illustrating the widespread nature of the problem. Similarly large numbers of specific locations of parks and

174

open spaces, footpaths and cutways, subways, car parks and bus stops were identified. Other locations mentioned by respondents were those frequented by drunks, down and outs, gangs of youths and kerb crawlers and others that were either deserted or regarded as disreputable, derelict, poorly maintained or badly lit.

A number of other surveys have confirmed the findings from the major crime surveys and transport research studies already mentioned. For example, the Greater London Council (GLC) commissioned a survey of London women's opinions on a variety of issues which was carried out by Market and Opinion Research International (MORI) in January 1986. The main focus of the survey was on women's political attitudes and participation in public affairs. However, the unprompted questionning of women about their most important concerns showed fear of attack or robbery as the prime concern (32%) with safety in the streets if out alone or at night a close second (26%). When proferred a list of issues, 'safety on the streets' was selected as among the most important by 66% of women. Furthermore, the relationship between importance and the degree of satisfaction with the way the issue was being tackled by central and local government shows personal security in a class of its own (Figure 9.1).

Figure 9.1. **Issues for women in London: Importance versus satisfaction**

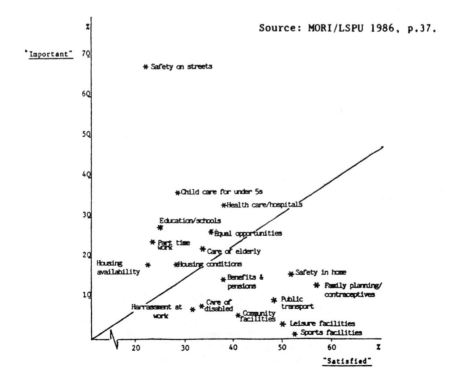

On 31 January 1987 Birmingham Junior Chamber of Commerce
conducted a 'City Pride' survey of public opinion in twelve
locations in the city. From 575 responses, 61% said they
were deterred from visiting the city centre in the evening.
This included 70% of women and 70% of people aged over 45.
the overwhelming balance of reasons given by respondents
related to personal security including comments such as
mugging, violence, crime, gangs of youths, unsafe subways
and car parks, hooliganism and vandalism. Again the
deterrent effect was related to frequency of visit (see
Table 9.7).

**Table 9.7. Whether feel deterred from visiting city
centre in evening by frequency of visit**

Frequency	% Deterred
Infrequently/ never	74
Moderate	62
Frequent	56

Source:Birmingham Junior Chamber of Commerce, City Pride
Survey Report, 1987.

Another survey concerning women's security fears, but
focusing on the workplace, was conducted by the Brook
Street Bureau and Elle Magazine following the disappearance
of London estate agent Suzy Lamplugh. Two thousand
magazine readers returned questionnaires, with a further
household survey of one thousand women. The major finding
was that personal security was the biggest fear for working
women, greater than cancer, losing their jobs or falling
into debt. Forty per cent were afraid of being attacked in
the workplace and only fifteen per cent felt safe while
'out and about' in their work. Over the previous twelve
months 73% of women had had unwelcome approaches (3).

3.   Review

These surveys collectively provide incontrovertible
evidence of the widespread and serious nature of women's
fears about travelling, particularly at night. The
principal factors affecting levels of apprehension are now
reviewed: firstly, personal characteristics are considered,
then environmental factors and finally frequency of travel.

a)   Age

Many of the surveys show higher levels of fear among young
and elderly women. It seems likely that this is related to
perceived vulnerability. the elderly are generally less
able to counter attacks and are often more fearful
generally. It is suggested by Hough and Mayhew (1985) that
the greater fears among young women relate to anxiety about
sexual assault. Jones, Maclean and Young (1986) note that

fear of crime among elderly women is the product of accumulated experience of attacks and harassment.

b)   Race

Women from ethnic minorities can be subject to racially motivated attacks and harassment. The GLC transport survey targetted a special supplementary survey on ethnic minority women. This showed feelings of safety among Afro-Caribbean women to be at a similar level to white women, except for travel by tube at night when Afro-Caribbean women felt very much less safe.

Asian women were consistently more fearful than other racial groups with 95% saying they did not go out at night (GLC, 1984-1986, Women on the Move, Booklet 5). Although there may be some cultural factors influencing this very high figure, fear of attack was also a commonly mentioned factor (70%). The Islington Crime Survey also considered race but, although there were differences between racial groups, it was noted that gender is a much more important determinant of perception of risk than race (Jones, Maclean and Young, 1985:162).

c)   Sexual orientations

Lesbians can be subject to additional intimidation simply because their behaviour or appearance may not conform to conventional stereotypes. While 'queer bashing' is often regarded as being directed at male homosexuals, there are very many examples of lesbians being particularly singled out for aggressive intent. The GLC Women and Transport survey did consider lesbians but this research has not yet been published.

d)   Economic status

The safest modes of travel are perceived to be cars and taxis. Women, with fewer financial resources, will be less able to use these modes and are, therefore, more reliant on modes perceived as less safe, particularly walking. Thus, the travel patterns of women with fewer economic resources are likely to be more constrained by security fears. There is some limited evidence to support this theory from the Islington Crime Survey (see Table 9.8).

Table 9.8. Women's fear of crime by economic status

Income (f)	Feeling there are serious risks for women after dark	Feeling worried about self after dark
Under 3,000	65.4%	75.2%
3,000-7,999	64.5%	74.5%
8,000-11,000	60.3%	68.7%
12,000 plus	51.9%	67.7%

Source: Jones, Maclean and Young, 1986. Table 4.7.

e)   Activity levels

The reduction of crime, and fear of crime, through the presence of other people, through public surveillance, is a major feature of the seminal work of Jacobs (1961) and Newman (1972).

"...a well used city street is apt to be a safe street, a deserted city street is apt to be unsafe." (Jacobs, 1961)

Despite these generalities, most recorded crimes take place where people are found, for example, on the principal streets in a town centre where the popular pubs, nightclubs and restaurants are often located. These are frequently the locations for violence, clashes with the police and personal theft. However, these areas may be relatively safe for women because of late night surveillance. For example, in Southampton, the Derby Road area (a notorious 'red light' district) was found to be relatively safe:

"The existence of numerous houses utilised by prostitutes in the Derby Road area seem only to be linked, at least directly, to a comparatively small tally of crimes. It is the prostitutes who are most at risk - inside their houses." (Ramsey, 1982)

f)   Time of day

As is obvious from the data given above, travelling in darkness is perceived as being much less safe than travel during the day. This is probably due not just to the difficulty of effective surveillance at night but also to the reduced presence of other people. It is interesting to note that in the GLC transport survey the reported attacks on women occurred as follows: one third between noon and 4.00 p.m., one third between 4.00p.m. and 7.00p.m and one third between 7.00p.m and 1.00a.m. However, consideration of the numbers of women travelling at these times (the exposure rate) means that the risks of being attacked are correctly perceived as being greater at night.

g)   Lighting

Surveillance is more effective if there is adequate street lighting. However, street lighting has traditionally been designed with the primary aim of promoting road safety, particularly for vehicular traffic. Policies are changing, however, and many local authorities, for example, City Councils in Leicester and Southampton and the London Boroughs of Islington and Wandsworth, are improving street lighting with the aim of crime prevention.

h)   Graffiti and cleanliness

Desolation, disrepair and untidyness create an unpleasant atmosphere which itself constitutes a deterrent to the use of, or passage through, an area. More importantly, however, if graffiti writing and vandalism are possible then similar conditions of non-surveillance apply in which women can feel threatened.

i)   Frequency of travel

A consistent finding from many surveys is a relationship between perceived safety and travel frequency. Those who go out more find travel less fearful than those who travel little. Those who use a mode often feel more safe using it than those who travel by it less frequently. Obviously, people who perceive a mode to be unsafe are likely to avoid using it, and those who do use a mode are likely to justify their choice by reporting it to be safe. However, it also seems probable that perception is influenced by frequency of use; initial apprehension and simple fear of the unknown is replaced by confidence after repeated safe passage through feared locations.

An important corollary to this relationship between apprehension and frequency of use is that increased use of a particular mode by women is likely to improve their perception of its safety. Furthermore, as increased activity and the presence of other travellers also improves the perceived safety of the mode (see above), the increased use of travel facilities by women should have synergistic effect of generating higher levels of mobility; there should, thus, be an upward spiral in women's travel behaviour. For this reason, measures to improve the security characteristics of transport systems could have considerable influence.

4.   A well grounded fear?

In studying the influence of personal security on women's travel patterns and personal mobility, it is fear and apprehension that are the relevant considerations and not recorded crime levels. However, many reports and several

179

transport operators point out that the actual number of recorded incidents of attack or violence is in fact very low. Indeed, recorded crime statistics often suggest that men are more frequent victims of mugging and assault than women, yet men are less apprehensive. The unwillingness of men to report fear for reason of self esteem has been considered, but a more common suggestion, either implicitly or explicitly, is that women's perceptions of risk are wrong. Are women's fears therefore 'unjustified'? Should the target for action be women's unrealistic perceptions of the risks they face, rather than, or perhaps in addition to, the direct causes of those fears? (4)

Such analysis of women's travel experience disregards several important factors. Firstly, it fails to consider the frequency of incidents other than those which are recorded. As shown earlier, non-criminal street violence and harassment are widespread and the frequency of these incidents contributes to perceptions of frequency about more serious attacks. Indeed, it might be more helpful to consider an uncategorised continuum of anti-social behaviours. Certainly Jones, Maclean and Young (1986) conclude that the ICS results show that: "the perceptions of risk are probably more accurate than other research suggests" (1986:166).

Secondly, it fails to recognise the very great psychological impact of attacks and harassment, which can often be very long lasting. While rape trauma is now recognised it should also be noted that even 'minor' incidents can be extremely upsetting and disturbing, given the uncertainty of the outcome of any particular incident. The effects influence personal behaviour, including travel decsions, but can also have a very profound influence on the way victims view society, even changing or modifying personality. A contributory factor is the way victims are treated by society. A lack of appreciation and understanding is common, together with a presumption that such incidents are an everyday, normal occurrence and should be accepted as part of urban living for females. The treatment of victims by police can be unsympathetic and this general lack of institutional support for victims contributes to feelings of powerlessness which exacerbate fears.

Finally, such limited analysis fails to give credence to risk aversion behaviour which is generally treated as being entirely logical in other contexts. Insurance companies rely on the fact that most people are unwilling to accept even a very small degree of risk if the possible consequences are very serious. Considering both the high probabilities of encountering disturbing incidents and the potentially serious consequences of at least some of those incidents, high levels of expressed fear should not be considered either surprising or unrealistic. In contrast, street violence against men is often related to specific flash point locations, such as outside pubs and clubs, and this implies a certain degree of choice.

It remains true, of course, that some people may have erroneous perceptions of risk, and the contribution of media reporting deserves some attention. Although extremely violent incidents are still a rare occurrence in most locations, they way that the media focusses on the most extreme cases can give rise to misleading impressions. Often a single incident may be reported three times, first when it occurs, second when the offender is apprehended and third when the case comes to court. Television, in particular, provides such powerful images that some people, particularly those more susceptible to fear, are encouraged to adopt extreme precautionary tactics that are probably unnecessary, yet affect their lives in substantial ways. However, it is also relevant to consider the opposite argument. The reduction of apprehension among women without tackling its root cause could merely encourage women to be less cautious and perhaps place themselves at greater risk. Many of the suggested proposals to improve travel conditions set out in the next section do indeed principally tackle the causes of fear, rather than the causes of violent behaviour. As one woman in the Southampton survey put it: "It's the people not the streets that need attention" (Lynch and Atkins, 1987).

5.   Proposals to reduce women's travel fears

The solutions proposed to counter the problems described in the previous sections can be categorised into four main groups. First, there are those suggestions concerning the policing and staffing of streets and transport systems. Second, there are proposals related to changing the environment in the locations where women feel most threatened, the 'situational crime prevention' approach. Third, there are actions which are targetted at social attitudes and the more fundamental social causes of crime. Finally, there are schemes concerned with improving the level and quality of transport service provided for women.

a)   Policing and staffing of transport systems

Among women concerned about personal safety, the most common call is for increased presence of people, particularly those with some degree of responsibility for maintaining order. Women ask for more and better policing, for greater staff presence on both the stations and vehicles of the public transport system, for park wardens and dog patrols, for attendants in multi-storey car parks.

Requests for greater police presence are often associated with calls for that presence to be more sensitive to women's requirements. Many women call for police to be put back on the beat on foot, rather than drive around in cars.

Sexist attitudes are still prevalent among police officers. In some inner city areas, community confidence in the police is low; greater police presence may even give rise to increased alarm in anticipation of trouble. There is also some recognition of the relatively low priority afforded by some police officers to their so called 'social' order maintenance duties in contrast to the high esteem accorded to apprehension of criminals involved in crimes against property (5).

On many public transport systems, the trend is towards the employment of less staff with more automation and greater use of high technology equipment. The introduction of one person operated (OPO) buses and trains and the de-staffing of stations especially at times of low usage exacerbate feelings of insecurity. Many jobs are also being deskilled, leading to lower grades of employment. With low levels of pay and responsibility, staff have little incentive to intervene in an incident which may be threatening to them as well as to the passengers. Programmes of training to foster a more caring attitude towards customers are being adopted by several public transport operators. Training in how to deal with aggressive situations and how to give or gain assistance could be beneficial.

The principal reason for seeking increased staff presence is not simply that such presence acts as a deterrent to potential wrong-doers, but the belief that it also provides some possibility for attacks to be interrupted, assistance offered and, perhaps, offenders apprehended. Women's perceptions of the contrast between staffing solutions and passive security systems such as closed circuit television (CCTV) is significant.

b)   Situational crime prevention

A second group of remedial proposals concern changes to the environment in which women feel most afraid. The most obvious of these is the virtually unanimous request from women for improved lighting. Traditionally street lighting has been designed with the primary aim of illuminating the carriageway as an aid to road safety. The contribution of street lighting to crime prevention has always been known to lighting engineers but only recently has there been greater discussion of this function and more stress laid on the lighting of footpaths, alley ways and pedestrian routes. Lighting at bus stops and on stations is often criticised, although many women also drew attention to poor lighting on the approaches to or in the vicinity of isolated rail stations.

Other proposals relate to changes in design layouts to promote surveillance. These include suggestions to cut back vegetation, the avoidance of hidden corners in subways and tunnels, the closure of under-utilised passageways in the London Underground at night and the provision of secure waiting areas at rail stations.

CCTV has been introduced in some locations, although sometimes for operational reasons (e.g. for OPO drivers of underground trains to view platforms) rather than as a security measure. CCTV has the potential to provide greater surveillance capability, particularly in the context of de-staffing. However, the feasibility of control room personnel scanning numerous television monitors with sufficient frequency to detect incidents may be unrealistic. Making the control room visible to passengers has been suggested to promote deterrence effects. While CCTV cameras may detect, and in some cases even record the images of offenders, they provide no direct assistance to the victims of assault. However, some experiments with CCTV on buses to counter graffiti damage have proved successful, for example, in Coventry.

Alarm buttons for passengers and improved communication systems between travellers and staff and between staff and control rooms can increase confidence. Communication systems for passenger information or emergency use are provided on stations of London's Docklands Light Rail and at some stations on the Newcastle Metro, both systems having a general policy of unstaffed stations. Many buses have radio links to control rooms, in some cases with 'panic' buttons to override other messages. However, most such systems are regarded by women as mere palliatives compared to the presence of uniformed transport staff.

Many of these proposals come under the general heading of 'situational crime prevention' (6). This has become a popular, even populist, concept with the work of Coleman (1985) on housing estate design becoming perhaps the most controversial example. Situational crime prevention (SCP) aims to reduce the opportunities for offences to take place by modifying the crime environment, either through physical changes or operational practice. SCP includes ideas like target hardening or target removal and improving formal and informal surveillance. It thus encompasses matters like improved locks, bolts and shutters, marking of property and neighbourhood watch schemes, as well as aspects of physical layout and design.

One criticism of the SCP approach is that by increased formal security measures such as locks and barriers and through certain design constraints like avoiding vegetation which could provide opportunities for concealment, a more closed and hence hostile environment may be created. Heightened awareness of crime prevention tactics increases concern and fear about crime. Recognition of this problem and greater sensitivity and ingenuity in design should minimise this difficulty.

A more trenchant criticism of SCP concerns displacement: crimes are not prevented but merely moved in time, location or nature. Healy and Laycock (1986: 127) note that SCP is most influential on opportunistic or acquisitive crimes like criminal damage, vandalism, burglary and 'auto' crime. Trasler (1986) goes further and suggests that SCP is likely to be less effective on expressive crime like assault, where the underlying violence is less likely to be deterred and more likely to be displaced.

However, while displacement may limit the overall effectiveness of SCP measures for offences against the person, in specific areas (or for transport, on specific routes), SCP may provide localised security gains. The establishment of safe areas or safe routes could provide considerable social benefits for women. There is, however, a real difficulty in providing safe routes given the dispersed nature of travel patterns. Vulnerability at the beginning and the end of the journey will be hard to overcome, and SCP solutions would be costly.

Even is all that could be guaranteed were displacement, such measures could be worthwhile. However, another concern is that design changes such as improved street lighting do not tackle the real problem and could merely provide synthetic and unjustified changes in perception. By making an environment appear safer women may be encouraged to take unjustified risks. It is, therefore, highly relevant to consider other measures aimed at changing behaviour under the general heading of social crime prevention.

c)   Social crime prevention

Women's suggestions to alleviate personal security fears also encompass the usual range of penal policies from advocating more severe sentencing policies to requesting provision of more activities for youths to do (Southampton City Council 1987). A harsher penal regime, including the 'short, sharp shock' treatment for youth offenders', has been promoted by the current Conservative government in the U.K. There is little evidence to suggest that this has led to any reductions in crime and widespread feelings that the situation has, if anything, become worse. Indeed this lack of success has perhaps stimulated greater interest by the government in the situational crime prevention approach.

The limitations of penal policies in the context of transport crime is already recognised by some European operators outside the U.K.

"We cannot respond to the sense of insecurity soley by providing more police and prisons, since to do so is to move towards a different type of society....(I)t is necessary to beware of an attitude that leaves room for law enforcement alone......(L)aw enforcement sometimes simply indicates a failure to communicate and so prevent acts of assault and vandalism, perhaps a sign that the

(transport) undertakings have become too inward looking".
(Quidort, 1987: 7-8)

An approach to crime prevention through tackling the root social causes of crime is one that has been applied in the U.K., most notably by the National Association for Care and Re-settlement of Offenders (NACRO). In their 'Safe Neighbourhood Unit' work on housing estates, NACRO has promoted a multi-agency approach to crime prevention but firmly based on local community participation. Tackling social, housing and environmental problems on 'negatively coded' inner city estates, NACRO's techniques have begun to pay dividends. The methods used involve resident opinion survey, community stimulation, community involvement and the obtaining from both public and private agencies of commitments to provide resources. The target is to improve both physical and social conditions, to tackle despair and deprivation, and to promote confidence and self esteem of estate dwellers in their neighbourhoods. With some reservations on the role of outside agencies, similar resident participation schemes have been adopted by several local authorities (LSPU, 1987b).

In the context of transport systems some interesting experiments in social crime prevention have been undertaken in France (King, 1988), Denmark and West Germany, mainly targetted at vandalism and graffiti. Brog (1987: 30-31) characterises vandals as young people feeling excluded or not accepted by society and hence expressing their aggression against 'the system' as a way of drawing attention to themselves. Public transport is a prime target because it is perceived as anonymous; no one apparently suffers from acts of vandalism. Preventative action has been targetted at making young people feel at home on buses. Measures include publicity campaigns with schools, letting young people paint and internally re-design buses, the provision of pop music and a series of competitions and games relating tom music and films (Quidort, 1987: 11). Establishing a bond between the young and the bus company has had an inhibiting effect on vandalism. In Marseilles, the operator has, with police co-operation, identified offenders but then approached the leaders of the relevant social group in attempts to persuade the ringleaders to stop damaging public transport. Obtaining a dialogue in this way between the operator and community groups has had some success (Quidort, 1987:15).

In Denmark, the Copenhagen operator is said to be 'very aware of the fact that aggression spawns more aggression' (Hauber, 1987: 13) and has instituted peaceful action programmes. These are designed to show the public that the operator is doing all it can to fight vandalism and includes cleansing teams dressed in white overalls cleaning tram cars during journeys, publicity, pop songs and television commercials using popular Danish figures. It is hoped that passengers will be encouraged to exercise informal social control over anti-social behaviour.

Initial results are promising (Hauber, 1987: 14). In Germany, persistent fare dodgers have been placed under the supervision of public transport employees and counselling has been used to promote changes in attitude and behaviour (Hauber, 1987: 7).

In seeking to change social attitudes perhaps the most crucial educative process is to change men's attitudes towards women as sexual objects. A small contribution to this was the ban on sexist advertising introduced by London Transport when controlled by the Greater London Council. Posters depicting women in sexually provocative or submissive positions were not accepted. London Regional Transport, now under central government direction, has recently rescinded this policy, a decision reported with much glee in the London Evening Standard (7).

d)   Quality of transport services provision

A final group of proposals to eliminate or at least ameliorate women's security fears are those associated directly with transport service provision.

More frequent buses, better reliability and better time keeping would reduce waiting times at bus stops and reduce risk exposure. Better information on routes and timings would also be beneficial. A London experiment on the 36 bus route provided bus stop displays of the estimated time to the arrival of the next bus, similar to the London Underground dot matrix displays. This was widely appreciated, but the high cost of equipment and difficulties with allocation of radio frequencies has prevented its continuation. A proposal strongly supported by women in London was the guaranteed availability of taxis at remote stations at night (GLC, 1986 Booklet 6).

However, the proposal most favoured by women for night time travel is women's safe transport (WST). Two WST schemes currently operate in London in the Boroughs of Lambeth and Lewisham. Established, managed and operated by women these schemes provide safe door-to-door transport for women at night. Popular for educational, social and recreational trips by women unable to afford or unwilling to use taxis, both schemes can not cope with existing levels of demand (Brewer and Davies, 1988). Although receiving some local authority support, both schemes have very restricted and uncertain resources and can offer only limited services.

6.   Conclusion

It is still possible for major transport operators in the U.K. conurbations to declare that personal security among passengers "is not a problem here". There is a need to promote greater awareness among those responsible for transport provision of the scale and significance of the problem as shown earlier in this chapter. However, given the widespread public concern, it is relevant to ask just why so little attention has been given to the issues in the past. There are a number of possible reasons to explain why this is so.

First, it might perhaps be suggested that crime and violence have nothing to do with transport planning; transport merely reflects society's ills and violence on transport is a problem for the police, for the criminal justice system, for sociologists. This cannot be so. Transport is an integral part of society and cannot be treated in isolation as a technical engineering or economic enterprise. Just as the wider social effects of transport, such as environmental impacts, are a legitimate concern, so should transport play its part in facilitating solutions to broader social issues such as unemployment, poverty, equality of opportunity and community safety. This view is borne out in a recent Home Office publication which concludes that it is desirable to target "departments and organisations providing services for the public sector" in order to "establish a belief that a satisfactory public service should meet not only traditional criteria....but also contribute to the reduction in crime. Thus it is not sufficient to ensure that people are transported from A to B; it is also important (and part of service) that they are not assaulted on the way (Heal and Laycock, 1986).

Second, official failure to notice the issue is probably to be explained in terms of the social characteristics of those affected. Those most affected by fear; women, elderly people, people with disabilities and people from ethnic minorities, are the least powerful in society and are least able to effect change. These groups are not just disadvantaged in terms of political influence, they are also under-represented in the transport planning profession.

Third, the issue has not gained attention because of the methods generally adopted by transport planners. Transport planning has usually operated on the basis of observed demand and current travel behaviour patterns. It has disregarded the different nature, abilities and resources of separate groups within society. However, to be gender free (for example) is not to be gender neutral. Women's travel needs have not been addressed. The travel needs of elderly people or those with disabilities have been pigeon holed as 'special needs'. Their needs are not special. They are perfectly ordinary needs for access to people and activities, but needs which are not met by current transport provision. If people do not travel, for whatever reason, they are not considered in the demand orientated planning approach. In contrast, a needs based analysis reveals not only the existence of suppressed travel demand, but also the barriers to its expression. It is only through the adoption of a wider needs based approach that

issues such as that of personal security will reach the
agendas of transport planning.

Notes

1. For a broader analysis of social control effected through violence or threats of violence against women see Hanmer and Maynard (1987).

2. See, for example, McNeill, S. 'Flashing: its effects on women' in Hanmer and Maynard (1987). In the Leeds study by Hanmer and Saunders, it is reported that the type of incident was not as frightening as the uncertainty of the outcome (Hanmer and Saunders, 1984).

3. See London Evening Standard, 16 June, 1987; Elle Magazine, July, 1987.

4. For a deeper analysis of this and other related issues see Stanko, E., 'Typical violence, normal precaution'. in Hanmer and Maynard (1987).

5. See Kinsey, Lea and Young, 1986. pp 60-61

6. For a wider view of the situational crime prevention approach see Clarke and Mayhew, 1980; Heal and Laycock, 1986; Hope, 1986 and Poyner, 1983.

7. See London Evening Standard, October 1987 for news item and letters in response.

10 The European Parliament, travel and equal opportunities

CLARE WELLS

1.   Introduction

It is generally recognised that equal opportunities can not be realised in the absence of adequate child care facilities (Pickup, Ch.11 for a fuller statement of this argument).   This is particularly true where a parent's occupation involves travel away from home; and still more so where working parents live far from their natural support networks (Whipp and Grieco, Ch.1), as well as from their linguistic roots.

The radical circumstances of frequent official travel, distance from family and friends, and remoteness from country and language of origin are all combined in the case of the European Parliament, the institution created to ensure democratic control over the processes of European integration.   Although the case may be extreme, it nevertheless illustrates problems common to many occupations - whether in business or diplomatic circles- involving regular travel away from home for longer or shorter periods of time.

This chapter describes the work and travel conditions of staff of the European Parliament, discusses the way these effect achievement of equal opportunities within the institution, and indicates the further research needed.

2.   The European Parliament: and its work organisation

a)   The European Parliament's three workplaces

For political and historical reasons, which it is not the purpose of this chapter to explore, the European Parliament has what are termed three 'usual' workplaces: Luxembourg, Brussels and Strasbourg.

The bulk of the 3,000 or so officials making up the Secretariat are based in Luxembourg, with a small outpost of some 20 staff members in Strasbourg and approximately 300 staff based in Brussels.

Meanwhile, virtually all parliamentary activities proper take place in Brussels and Strasbourg. The full house normally sits for one week each month in Strasbourg with the exceptions of August, when the Parliament recesses, and the months of March and October - which usually include an additional week long sitting each devoted to negotiations, respectively on agricultural prices and on the European Community Budget. Meetings of the Governing Bodies of the Parliament (Bureau, Enlarged Bureau and Quaestors) also take place in Strasbourg as do some meetings of the Parliamentary committees.

The eighteen standing Parliamentary committees meet on average once a month for two to three days in Brussels. Some meetings of the governing bodies of the Parliament are also held in Brussels, as are the majority of the meetings of the Parliament's nine political groups. In addition, each committee is entitled to meet once a year outside the three usual workplaces. The twenty four delegations for contacts with parliaments in countries not belonging to the Community meet in both Brussels and Strasbourg.

The fact that most Parliamentary activities occur in cities other than those where the officials who service them live imposes a requirement of geographical mobility on the staff members concerned. While some departments (e.g. translation, typing pools, various administrative units) are barely affected, several hundred key Parliamentary staff are expected to travel on average twice a month and to spend between 2 and 10 nights away from home every month except August.

b)   The European Parliament and equal opportunities: its designation as an exemplary institution

The European Parliament, like the other institutions of the European Community, has expressed explicit commitment to the achievement of equal opportunities not only in the wider Community but also - given its exemplary role- within the institution itself. The Ad Hoc Committee on Women's Rights set up by the European Parliament in 1979 gave rise in turn to the creation of a Committee of Enquiry into the Situation of Women in Europe and subsequently of a standing Parliamentary Committee on Women's Rights. The two latter committees have adopted reports bearing on equal opportunities within the Secretariat, on the basis of which the Parliament has in turn adopted resolutions (1). One result was the setting up with effect from 1 January 1987 of a Joint Committee on Equal Opportunities for Men and Women in the European Parliament comprising representatives of the Administration and of the Staff Committee. The Joint Committee (2) has, among other things, called attention to the question of child care during parents' official travel and to the need for a thorough survey of the problems raised and of possible solutions.

3.   Missions and child care

The fact that the European Parliament's activities are spread over three workplaces means that staff have to make child care arrangements catering for frequent and regular over-night absences from home. The range of problems involved depends of family circumstances, social and cultural factors, and financial circumstances.

a)   Family circumstances

Where both partners in a household are employed by and travel for the European Parliament, which is not infrequent, there may be no family member left in Luxembourg to care for children. The same may apply where one partner has a different employer but also has travel obligations and, very importantly, in the case of single, separated, divorced or widowed parents.

b)   Social and cultural factors

The European Parliament employs staff from twelve member states of the European Community (3). Some come from the 'heartland' countries of Europe and live within reasonable reach of family and friends who are able and willing to help with child care during parents' absences from home. But many others come from much further afield and may have no family near to hand. Initially at least, they may have few close friends (and those probably drawn mainly from workmates who are frequently obliged, by the jointness of their business, to travel at the same time as them) on whom they may call for support.

Added to the relative distance from kin and friendship support networks are language difficulties. Although couples sharing a single language exist, mixed language households are common. The combinations do not always include the language of the country in which the household lives. Luxembourg, where most of the European Parliament's Secretariat is based, has its own language - Letzeburgesch

192

- as well as two official languages (French and German) spoken in a characteristically local fashion by the Luxembourg population at large. A Danish-Greek or an Irish-Italian household may be reluctant to entrust their children to a local child minder speaking yet another language.

c)   Financial circumstances

Household income also obviously affects the choice of child care arrangements. Best able to pay for help meeting the relevant quality and language criteria are households with two salaries in the Administrator A category and above. Least able to afford such help are one parent families bringing home a salary in the clerical, secretarial and manual worker (B, C and D) categories.

Taking all the various factors into account, those best able to cope with the problems of child care during missions are officials with a partner who stays at home (typically a male staff member with a non-travelling wife) and households comprising one or two staff members in the A category from the heartland countries (Belgium, France, Germany and Luxembourg). Also reasonably well-placed are officials from countries such as Italy and Portugal: these countries are the source of a large pool of migrant domestic labour in Luxembourg which fellow nationals can tap to solve at least the language problem posed by the mobility requirements of Parliamentary employment. Worst off are single parents holding posts in the secretarial grades and lower, and coming from the remoter member states: typically the Danish, Irish, Greek or British (female) secretary.

d)   Moral problems

Practical aspects aside, the question of child care during missions raises moral problems. Regardless of their ability to find and finance reasonable arrangements for the care of children during missions, many officials find it personally objectionable and morally wrong to be continuously separated from their children and to have to leave them with paid outsiders. The traditional moral qualms experienced by working mothers are writ large when day time separation from family extends into overnight and even week long separations. Problems of this order can not be removed simply by the individual parent throwing money at them and buying the most expensive kinds of trained, live-in help but require, for their solution, more fundamental changes in the organisation of European Parliamentary work. The problems can not be resolved at the level of individual domestic arrangements.

3.   The range of solutions

Solutions to the problems of child care during missions include: taking the children along; leaving them behind; and reducing or eliminating missions for those with child care responsibilities, at no cost to their career development.

a)   Taking the children along

The option of taking children along on mission, which in any case applies only to pre-school children, is only readily available to the few officials with support systems on the spot.

Pre-school child care facilities run by the European Community Institutions for their staff are only available in two of the three 'usual' workplaces of the Parliament. In terms of quality they meet high standards and are designed to reflect the needs of European Community staff as regards working hours and language spread. But they are conceived on a safety net basis and as such cater only for a minority (the European Community run day nursery in Luxembourg, for example, provides only 120 places for all the children below three and a half years old of the 6,500 or so officials posted to that city). European Community run day nurseries operate in Brussels and Luxembourg, but at present each caters only for children of staff posted to the relevant workplace. No arrangements have been negotiated to take in, on a 'transit' basis, the children of staff on mission from another workplace. In practice, therefore, pre-school children of European Parliament staff based in Luxembourg have no access to an European Community run child care centre in Strasbourg.

Local child care facilities in Brussels and Strasbourg, meanwhile, are geographically scattered in relation to the Parliament's premises, their hours of work do not match those of the Parliament and, naturally enough, they do not offer the necessary spread of languages.

If child care facilities offering the requisite hours and languages were available in each workplace, parents who wished to take their small children with them on mission could look after them at night themselves. Such a solution, though doubtless tiring, would make it possible for parents to maintain daily contact with their children and monitor their well-being. Given the absence of such facilities, however, few parents attempt to take children with them on mission.

b)   Leaving children behind during missions

At present, most staff who travel on mission leave their children in the city where they are based. Private

arrangements for overnight child care are the rule.   The
European Schools, created to offer mother tongue
instruction to the children of European Community officials
and attended by the majority of such children, provide no
boarding facilities.   Nor is a night service available at
the Community run pre-school child care centres to cater
for parents' absences on official travel.   Children are,
therefore, cared for during a parent's absence by another
family member (if any), by live in help (au pairs or
trained nannies), by child minders in the latter's homes,
or in some similar way.

The advantages of individual arrangements of this sort,
as compared with Community run systems, are that they may
involve less physical upheaval and more individual
attention for the children; they may also lend themselves
to more flexible tailoring to the travelling parents'
requirements.

On the other hand, they may be costly in financial terms,
especially if they are additional to the cost of day care
arrangements and if they require a move to larger and more
expensive accommodation.   They cost time and energy to
organise, and usually need to be reorganised at frequent
intervals.   They may depend on untrained personnel.   Above
all, depending as they usually do on one person's presence,
health and reliability, they are fallible.   There are, at
present, no additional allowances provided for parents in
respect of the costs of child care imposed upon them by the
mobility of Parliamentary work.

c)   Reducing or eliminating missions

As an alternative to either taking children along on
mission or leaving them behind, there is the option of
cutting down on missions.   This may be achieved in one of
three ways.

Not travelling in a travelling post: Some staff members
occupy a post normally involving a requirement to travel
but elect to travel seldom or not at all.   This is a course
most often resorted to by secretaries who are to an extent
more interchangeable than staff in the administrative and
managerial grades.   Officials choosing this solution are
within their rights under the terms of an agreement
negotiated between the Administration and Staff Committee
in 1981 which specifies that no staff member may be forced
to travel against his or her will.

Nevertheless this course of action, which is inefficient
for the system as a whole, may entail a personal sense of
letting workmates down, and/ or active disapproval and
pressure on the part of colleagues and hierarchical
superiors to move to another post.

Transferring to a non travelling post: Some staff members may opt to transfer to a post requiring less or no travel. This approach may more often be selected by administrative and managerial staff, of whom there is a greater expectation that they will comply with the travel obligations of the post they occupy.

But the choice of non-travelling posts in a travelling institution, as it is presently organised, is necessarily limited. For secretarial staff, the shift may be from the staff of a Parliamentary body to the typing pool - a move not calculated to enhance career development. For administrators, too, the shift normally means a move away from direct servicing of frontline Parliamentary activities and, to that extent, diminished prestige and career prospects.

Transfer to another workplace: A variant on changing posts is to transfer to another workplace. A posting to Brussels or Strasbourg cuts out the need to travel in order to follow the Parliamentary activities which occur in that workplace and may also have the effect of reducing the length of missions to the third workplace.

For legal and political reasons, however, there is at present a strict limit on the number of posts which can be transferred away from Luxembourg. Although moves are afoot to bring about a wholesale removal of the European Parliament to Brussels, the decades' old issue of the seat of the Parliament is unlikely to be settled in the immediate future.

In the meantime, those choosing to move to Brussels or Strasbourg bear the principal penalty of exile; isolation from the centre with all that that entails in terms of diminished access to information, not least in respect or career prospects.

4.   Conclusion

The organisation of the European Parliament's work over three workplaces gives rise to acute problems of child care during the periods of staff travel which, at present, are left to the parents alone to resolve. As with elsewhere, it is the women staff members who would seem to experience the problems of reconciling work (and in the present case, travel as part of work) obligations with family commitments in their starkest form.

As has been suggested above, there is no single ideal solution to the child care problems posed for European Parliament staff during missions for as long as the institution's activities continue to be spread between three workplaces. Taking children on mission is at present scarcely feasible in the absence of suitable on the spot child care facilities and would in addition be wearying, while leaving them behind is worrying. Both have consequences for the efficiency and professional reputation of the individual staff member concerned. Meanwhile opting out of travel in a travelling institution effectively marginalises those who select this path, as may the alternative of moving away from the main secretariat location to one of the other two workplaces.

Nevertheless, diversifying the range of child care facilities to children of European Parliament officials during missions would give working parents on the staff, and especially mothers, a wider choice of solutions to the specific problems they face. It is probably necessary to envisage a mix of solutions including provision not only of a wider range of day care facilities, but also of boarding arrangements for both pre-school and school-aged children, in each workplace. In view of the complexity of the situation, it would be necessary as a first step for survey to be conducted under European Parliament auspices as a means of identifying more precisely and of quantifying the range of child care problems confronting staff as a result of the institution's specific working conditions.

Efforts to make it easier for working mothers among the staff to take on travel commitments would no doubt also encourage them to adopt a more positive approach to their careers. Such efforts would represent a cocrete move towards equalising opportunities for women and men staff members. At the same time, this would improve the overall efficiency of the secretariat.

Attempts by the European Parliament as an employer to adapt child care provision to match its own particular circumstances more closely would also set an example to employers at the national level whose staff are called upon to reconcile occupational travel with family responsibilities.

Clearly no two situations are likely to be identical. But at the level of social infastructure, as at other levels of policy in the area of equal opportunities, it is the political will to tailor solutions to suit the specific set of working conditions which in each case will determine the prospects for progress.

Notes

1. See, especially European Parliament Resolutions of 17 January 1984 on the situation of women inEurope, **Official Journal of the European Communities** (OJ), No. 46 of 20 February 1984, p.42; and of 18 June, 1987 on the situation of women in the institutions of the European Community, OJ, No. C 190 of 20 July, 1987, p.117.

2. Chaired by this writer.

3. Belgium, Denmark, France, Germany, Greece, Ireland, Italy, Luxembourg, Netherlands, Portugal, Spain and the United Kingdom.

11 Women's travel requirements: employment, with domestic constraints

LAURIE PICKUP

1. Introduction

The concern to better meet the travel requirements of women arose from the 'social relevance' debate which encompassed all areas of planning activity in the early 1970s and which, in transport studies, concentrated on a concern for those social groups lacking access to cars. In transport planning studies up to this period, the position of women's needs had been largely hidden by considerations of 'households'.

Since the late 1970s, a body of research has appeared in social geography, land use planning and transport social science which has explored the relationships between **social position and travel disadvantage**. Ad-hoc travel surveys documented the differences in the **travel mobility** of men and women (e.g. Hillman et al, 1974). Activity based research emphasised the complex inter-relationships that occur within households in the **scheduling and organisation of activities and travel** (Jones et al, 1983).

In earlier papers (Pickup, 1985a, 1985b), the relevance of analysing women's travel needs explicitly against a background of their **gender** role has been explored and is summarised in this chapter. Whereas for other social groups, it is physical frailty or dependency or income which limits travel opportunities, in the case of women, it is aspects of the gender role which determine their travel patterns. These latter essentially hinge on the problems of activity organisation within the home and the ability to budget activities within **time and space**. This chapter outlines the changing position of women against parallel changes in land use patterns and travel mobility. Specific emphasis is given to empirical work undertaken in the United Kingdom.

In a society which has become increasingly reliant on car use, women are a disadvantaged group in the population. In the 1978/1979 British National Travel Survey (NTS), only 30% of women held a driving licence compared with 68% of men. Furthermore, while according to the NTS, two thirds of women reside in car-owning households, evidence from a number of studies (reviewed in Pickup, 1981) shows that most of these women rarely have a car available to use whether they hold a driving licence or not. Women are far more reliant on using public transport and, therefore, in general, they have lower travel mobility compared with men.

Despite women's low travel mobility, it can be argued that their **travel requirements** have grown in recent decades. Their situation needs to be seen against radical changes which have occurred in women's life style over the last thirty years or so (Whipp and Grieco, Ch.1). Women now have considerably more control over fertility and childbirth than in the past. By the extension of this control, they have significantly reduced the proportion of adult life spent in maternity and child care. As a result, there has been a growing **participation of married women in the labour market**, a reduction in child care time yet a **negligible change in the balance of domestic tasks** undertaken by wives and their partners. Thus working women are now increasingly assuming a dual role within society; a role which, it will be shown, involves a complex and intricate budgeting and scheduling of activities in both time and space.

2.   Changing lifestyles

There has been a rapid growth in working women in most OECD nations (Rosenbloom, 1985), with the expansion in service, tertiary and light manufacturing sectors of the world's economy. In Britain in 1981, 40% of the workforce were women (Office of Population Censuses and Surveys, 1982). The rise in women workers has been fastest among married women who in 1981 formed 66% of all women workers and, within this group, there is a growing proportion of working mothers with very young children. In 1976, one in four children in Great Britain aged four years or less had a working mother (Central Policy Review Staff, 1976).

Much of the impetus for the growth in working mothers has been the **growth in part-time job** opportunities. Essentially, the increase in women's paid employment has been of a type which would not adversely affect maternal and other domestic commitments. Though the growth of such part-time work offers greater economic and social independence to women than that provided by domestic existence alone, these jobs form a **secondary labour market** to that of men, more poorly paid and of lower skill (Joseph, 1983).

Despite the limited range of jobs presently **compatIble with domestic commitments**, there remains a significant **latent demand for work** among housewives. One third of housewives questionned in the 1976 British General Household Survey said they would work if **adequate child care** was available (Office of Population Censuses and Surveys, 1978). Therefore, the non-working 'housewife' role is increasingly becoming the typical life style of women only during their immediate child bearing years.

The housewife role has changed with the growth in working women, smaller families, new social services and consumer goods. Mackenzie (1988) notes the manner in which housework tasks have changed in the past decades. Housework, for most working women, remains a demanding job. However, many of the activities which were undertaken in the home are now provided in shops or other facilities away from the home. Thus, in-home housework time has been **partially substituted** both into the service sector and into **additional travel time** required to gain access to these services.

Where planning agencies are continuing to centralise activities, e.g. the construction of District General Hospitals on urban perimeter green field sites, the additional costs imposed on individuals are not fully taken into account. These costs not only involve travel costs and the amount of time consumed but also the increased problems in the scheduling of activities to gain access to more dispersed facilities. For gaining access to some facilities, such as hospitals, additional problems in rescheduling activities can lead to additional anxiety and stress (Pickup, 1987).

Despite women's low mobility, the rise in the number of working women, particularly working mothers, has substantially increased women's travel **needs**. Table 11.1 compares the daily journey frequencies for different **activity categories** made by housewives and women working part-time and full-time from the 1975/1976 NTS. It shows that housewives returning to part-time work increase their daily travel by 30%. In the decision to re-enter the labour force resolving the time and space conflicts associated with combining home and work activities include an important travel time component.

Table 11.1. The frequency of travel for selected purposes by working women and housewives (journeys per person per day)

Working status	Work	Shopping	Journey purpose Personal business	Social	Escort	Other	All
Women employed full-time	1.33	0.45	0.18	0.42	0.09	0.45	2.91
Women employed part-time	0.96	0.70	0.22	0.41	0.28	0.40	2.97
Housewives	0.0	0.88	0.28	0.47	0.37	0.29	2.29

Source: 1975/76 NTS (cited in Pickup, 1981).

3.   Geographical pressures

The development of women's dual role has taken place alongside a growing **spatial separation of home and workplace**; suburbs have grown and many jobs have decentralised to suburban sites (Evans and Eversley, 1980). In addition to this, changes in **retail provision** have reduced the number of small local stores and supermarkets in favour of larger town centre developments of peripheral hyper-markets (Bowlby, 1978); new schools also are increasingly spreading to 'green field' sites (Levin and Bruce, 1967) and similar developments have taken place in health provision.

One of the consequences of the development of large retail outlets has been the lack of convenience shopping facilities in locations close to employment centres where trips can be easily accommodated into daily routines (Guy, 1985).

At the same time, the growth in women's employment has not been evenly distributed throughout different sectors but has largely occurred in clerical and service jobs in town centres and in a mixed market of local white collar or unskilled manual jobs. This degree of sectorial and spatial clustering has been less apparent among working men and may be attributed to differences in travel mobility between the sexes.

While the organisation of household activities underly the differences in mobility between men and women, it is, nevertheless, also affected by the occupational structure (Hamilton and Jenkins, Ch.2). The growth in company car ownership and use is one example of this. Access to such cars have primarily been the province of male workers rather than the female workforce; company cars have also had a secondary effect on the patterns of household car ownership and women's car availability in such households (Potter and Cousins, 1983).

When the factors contributing to women's changing lifestyles and activity needs are studied in the context of ever-increasing household car ownership and increasing pressure on public transport finance, it becomes pertinent to ask whether women's increasing travel needs are as well met today as was the case ten years ago when the first articles on travel mobility among different social groups emerged (see for example, the Independent Commission on Transport, 1973).

Several studies (e.g. McDowell, 1981) have argued that the built environment has been slow to respond to the spatial implications of the growth in working women. By changing the content of their lives, women have placed new demands on the planned environment. For example, the increasing number of working mothers has radically altered patterns of family life and the whole pattern of social interaction within residential areas. In addition, the previously 'private' domestic role has been partially transferred into the 'public' sphere changing the travel requirements of women and the timing and location of the journeys they make.

4.   Changing mobility

It should be noted that the dramatic rise in working women, particularly working mothers, although it has substantially increased women's travel needs, has not been met by a commensurate rise in the level of women's mobility (Pickup, 1988). There are a number of institutional factors which account for this discrepancy.

a)   Car use

Within households, there would appear to be a growing latent demand for car use among wives. For example, a report of a car sharing and car pooling experiment in Leeds by Vincent and Wood (1979) found that 45% of all husbands participating in the pooling scheme said that their wives used the household car on those weeks when it was available. Furthermore, this sample of husbands included a majority whose wives could not drive; thus it could be assumed that among licence holding wives, when a car was available it was used. However, these arrangements would still deny women the use of the car for regular commuting needs.

The reasons for and against women acquiring driving licences have been discussed earlier in this volume based on the London experience (Focas, Ch.8). In addition to the independence and convenience which accrue from car availability, safety emerges as a significant factor

(Atkins, Ch.9). Access to a car provides women with a 'defensible space' for travelling. It may free them to make journeys to certain locations and at certain times of the day when journeys would not otherwise have been undertaken. Furthermore, the trends towards more women acquiring driving licences are occurring at a faster rate among certain social groups. For example, Focas (Ch. 8) draws attention to the rapid rate of driving licence acquistion among Asian women relative to those of Afro-Caribbean origin or of women in general. These changes in the transport behaviour of the Asian community may usefully be examined with the aid of Hosking's model (Ch.6); perceiving the existing environment as threatening, Asian women have acquired the driving skills necessary to make that environment personally safer.

While many women do organise lifts to work, the very flexibility in working hours which has provided women with greater job opportunities militates against organising regular lifts. If women are to obtain a better matching of work and domestic timetables, this will inevitably lead to a demand among working mothers for greater parallel flexibility in commuting mode of the sort that only private transport can currently offer.

Is women's car availability likely to increase significantly in the future? The trends would appear to be positive; while licence holding among women remains low relative to men, Table 11.2 shows that it has grown from 10% to 30% in fourteen years (Tanner, 1981) and the rate of increase is faster than men in all age groups under 60 years. The proportion of licence holders among women in younger age groups is more than twice that of those in late middle age and old age. So it may be that, present trends continuing, women's licence holding in Britain will converge with that of men in roughly thirty years.

Within this general rise, the apathy among young mothers toward licence acquisition reported in Hillman et al. (1974) may continue given their limited car availability and due to the additional costs of purchasing a car. For example, Focas (Ch.8) reports that almost one in five of those women not holding a driving licence in the GLC survey had no interest in learning to drive.

For commuting requirements, however, the apathy towards licence acquisition among women might be lower than among housewives. Indeed, among working women, perhaps exerting their greater economic independence, licence holding is higher than among housewives. It has been shown elsewhere (Pickup, 1981) that the proportion of licence holders among women working full-time for all age groups under 50 years averaged 15% higher than the equivalent proportion of housewives of the same age. So the demands of women's employment do seem to encourage a greater wish for women to

Table 11.2. Driving licence holding by age and sex in Great Britain: 1965-1979

Age group		Great Britain Per cent holding licence in		
	1965	1972-73	1975-76	1978-79
Men:				
17-20	29	35	37	35
21-29	60	72	77	72
30-39	68	79	84	84
40-49	62	74	82	82
50-59	54	68	75	73
60-64	41	60	64	65
65+	19	31	41	42
All 17+	50	63	69	68
Women:				
17-20	6	13	19	17
21-29	15	32	42	42
30-39	18	34	47	49
40-49	13	27	38	39
50-59	9	19	25	26
60-64	6	10	18	19
65+	2	4	7	9
All 17+	10	21	29	30

Source: Tanner, 1981.

learn to drive. One important probable trend is that, with the growth in two car families, women's licence acquisition will be a response to having a car available as a main user rather than as a secondary, occasional user. In the 1978/79 British NTS, roughly one half of all women licence holders had the main use of a car and this proportion has risen from one third since 1965. Women in younger age groups owning cars may be much more reluctant to surrender their travel mobility after marriage than in past years.

b)   Public transport

While all the evidence suggests that women's access to cars is likely to increase in coming years and that this will both help and be a response to their employment circumstances, a majority of women still cannot drive a car. The more optimistic picture among those households where wives are main car users must not cloud the poorer situation of the majority of women who cannot drive.

In the United Kingdom, bus patronage has been falling since the mid-1950s when car ownership began to accelerate. Operating subsidies have been increasingly necessary since the 1960s. As a result of increased car ownership and an increase in women's travel needs, women have assumed a growing proportion of the shrinking bus market, both in terms of the proportion of women who are bus users and the proportion of full fare paying passengers. This increasing dominance of women in the bus market corresponds with changes in the use made of buses. In the 1978/79 NTS, shopping overtook commuting as the main journey purpose among bus users (Mitchell, 1981).

While increasing numbers of working women rely to a greater extent on public transport than do men to meet their commuting requirements, various trends (e.g. suburban growth, rising car ownership, higher costs in the bus industry) have made it more difficult to maintain levels of public transport without increased government subsidy. In order to reduce government subsidies on public transport, countries have, for example, tied subsidy increases to improved productivity (Italy), have taxed local employers to fund public transport (France) or have deregulated bus services to inject free market competition (United Kingdom).

In general, subsidies are now being held constant or reduced slightly at the expense of fares rather than of service levels. In the United Kingdom, recent deregulation of the bus industry has maintained the overall vehicle miles operated, though redistributed it with a reduction in services at fringe times of the day, weekends and at fringe locations, while increasing services on the most heavily used routes during both peak and inter-peak periods. The introduction of mini-buses has indeed improved the penetration of bus services into many suburban areas, increasing patronage among women residents, though causing some problems for them when escorting young children and carrying shopping due to the limited space available as a consequence of the bus design.

In British local planning authorities, methods have been developed in the past decade to take account fo the travel needs of various population groups, including women. In the County and Regional Councils, the 1978 Transport Act required authorities to make specific statements on the relationship of travel needs to service levels which led to a variety of **need measurement** and **accessibility** criteria to shops, schools and so on. However, a concern for the particular needs of women were not explicit in considerations of transport need, rather the focus was on the need to maintain access to particular facilities with minimum prescribed levels of services. Following deregulation, the legal requirement to meet these particular **social considerations** has disappeared; the new mode of servicing operates on the stated understanding that, on commercial services, if women have certain travel needs, it will be in the interests of bus operators in free market competition to provide what the market desires (e.g. mini-buses). On non-commercial **socially necessary services**, local authorities may distribute subsidy according to their own need criteria. Although TSU, Oxford are currently assessing the **social implications** of

deregulation in Great Britain, it is as yet too early to assess the detailed implications of this legislation on the travel requirements of different groups of women.

5.   The relationship between gender role and transport

It is argued that women's low mobility is a product of their gender role, a role which affects all areas of their life style and not merely their travel circumstances. The emphasis here is upon a gender differentiated role and not a sex differentiated role for, "the role of women within the family can not be described as a sex differentiated role since it is not directly related to the function of biological motherhood. Rather the female 'role' is a cultural phenomenon, a result of the gender differentiation of roles, socially ascribed, bearing no necessary relation to the individual's abilities or attributes." (Tivers, 1976: 8)

While social studies in transport have implicitly assumed that women's low mobility is a product of, and a response to, their social role, few studies have placed an evaluation of their travel circumstances explicitly in this wider context or taken account of women's changing roles and aspirations. Some feminists have argued that this lack of an explicit recognition of women's social position in research has led to a false assessment of their circumstances.

There are three types of low mobility which arise among women as a result of their gender role. The first derives from the impact **family role playing** exerts on patterns of women's car availability. The second relates to the impact of **gender related tasks** (both home and non-home based) on women's access to opportunities. The third relates to the problems deriving specifically from the **conditions under which women travel**; for instance, the problems of coping with children while travelling and women's growing fear of physical assault which deters many from going out at all particularly by public transport.

a)   Family role playing and car availability

Irrespective of whether domestic tasks are redistributed between household members when women start work, sociologists and social psychologists (notably, Oakley, 1974; Hosking, Ch.6; Rhodes, Ch.5) have argued that marriage partners relate to one another along traditional lines. In turn, this is reinforced by the limited types of jobs women have had access to. Like other areas of women's life style, the subordinate gender role extends itself to inluence the **distribution of household travel mobility.**

In the 1975/76 NTS, a third of women resided in households without cars where low mobility results primarily from low income. However, of the remaining two thirds of women residing in car owning households, 85% had one car only. In these households, patterns of car availability and use are quite different. While research by Dix et al. (1983) in Coventry has shown that car use decisions between partners in roughly one third of households are the products of 'objective reasoning' (for example, the journey was impossible using public transport), for a majority of car owning households, decisions as such are made primarily on the grounds of gender role.

In their study of travel patterns in London's Outer Metropolitan Area, Hillman et al. (1974) found that only 29% of the sample of women with children aged 11 years or less residing in households owning one car had the use of the car at all times as a driver or a passenger. They noted a strong relationship between the husband's mode of travel to work and women's car use. The general pattern was for husbands to have first claim on car use, usually for commuting and for wives to rely on public transport or receiving lifts to meet their travel needs. This situation reduces the incentive for women to travel far, particularly if escorting young children and it also discourages women from learning to drive if their access to the car is minimal.

b)   Managing activities in time and space

Women's domestic role involves activity commitments with a variety of obligations attached to them. While activities like child care and school escort journeys are 'time-fixed' unless delegated to another adult - and must be viewed as **hard constraints** on scheduling - many housework tasks or shopping journeys allow more discretion as to when or where they may be carried out - and ought to be viewed as **soft constraints**.   Both types of activity, hard and soft constraints, are vital issues in women's job choice.

Considerable **reallocation**, delegation or loss of tasks is necessary when women consider returning to the labour market; even a part-time job requires reallocation up to 30 hours of domestic activities each week. While the relationships between the time spent in child care and employment is strongly negative for women (Jones et al, 1983), the relationship between domestic soft constraints and their job choices is less clear. Some housework activities can be easily rescheduled between fixed activities.   Others, like preparing meals, assume the importance of a fixed constraint against job choice. Here a quote will serve to indicate the extent to which such factors limit married women's access to employment:

"He didn't want us to work.....I think because it would inconvenience him more than anything else to be honest...it wasn't because he didn't want us to buy lots

208

of things for the house or anything because that is where the money went. I think it was because he did used to come home for his dinner. When I was working he naturally couldn't, he had to go to the canteen. But he didn't like that for a start, you know, and then, as I say, it was this problem of the evening time meal, where I used to have to run, and though I had prepared the meal the night before - did the potatoes and cooked the meat and that - it was because he was used to coming in and having the meal put on the table as he came through the door......He found he didn't like it at all.. Well I used to get in by the skin of my teeth, just in front of him, you know. My sister-in-law used to have the baby in the pram and bag packed and that for us, you know. She'd seen to her tea, I just had to come home and see to him really. But I mean, you know, I didn't earn that much.....by the time I got home and cooked the meal, I'd taken too heavy a burden. Like I say, it wasn't worth the money I was getting, you know..." (North Tyneside CDP, 1978).

Clearly, where travel time consumes an increasing proportion of the daily activity budget, the reallocation or cancellation of tasks is necessary. This situation has been most acute among those women workers commuting for long durations. Research in European Community member states (Pickup and Town, 1983; Pickup, 1987a, 1987b, 1988) has shown that, on average, individuals have 4.3 hours per day leisure assuming a mean travel time budget of 25 minutes in each direction. Where commuting times were increased to one hour in each direction, travel time now consumed the equivalent of a half leisure time and one third of working time. The duration of commuting journeys were shown to significantly reduce the number of trips which were made for shopping, social and leisure reasons. Women, because of dual roles, had greater problems coping with domestic issues than men. The main way in which women workers adjusted their time budget was by **reducing their amount of sleeping time**. Domestic tasks and poor access to mobility resources were thus increasing the pressure on working women to obtain jobs within easy access of home.

The consequence of activity organisation for the well being of women should not be underestimated. It is clear that tightly scheduled activity patterns have **adverse effects on the well being of women** both in the short term and potentially on longer term health conditions. A body of work is emerging on this issue (Pickup, 1987a, 1987b). In 1986, studies were undertaken in the Netherlands and Italy of the effects of long and short work journeys on the health of workers (Pickup et al, 1987; Pickup, 1987b). In addition to medical effects, measurements were also obtained on a variety of indicators of well being. Table 11.3 shows the results of the survey of Italian workers.

Table 11.3. Commuting duration, indicators of well-being

	Commuters 45 mins+		Commuters less 20mins	
	Men	Women	Men	Women
Sample size	329	94	126	99
Average commuting duration (mins)	73	56*	16	17
Waking time	05.58	05.54	06.46	06.23
Number of late arrivals at work within the previous year	8.2	8.5	1.3	0.5
Amount of sleep (hrs/mins)	6.54	6.40*	7.20	7.04*
Problems with domestic tasks/ family activities (per cent)	64.2	77.1*	36.4	52.4*
Not satisfied with current job (per cent)	29.9	40.2*	26.1	33.3
Prepared to commute further for better job	48.2	36.6*	69.5	24.6*

* 95% significant difference between men and women commuters travelling for the same duration.

Source: Pickup, 1987.

The table confirms that those commuters making longer duration journeys to work of over 45 minutes each way rose earlier, slept significantly less, reported higher rates of sickness absence at work and more late arrivals than did those workers residing within 20 minutes commuting time. The table also shows these effects were more marked among women workers than their male counterparts with a greater incidence of domestic problems, lack of time and fatigue. At work, women commuters travelling longer durations were also less satisfied with their jobs than men travelling similar distances. They were also more reluctant to increase their commuting times in order to seek a more satisfying job.

Medical results also confirmed that the incidence of **reported health complaints** were greater among women travellers. Most complaints were psychosomatic indicating the presence of an overall more stressful situation. Analysing medical records, while it was difficult to ascertain differences in the states of health of long and short duration, commuting women showed a significantly higher consumption of tranquilisers. Other research in France has also documented that regular exposure to certain travel conditions can increase the likelihood of pregnant women having premature births.

When women consider returning to work, after child rearing, the number of **accessible job locations** are crucially determined by the time and space conflicts between gender role activities and available working hours. A **time-geographic accessibility analysis** of women's access to a sample of 89 job location in Reading employing 100 women or more illustrates this point (Pickup, 1983).

Figure 11.1 compares the numbers of job locations accessible by different travel modes from three areas of the Reading district; Newtown, a working class residential district relatively close to central Reading with a frequent bus service; Woodley, a typical more affluent modern outer suburb with high car ownership and below average bus provision; and Sonning Common, a village six miles north of Reading with high car ownership and an hourly bus service. For each area, Figure 11.1 compares the number of accessible job locations without time restrictions to the number of accessible job locations when the time constraints associated with nursery and school hours are taken into account; it provides a good illustration of the relative importance of time and space constraints on the job choice available to women.

The figure shows that once the time constraints of working hours were considered, women with child care commitments were barred from the full-time labour market. Allowing for creche opening hours, only 21 of 89 job locations were temporally accessible and only 25 of 89 job locations were within school hours; all these jobs were part-time. Even within these smaller sets of available part-time jobs, the actual number of potentially accessible job locations is crucially related to travel mobility. So while higher status jobs usually required longer journeys and, therefore, higher travel mobility (Pickup and Town, 1983), low travel mobility per se is of secondary importance to the constraints of gender roles. However, within the limited labour market offered by such time constraints, access to a car is an advantage for reaching a greater range of jobs; for mothers seeking work from villages such as Sonning Common, it is a necessity.

It is clear that local job choices among women and the locally oriented activity pattern of housewives result from a combination of all of the three aspects of gender related travel mobility - limited car availability, problems of scheduling domestic and work activities, travel safety and personal security - but particularly important are the activity time constraints.

A further analysis of samples of activity diaries among working women and housewives in Reading (Pickup, 1983)

Figure 11.1.   **Accessibility to job locations* for women in Reading – comparison of simulation experiments from 3 areas**

*Employers employing 100 women or more

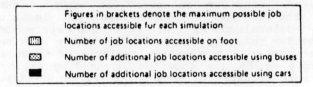

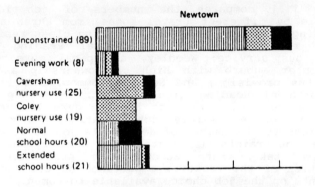

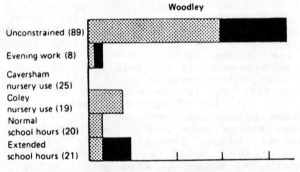

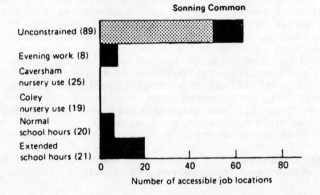

showed that child care commitments and domestic tasks not only affected working status and working hours chosen but also the job locations taken. Classified into 7 life cycle groups, it was working women in those groups most associated with the largest child care time commitments that had the shortest commuting journeys.

The pattern was for young single and married women to commute by bus to jobs in central Reading and work normal hours. Mothers with pre-school and primary school children who worked did so in the local area at a variety of hours, though particularly in the evenings when husbands could care for children. Most of these women commuted on foot; only a few used cars but when mothers did have use of them their commuting distances were longer. As the age of children increased, mothers took on more stable part-time jobs within school hours usually in the local area. Among middle aged women, the pattern of employment reverted to working full-time, commuting to jobs in central Reading but (in contrast to younger women) travelling to work as a passenger in a household car when available rather than by bus.

The analysis above underlines the importance of seeing women's travel issues in terms of their management of time and space as resources for scheduling activities. Traditionally, the theories on **travel decisions** centred on notions of the generalised costs of travelling by different modes (for a summary, see Madden, 1981). Also, within economics, studies centred on the costs of time allocated by women to housework and child care in their decision to re-enter the labour market. Madden, for example, has developed the economic argument to estimate the differential spatial wage gradient of men and women. He (1981) argues that women work closer to home than men because they receive lower wages and because there is a low probability of them earning more by commuting further given the lower grade jobs they do. However, contrary to these explanations, an analysis of commuting patterns using 1975/76 NTS suggests that women's local job choices relate to gender role constraints and not to travel costs or, to a lesser extent, travel modes.

In the NTS, a higher proportion of women than men worked within 1.5 km of home; 44% and 27% of work journey stages respectively. While a higher proportion of men commuted long journeys over 8 km, the proportions of men and women commuting intermediate distances were broadly equal. The NTS shows that even within occupational groups and at any commuting distance, women's mean weekly incomes were only just over half those of men's.

While there was a tendency among all workers for longer commuting journeys to include a larger proportion of higher income workers (and thus agree with Madden's thesis), large enough proportions of women workers (including part-time workers) were commuting relatively long distances for low wages to suggest that **travel costs** for the majority of women workers were **not an important constraint** on job choice; indeed a higher proportion of women than men commute to town centres to work. It was also clear that neither travel mobility nor travel costs in general influenced women's decision to work full-time or part-time, indeed the commuting modal split of full and part-time women workers were similar, as shown in Table 11.4.

Table 11.4. Modes of travel to work by men and women (%)

	Car driver	Car passenger Household car	Other car	Bus	Cycle	Walk	Train	Other	Total
All working women	13%	7%	5%	18%	3%	48%	2%	4%	100
No. of respondents: 8486									
All working men	39%	1%	5%	9%	5%	30%	2%	9%	100
No. of respondents: 12347									
Working women:									
Full time	13%	8%	6%	19%	2%	45%	3%	4%	100
No. of respondents: 5490									
Part time	12%	6%	4%	17%	5%	52%	1%	3%	100
No. of respondents: 2922									

Source: 1975/76 NTS Stage Data.

While the overall spatial wage gradient among women was flatter than men's, there was a steep wage gradient among women commuting to local jobs. The mean incomes of women commuting between 1.6 and 3.2 km from home were 27% higher than those commuting under 1.6 km. This suggests that within women's limited labour market opportunities, they can substantially improve weekly incomes if they are able to commute beyond the local labour market and that they are constrained from doing so by gender role constraints rather than by travel costs. The Reading studies also showed that while car use did encourage women to make job choices over a wider area, it did not act as the main factor persuading women to choose between local and town centre employment; rather the lack of car use defined those areas where women did not seek jobs (i.e. jobs requiring journeys across suburbs, jobs on the urban fringe and jobs requiring inter-urban travel; jobs much less accessible to the public transport user).

c)   Gender roles and travelling difficulties

Rather than having poor relative access through activity constraints or low car availability, many mothers are deterred from travelling as a result of the difficulties encountered escorting children; some women are deterred by their perception of the risks to themselves involved in trip making. Escorting very young children is particularly disadvantageous to mothers. While some paratransit services for the disabled admit women in the advanced stages of pregnancy, young mothers escorting children with prams or folding push chairs also have many difficulties using conventional public transport.

The studies in Reading showed most women with children did not consider using buses due to the difficulties in coping with them. A study by Hillman et al. (1974) on London's outer metropolitan area found that the age of children affected the frequency by which mothers used public transport. Housewives whose children were young enough to need prams or pushchairs used the bus on average once a week whereas those with children of three to five years patronised buses twice weekly. As well as problems of unreliability, poor frequency and high fares, which were cited by all women bus users, those escorting children mentioned inadequate routes and distances to bus stops more frequently. While better shops or creche facilities may be available by using public transport, the added problems of escorting children lead to a preference for fewer, more local journeys which is not the case for women car users (Pickup, 1983). The problems posed for women by escorting, coupled with the reliance many women have on public transport, leads to them preferring the immediate local environment which, for housewives, can contribute to the **problem of social isolation**. The reading studies showed that, in such circumstances, daily local trips by housewives to shops and schools had an important social function for them in contrast to employed women for whom such journeys are purely functional.

Another important aspect of women's travelling difficulties is the fear of physical assault or sexual harassment while travelling; women require **defensible space**. Such fears prevent many women from going out unaccompanied and particular fear exists over the use of public transport. The scale and extent of such perceptions is important (Atkins, Ch.9; Rhodes, Ch.5) given the 'necessary' economies in staffing that operators are making on their services. To combat these problems, there have been a few experiments to introduce 'safe taxi' schemes for women (Connally, 1982) and also women only cars have been provided on some metro systems (e.g. Mexico City).

Recent work by this author on a low income housing estate in Merseyside (Pickup, 1987/88) has also underlined the importance of the safety threat in women's use of public transport - restricting bus use to certain times, ensuring all trips are escorted, foregoing evening journeys due to previously unreliable bus services and long waits at bus stops, not going upstairs on the bus, not using local rail services, etc.

The evidence cited in this volume by both Atkins and Focas indicates a number of guidelines and measures which, if effected (Coleman, 1985), would improve the travelling environment for women; staffing on public transport and at termini to intervene in attacks, removal of sexist advertising, improvements in bus design, alarm buttons, park wardens, street policing, improvements in footpath siting, better lighting, greater participation of the community in safety issues and so on.

6. Discussion and conclusion

The extent to which women feel a degree of travel deprivation depends on their own attitudes towards and beliefs about their domestic and working lives; three different standpoints can be identified. In the first case, the housewife role and low travel mobility is an accepted life style: a choice. If, given domestic duties, a job opportunity, accessible in terms of location and hours, arises it is taken and assumed to be a 'bonus' role in the life style of the woman concerned. In this case, travel deprivation is neither felt nor explicitly realised.

The second case most closely approximates to a **constrained choice**. The domestic role is not so much a consciously accepted life style here, rather it is seen as part of life. Even though they may feel somewhat constrained in their present roles, the women concerned are not aware of the child care alternatives that might exist; thus they adapt as best they can. Like the first case, any jobs are seen as a bonus and travel deprivation though sometimes felt is not explicitly realised.

The third case assumes that a **greater level of constraint is recognised by the woman concerned.** Employment is viewed as a more necessary part of the life style of these women. Such women faced with using public transport for combining domestic and work roles may be forced into local jobs and may feel this as some degree of travel deprivation.

Few studies have attempted to assess in detail the reasons for and the employment consequences of women's low mobility and the spatial impact of their gender role. The most notable study has been that of Hillman et al. (1974) but even here the analysis was limited to the study of licence holding and travel patterns only. Other early studies which touched on women's travel patterns, while implicitly recognising the existence of a gender role constraint, paid it little detailed attention. In many ways, this led to a false and simplistic assumption that women, as one transport deprived group, could be catered for by sympathetic transport policies alone.

More recently in the transport social sciences where the chief concern has been for particular deprived groups, the life cycle research became more concerned with developing more socially accountable methods of forecasting travel demand. Like other strands of transport modelling, the detailed travel circumstances of women become lost within the concepts of household or family life cycles. The lack of concern with a detailed examination of the travel implications of women's gender role arises partially from its seemingly difficult nature for generalisation or easy measurement; too often in social research, women's role is accepted as part of normal living, as natural. Feminists would argue that it is only when this acceptance of the gender role as normality is questionned that women's problems, including accessibility issues, are seen in a true light.

The studies undertaken in Reading did show that general statements about the travel context of women's gender role were possible once a time-geographic perspective was adopted. The strength of time geography is its ability to handle the time and space dimensions of human behaviour within a single analytical framework. Conventional spatial accessibility measures of access to shops or jobs were meaningless for women whose activity choices were continually facing additional time constraints from their gender roles. e. g. problems of **temporal accessibility**. For the analysis of men's job choices, such measures might have more adequacy.

It is the failure to properly conceptualise the notions of time and space in women's behaviour patterns that has led to problems of theory building in this area of work. Two notable examples of how women's gender role has had difficulty in being incorporated into standard bodies of theory exist. In economics, the growth in women's employment created an urgent need for economic theorists to include household production and consumption in models of employment participation. While it was recognised that time may be the measure of such processes, the subsequent models used the overall amounts of time spent on domestic activities and valued it at a given fraction of the alternative wage rate. The Reading studies showed that the use of the time concept in these models was crude and that housework time was much more complex in its constraints on job prospects than is allowed for in such approaches.

The second example relates to transport modelling which has been wrestling with notions of the **value of time** for many years. Despite ten years of social science input in transport, the time value of those journeys connected with women's gender role such as shopping or escorting children are still often valued the same as for leisure journeys. Perhaps the lesson arising from these two examples in economics and planning is that it is difficult to incorporate a rise in women's employment into existing models as they have developed on **essentially male constructs.** Successful incorporation will only occur if theories are rebuilt, starting with women themselves (Tivers, 1976).

a)   Social change

As society increasingly encourages a domestic role for women, women themselves attach much less emphasis to it. Partly as a result of the tensions which arise from both the activity constraints and from the lack of male involvement in household activities, family cohesion would appear to be threatened; divorce rates are increasing and the proportion of nuclear families is falling relative to the rise in single parent families (where a majority of parents are women).   The increase in women working is fastest among mothers in suburban jobs, i.e. the trend is towards increasing the number of those working women whose domestic and work activity constraints are greatest and where the   reliance on slower and less reliable travel modes is most felt; and where access to a car is of most benefit.

b)   A multi-faceted policy issue

The contributions to this book have demonstrated that the issue of gender constraints in travel behaviour can not be explained by reference to the transport structure alone, for transport problems essentially reflect the wider social planning environment. This is not to argue that transport policy has no role to play in facilitating female mobility or achieving **distributional equity** but to indicate that other social policy areas have an important part to play, along with transport, in improving the mobility opportunities of women.

c)   The well-being of women

In addition to the problems of poor mobility and accessibility which confront women, this chapter has also underlined the effects that tightly scheduled, busy activity patterns can have on levels of anxiety and stress. There is a growing body of research documenting the harmful effects of women's lifestyle on their health and well being.   In the future, this position may be compounded by current social policies which favour an even greater caring role for the community as the population ages. The levels of daily anxiety and stress are evidence of a congested lifestyle; they also involve **hidden costs to the community** at large, for example, the cost of treating related illnesses in the health service or in lost production at the workplace.

d)   Safety and personal security

The issue of providing women with a defensible space while
travelling has emerged as an important topic in this
volume. It is clear that many women feel unsafe while
travelling and that such fear is also compounded by other
factors such as old age or **ethnicity**; the latter was an
important reason for driving licence acquisition. Women
are limiting their travel as a result of their perception
that the travelling environment is unsafe. The current
reliance on escorts for some trips clearly limits social
opportunity. While increased fear of personal attack or
harassment is symptomatic of general social trends, the
chapter by Atkins in this volume suggests a wide range of
policy options which planners and transport operators could
usefully adopt to enable women to move around more freely.

e)   Accessibility

A variety of policy palliatives are available to improve
the provision of facilities to women where and when it is
most convenient for them to use it, such as the provision
of convenience shopping at transport interchanges. For the
least mobile, there is merit in planning to provide the
basic necessities within locally defined neighbourhoods.
It is crucial that the provision of better facilities also
takes account of women's time constraints.

The Reading studies clearly demonstrated that in many
cases policies to provide women with greater use of time
must take priority over transport initiatives. For
example, if a local authority wished to increase women's
access to jobs, the money would be better used by
increasing child care facilities in the suburbs rather than
by increased accessibility through better public transport
provision. Considerations of temporal accessibility may
prove to be more significant than considerations of spatial
accessibility to the improvement of employment
opportunities for women.

f)   Mobility

In spite of promising trends in women's access to cars,
most women still cannot drive and rely on public transport
for their travel requirements beyond the immediate
locality. While public transport services currently
provide reasonable accessibility to job and facility
locations within urban cores, they face problems in serving
more **dispersed locations**.

Perhaps, the best prospect for increasing women's travel
mobility is to come from redistributing car use within more
egalitarian households. However, trends in task sharing
within households are not promising in this respect. It is
clear that limited car availability will be inadequate to

women's commuting needs outside the locality. The very
flexibility in working hours which has provided women with
greater job chances requires a parallel flexibility in
commuting modes of a a type only private transport
currently offers. Positive policies have been suggested in
this volume to encourage more women to learn to drive.
While women's licence holding will continue to increase and
converge with that of men, their future levels of car
availability remain uncertain. It may be that a growing
number of women drivers are more reluctant to forego their
use of a car when they marry.

g)   Social equity

Transport policy clearly can not be neutral; there will be
gainers and losers. Despite over ten years of social
studies in transport, a recognition of the outcomes of
policies for different social groups is still not
explicitly made. There is a need to make a **social
evaluation** more prominent alongside the technical
evaluation of policy alternatives, one element of which
should be the implications for women. Hamilton and Jenkins
(Ch.2) stress the effect of current transport and social
policies as compounding the differences in mobility which
exist between men and women; other contributions to this
book have outlined a variety of ways in which progress can
be made in this area.

   There are pressures for women to develop a greater
'community' role in child care and in the care of the aged,
coupled with a limited dispersal of home or neighbourhood
based new technology jobs. Whether their social role is to
develop in this direction will be much debated in future
years. While this would lower women's travel needs, as
presently envisaged, it could also merely signal a re-
emphasis of their current inferior social position and
access to resources. Given the current trends in women's
employment, they are unlikely to accept such a role, in
which case their demands on the transport system to combine
work and home roles will grow.

Conclusion

It has been argued that transport palliatives merely
scratch the surface of women's gender role constraints and
that more fundamental social changes are required before
women's employment circumstances improve. However, the
research reported here has shown that people develop
behavioural patterns and expectations within the time and
space limitations of their environment. By improving
accessibility in the short and medium terms, expectations
will increase which will influence gender roles in the
longer term. In such a scenario, transport clearly has a
role to play.

At the beginning of the 1980s, an assessment was made of the social science methodologies being used in mainstream transport planning to assist the policy process (Pickup and Town, 1981). One of the key conclusions to that assessment remains true today: that more sympathetic transport planning could be achieved by professionals adopting a broader social perspective of the travel requirements of different social groups. Such a development could be achieved by a closer working relationship with mainstream sociology. Similarly, it is the case that those engaged in the development of social policy would be wise to give more explicit attention to the transport and spatial implications of daily life in the assessment and analysis of social interaction.

Building bridges between disciplines is never easy, yet many important social issues such as those of gender make multi-disciplinary research all the more necessary if sensible policy packages are to result. This volume has demonstrated the value of such an approach by increasing our awareness of the practical issues confronting women in the conduct of their daily lives and by suggesting potential ways by which their well being can be enhanced. Gender is of critical concern for any thorough analysis of transport behaviour.

Consolidated bibliography

Abrams, P. (1980), 'Social change, social networks and neighbourhood care', <u>Social Work Service</u>, 22, pp.12-23.

ABSWAP (1983), First National Conference on Black Children in Care, Friends Meeting House, London, 15.11.83.

Allen, S. and Wolkowitz, C. (1987), <u>Homeworking: myths and realities.</u> Macmillan: London.

Archer, J. and Lloyd, B. (1982), <u>Sex and gender</u>. Cambridge University Press: Cambridge.

Balcombe, R.J., Hopkins, J.M., Perrett, K.E. and Clouch, W.S. (1987) <u>Bus deregulation in Great Britain: a review of the opening stages</u>. TRRL: Crowthorne. Barrett, M. and Macintosh, M. (1982), <u>The anti-social family.</u> Verso: London.

Beckett, H. (1986), 'Adolescent identity development' in Ed. Wilkinson, S., <u>Feminist social psychology.</u> Open University Press: Milton Keynes.

Bernard, P. (1981), 'The Adelaide travel demand and time allocation study: questionnaire forms, interviewers and coding manuals'. <u>Australian Road Research Board</u>, Internal Report.

Birimingham Junior Chamber of Commerce (1987), <u>The city pride survey report.</u> Birmingham Junior Chamber of Commerce: Birmingham.

Block, J.H. (1984), <u>Sex role identity and ego development.</u> Jossey Bass: San Francisco.

Bowlby, S. (1978), 'Accessibility, shopping provision and mobility', in Eds. Kirby, A. and Goodall, B., <u>Resources in planning.</u> Pergamon Press: Oxford.

Brewer, M. and Davies, C. (1988), <u>Women's safe transport in London.</u> LSPU: London.

Broadbent, D. (1987), 'Skill and workload' in Ed. Warr, P., <u>Psychology at work.</u> Penguin: Harmondsworth.

Brog, W. (1987), <u>Delinquency and vandalism in public transport.</u> European conference of Ministers of Transport, Economic Research Centre, round Table 77.

Brown, H. and Hosking, D. (1986), 'Distributed leadership and skilled performance as successful organisation in social movements.' <u>Human Relations</u>, 39, pp. 65-79.

Buchan, M. (1977), 'The fisher girls' in Ed. Hunt, D., <u>The fisheries.</u> Robert Gordon's Institute of Technology, University of Aberdeen.

Buchanan, C. (1963), <u>Traffic in towns; a study of the long term problems of traffic in urban areas.</u> HMSO: London.

Buchanan, M., Bursey, N., Lewis, K. and Mullen, P. (1980) <u>Transport planning for Greater London.</u> Saxon House: Farnborough: Hampshire.

Burgoyne, J. (1987), 'Material happiness: are the joys of life reserved for the better off?' <u>New Society</u>, March 10.

Burgoyne, J. and Clarke, D. (1984), <u>Making a go of it: a study of step-families in Sheffield.</u> Routledge and Kegan Paul: London.

Burns, L. (1979), <u>Transportation: temporal and spatial</u> <u>components of accessibility.</u> Lexington Books: Lexington, Mass.

Butt, J. (1983), 'Working class housing in the Scottish cities'. in Eds. Gordon, G. and Dicks, B. <u>Scottish urban</u> <u>history.</u> Aberdeen University Press: Aberdeen.

Campaign to Improve London's Transport Research Unit (1987) <u>Free to move: a report on the transport needs of women in</u> <u>the London Borough of Southwark.</u> Campaign to Improve London's Transport: London.

Carlstein, T., Parkes, D. and Thrift, N. (1978), <u>Timing</u> <u>space and spacing time.</u> Vol 3. Edward Arnold: London.

Carpenter, S. and Jones, P.M. (Eds.) (1983), <u>Recent</u> <u>advances in travel demand analysis.</u> Gower: Aldershot.

Carroll, J. (1980), 'Using groups'. <u>Adopting and fostering.</u> 101, No. 3, pp. 20-24.

Central Policy Review Staff (1976), <u>Services for young</u> <u>working mothers with children.</u> HMSO: London.

Clarke, M., Dix, M. and Jones, P.M. (1981) 'Error and uncertainty in travel surveys'. <u>Transportation</u>, 10, pp.105-126.

Clarke, R.V.G. and Mayhew, P. (Eds.) (1980), <u>Designing out</u> <u>crime.</u> HMSO: London.

Coleman, A. (1985), <u>Utopia on trial: vision and reality in</u> <u>planned housing.</u> Hilary Shipman: London.

Collinson, D. (1988), <u>Barriers to fair selection.</u> Equal Opportunities Commission/ HMSO: London.

Connally, J. (1982), <u>Ann Arbor takes a night ride.</u> Ann Arbor Transportation Authority, Transportation Project 738: Ann Arbor.

Daily Mail (1984), 'Black, white and happy: the foster mother and the superstar who disprove the Left's latest theory on race', 25th Feb.

Davanzo, J. and Morrison, P.A. (1978), <u>The dynamics of</u> <u>return migration: descriptive findings from a</u> <u>longitudinal study.</u> Rand Corporation: Santa Monica, California.

David, M. (1986), 'Morality and maternity: towards a better union than the Moral Right's family policy', <u>CSP</u>, Summer 1986, No. 16, pp. 40-56.

Davidson, M. (1987), 'Women and employment', in Ed. Warr, P., <u>Psychology at work.</u> Penguin: Harmondsworth.

Davis, S. Morris, B. and Thorn, J. (1981), 'Task centred assessment for foster parents'. <u>Adoption and Fostering.</u>

Davies, C. and Rosser, J. (1986), 'Gendered jobs in the health service; a problem for labour process analysis', in Eds. Knight, D. and Wilmott, H., <u>Studies in gender</u> <u>and technology in the labour process.</u> Gower: Aldershot.

Dawson, H. (London Transport Technology Network) (1987), <u>Wrong tracks: a study of British Rail services in the</u> <u>South East.</u> Commissioned by the South East Economic Development Strategy.

Department of Employment (1984), <u>Family Expenditure Survey</u> <u>1984.</u> HMSO: London.

Department of Health and Social Security (1981), <u>Children</u> <u>in care in London: Report of the DHSS Social Work</u> <u>Service,</u> <u>London Region.</u>

Department of Health and Social Security (1982), <u>Press release: Children in care; growing numbers placed with foster parents.</u> 3.5.1982

Department of Transport (1978/79), <u>National Travel Survey 1978/9 Report.</u> HMSO: London.

Department of Transport (1986), <u>Transport Statistics Great Britain, 1975-1985</u>. HMSO: London.

Department of Transport (1986), <u>Crime on the London Underground</u>. HMSO: London.

Di Leonardo, M. (1987), 'Women, families and the work of kinship', <u>Signs</u>, Spring, pp. 440-453.

Dix, M.C., Carpenter, S., Clarke, M.I., Pollard, J. and Spencer, M. (1983), <u>Car use: a social and economic study.</u> Gower: Aldershot.

English, J., Madison, R. and Norman, P. (1976), <u>Slum clearance: the social and administrative context in England and Wales.</u> Croom Helm: London.

European Parliament Committee on Social Affairs and Employment, 'Family policy in the E.E.C.'. Working Document PE 70:147.

Evans, A. and Eversley, D. (1980), <u>The inner city</u>. Heinemann: London.

Fanshel, D. (1966), <u>Foster parenthood: a role analysis.</u> University of Minnesota Press: Minnesota.

Family Expenditure Survey (1983) HMSO:London.

Finch, J. (1984), 'Community care: developing non-sexist alternatives', <u>Critical Social Policy</u>, No. 9, pp. 6-18.

Focas, C. (Forthcoming), <u>Non-drivers in car owning households: constraints in mobility and access. The case for Greater London.</u> Gower: Aldershot.

Foster Care (1978), 'Patterns of Foster Care', 20.10.1978.

Foster Care (1983), Correspondent to Foster Care, No.33, March 1983.

Foster Care (1986),'NFCA calls for more realistic fostering allowances', January.

Foster Care (1986), Correspondent to Foster Care, March.

Foster Care (1986), 'Report on London Working Party on Teenage Fostering', September.

Foster Care (1987), 'Men can play an active caring role', March.

Friedan, B. (1982), <u>The second stage.</u> Joseph: London.

Galbraith, J. (1973), <u>Organisation design</u>. Addison-Wesley: London.

Game, A. and Pringle, R. (1984), <u>Gender at work.</u> Pluto Press: London.

George, V. (1970), <u>Foster care: theory and practice.</u> Routledge and Kegan Paul: London.

Gershuny, J. (1983), <u>Social innovation and the division of labour.</u> Oxford University Press: Oxford.

Gershuny, J. and Thomas, G.S. (1980), 'Changing patterns of time use: data preparation and preliminary results, U.K. 1961-1974/5.' <u>SPRU Occasional Paper Series</u>, No.13.

Giddens, A. (1985), 'Time, space and regionalisation', in Eds. Gregory, D. and Urry, J., <u>Social relations and spatial structures.</u> Macmillan: London.

Gill, O. and Jackson, B. (1983), <u>Adoption and race: black,</u> <u>Asian and mixed race children in white families.</u> Batsford Academic and Educational: London.

Gillespie, A.E. (1979), <u>Transport and the inner city.</u>Centre for Urban and Regional Development Studies: Newcastle.

Gilligan, C. (1982), <u>In a different voice.</u> Harvard University Press: Cambridge, Mass.

Gittens, D. (1985), <u>The family in question: changing</u> <u>households and familiar ideologies.</u> Macmillan: London.

Glendinning, C. and Millar, J. (1987), <u>Women and poverty in</u> <u>Britain.</u> Wheatsheaf: London.

Goodwin, P.B. (1985), <u>One person operation of buses in</u> <u>London</u>. GLC:London.

Greater London Council (1985), <u>GLTS 1981: Transport Data</u> <u>for London.</u> Greater London Council: London.

Greater London Council: Women's Committee (1985), <u>Women on</u> <u>the Move 1: Initial research preliminary to the survey.</u> <u>Women's group discussions</u>, Greater London Council: London.

Greater London Council: Women's Committee (1985), <u>Women on</u> <u>the Move 2: Survey results: the overall findings</u>. Greater London Council: London.

Greater London Council: Women's Committee (1985), <u>Women on</u> <u>the Move 3: Survey results: safety, harassment and</u> <u>violence.</u> Greater London Council: London.

Greater London Council: Women's Committee (1986), <u>Women on</u> <u>the Move 4: Detailed results: Differences between women's</u> <u>needs</u>. Greater London Council: London.

Greater London Council: Women's Committee (1986), <u>Women on</u> <u>the Move 5: Detailed results: Black Afro-Caribbean and</u> <u>Asian women.</u> Greater London Council: London.

Greater London Council: Women's Committee (1986), <u>Women on</u> <u>the Move 6: Ideas for action.</u> Greater London Council: London.

Greater London Council: Women's Committee (1986), <u>Women on</u> <u>the move 7: Methodology.</u> Greater London Council: London.

Gregory, D. (1982), <u>Regional transformation and the</u> <u>industrial revolution: a geography of the Yorkshire</u> <u>woollen industry.</u> Heinemann: London.

Grieco, M.S. (1982), 'Work organisation and hospital design'. <u>Work Organisation Research Centre, Mimeo.</u>

Grieco, M.S. (1985a), 'The role of grapevine recruitment processes in labour market discrimination: evidence from south east London'. <u>London Economic Policy Unit, Mimeo.</u>

Grieco, M.S. (1985b), 'Corby New Town: planning and imbalanced development.' <u>Regional Studies</u>. February.

Grieco, M.S. (1986), <u>Public transport requirements and</u> <u>the Surrey Docks area</u>. Transport Studies Unit, University of Oxford, Working Paper 363.

Grieco, M.S. (1987a), <u>Keeping it in the family: social</u> <u>networks and employment chance.</u> Tavistock: London.

Grieco, M.S. (1987b), 'Transported lives: urban social networks and labour circulation', in Eds. Vertovec, S. and Rogers, A., <u>Urbanism: conference proceedings in</u> <u>honour of J.C. Mitchell.</u>

Grieco, M.S. (Forthcoming, 1989), Workers' dilemmas:
recruitment, reliability and repeated exchange.
Tavistock: London.

Grieco, M.S. and Hosking, D. (1987), 'Networking,
exchange and skill', International Studies of Management
and Organisation, Vol xvii, No. 1, pp. 75-87.

Grieco, M.S. and Whipp, R. (1986), 'Women and the
workplace: gender and control in the labour process', in
Eds. Knights, D. and Wilmott, H., Studies in gender and
technology in the labour process. Gower Press:
Aldershot.

Grossin, W. (1983), 'Le temps de travail des salaries: vers
une diversification des statuts', Le Travail Humain, 46,
pp. 297-311.

Guardian, The (1985) Letter 24.2.1985.

Guiver, J. and Hoyle, S. (1987), Buswatch: the inital
findings. Transport 2000 paper presented at Conference on
Deregulation held by Transport Studies Unit, University
of Oxford, May 1987.

Gutek, B., Larwood, L. and Stromberg, A. (1986), 'Women at
work', in Eds. Cooper, G. and Robertson, I.,
International Review of Industrial and Organisational
Psychology. Wiley: Chichester.

Guy, C. (1985), 'The food and grocery shopping behaviour of
disadvantaged consumers: some results from the Cardiff
Consumer Panel', Transactions of the Institute of British
Geographers, 10, No. 2, pp. 181-190.

Guy, C. and Wrigley, N. (1987), 'Walking trips to shops'.
Town Planning Review. Vol. 58, No. 1, pp.63-80.

Hagerstrand, T. (1970), 'What about people in regional
science?' Papers of the Regional Science Association.,24,
pp. 7-21.

Hagerstrand, T. (1974), The impact of transport on the
quality of life. Fifth National Symposium on Theory and
Practice in Transport Economics, Athens.

Hakim, C. (1979), Occupational sergregation: a comparative
study of the degree and pattern of differentiation
between men and women's work in Britain, the United
States and other countries. Department of Employment
Research Paper No.9, November.

Hamer, M. (1987), Wheels within wheels: a study of the road
lobby. Routledge and Kegan Paul: London.

Hamilton, K. and Jenkins, L. (1987), Women and transport in
West Yorkshire: Phase 1, the pre-deregulation study; a
preliminary report. Transport Studies Unit, WYCROW,
University of Bradford.

Hamilton, K. and Potter, S. (1985), Losing track.
Routledge and Kegan Paul: London.

Hanmer, J. and Saunders, S. (1984), Well grounded fear: a
community study of violence to women. Hutchinson: London.

Hanmer, J. and Maynard, M. (Eds.) (1987), Women, violence
and social control. Macmillan: London.

Hanson, S. and Hanson, P. (1980), 'The impact of women's
employment on household travel patterns; a Swedish
example.' in Ed. Rosenbloom, S., Women's travel issues.
U.S. G.P.O.: Washington D.C.

Hanson, S. and Hanson, P. (1981), 'The impact of married women's employment on household travel patterns: a Swedish example'. Transportation, Vol 10, No. 2, pp. 165-183.

Hardy, J. (1986) 'Professional fostering: handicapped children.' Adoption and Fostering, 10, No. 2, pp. 19-21.

Hareven, T. (1982), Family time and industrial time. Cambridge University Press: Cambridge.

Harris Research Centre (1986), London Travel Survey: June 1986. The Harris Research Centre: Richmond, Surrey.

Harvey, J. (1987), 'New technology and the gender division of labour'. in Eds. Lee, G. and Loveridge, R., The manufacture of disadvantage. Open University Press: Milton Keynes.

Hauber, A.R. (1987), Delinquency and vandalism in public transport. European Conference of Ministers of Transport, Economic Research Centre, Round Table 77.

Headicar, P.G., Fisher, R.G. and Larner, T.C. (1987), The initial effects of bus deregulation in West Yorkshire. PTRC Annual Summer Meeting, Seminar B.

Heal, K. and Laycock, G. (1986), Situational crime prevention: from theory to practice. Home Office Research and Planning Unit, HMSO: London.

Hewlett, S.A. (1987), A lesser life: the myth of women's liberation. Michael Joseph: London.

Hill, S. (1976), The dockers: class and tradition in London. Heinemann: London.

Hillman, M., Henderson, I. and Whalley, A. (1974), Mobility and accessibility in the Outer Metropolitan Area. Political and Economic Planning Report to the Department of the Environment, Policy Studies Institute: London.

Himmelweit, S. and Ruehl, S. (1983), Economic dependence and the State. Open University Press: Milton Keynes.

Hope, T. (1986), 'Crime, community and environment.' Journal of Environmental Psychology. Vol. 6, pp. 65-78.

Hosking, D.M. (1988) 'Organising through skilful leadership.' The Occupational Psychologist, April.

Hosking, D.M. and Morley, I. (1988), 'The skills of leadership', in Eds. Hunt, J., Baliga, B., Dachler, P. and Schriesheim, C., Emerging leadership vistas. Lexington Books: Lexington, Mass.

Hough, M. and Mayhew, P. (1985), Taking account of crime: key findings from the second British crime survey. Home Office Research Study No. 85, HMSO: London.

Hoyenga, A.K.B. and Hoyenga, K.T. (1979), A question of sex differences: psychological, cultural and biological issues. Little Brown and Co: Boston.

Humphries, J. (1977), 'The working class family, women's liberation and class struggle: the case of nineteenth century British history', The Review of Radical Political Economics, 9, pp. 25-41.

Independent Commission on Transport (1974), Changing directions. Coronet Books: London.

Jacobs, J. (1961), The death and life of great American cities. Random House: New York.

Jayaweera, H. (1984), Afro-Caribbean women in Britain: a double oppression. Unpublished M.Phil. thesis, University of Oxford.

Jones, P.M. (1978), School hour revisions in West Oxfordshire- an exploratory study using HATS: HATS Technical Report 1.Transport Studies Unit, University of Oxford. Ref. 068/PR.

Jones, P.M. (1979a), 'New approaches to understanding travel behaviour: the human activity approach'. in Ed. Hensher, D.A. Behavioural travel modelling. Croom Helm: London.

Jones, P.M. (1979b), 'HATS: a technique for investigating household decisions.' Environment and Planning. A 11 (1), pp. 59-70.

Jones, P.M., Bradley, M. and Ampt, E. (1987), Forecasting household responses to policy measures using computerised activity based stated preference techniques. Paper prepared for the Fifth International Conference on Travel Behaviour, La Baume-Les-Aix, France. TSU Ref. 381

Jones, P.M. and Clarke, M.I. (1988, forthcoming), 'The significance and measurement of variability in travel behaviour: a discussion paper.' Transportation.

Jones, P.M., Clarke, M.I. and Dix, M.C. (1986), 'Household activity travel patterns in Adelaide: Stage 1b (HATS Surveys and Further Activity Analysis).' Report to the Director General of Transport, South Australia.

Jones, P.M. and Dix, M.C. (1978), Household travel in the Woodley/ Eardley area - report of a pilot study using HATS. HATS Technical Report 4. Transport Studies Unit, University of Oxford. Ref. 071/ PR.

Jones, P.M., Dix, M.C., Clarke, M.I. and Heggie, I.G. (1983), Understanding travel behaviour. Gower: Aldershot.

Jones, T., Maclean, B. and Young, J. (1986), The Islington Crime Survey. Gower: Aldershot.

Jordan, B. (1985), 'Children and care: was the real lesson of the Beckford case that social workers undervalue care?' New Society, 13th December.

Joseph, G. (1983), Women at work. Phillip Allan: Oxford.

Kam, B.H. (1982), Role situations and activity scheduling; an empirical analysis. Unpublished Ph.D., Urban Planning Department, UCLA.

King, M. (1988), How to make social crime prevention work: the French experience. NACRO: London.

Kinsey, R., Lea, J. and Young, J. (1986), Losing the fight against crime. Blackwell: Oxford.

Knapp, R.H. (1983)m 'Life cycle stages and national travel surveys.' in Eds. Carpenter, S. and Jones, P.M., Recent advances in travel demand analysis. Gower: Aldershot.

Knox, P.L. (1984), 'Community studies in geography: a review and select bibliography'. Paper presented to the SSRC Community Studies Workshop, Aston University, 11th-13th January.

Kotter, J. (1982), The general managers. Free Press: New York.

Lambert, L. and Streather, J. (1980), <u>Children in changing</u>
<u>families: a study of adoption and illegitimacy.</u>
Macmillan: London.

Laurance, J. (1983), 'Should white families adopt black
children?'<u>New Society</u>, 30th June.

Lester, N. and Potter, S. (1983), <u>Vital travel statistics.</u>
Transport 2000/ Open University Press: London.

Levin, P.H. and Bruce, A.J. (1976), <u>The location of primary</u>
<u>schools</u>. Ministry of Public Buildings and Works, Building
Research Station Note ED 71/67: Garston.

Lewis, J.D. and Weigert, A.J. (1981), 'The structures and
meanings of social time.' <u>Social Forces</u>, 60, pp. 432-462

London Boroughs Childrens Regional Planning Committee
(1982), <u>Survey of social fostering schemes in London</u>.
2.12.1982.

London Strategic Policy Unit/ Women's Equality Group.
(1986), <u>Women in London; a survey of women's opinions.</u>
Market and Opinion Research International: London.

London Strategic Policy Unit/ Women's Equality Group
(1987a), <u>Women on the Move Booklets 9 (Women with</u>
<u>disabilities)   and   10 (Implementing the survey's</u>
<u>findings).</u>

London Strategic Policy Unit (1987b), <u>Safety by design?</u>
London Strategic Policy Committee Report, LSPC (9), 11th
August.

London Strategic Policy Unit (1987c), <u>Women's safe</u>
<u>transport: the local authority role.</u> LSPU Transport
Group: London.

Lynch, G. and Atkins, S. (1987), <u>The influence of personal</u>
<u>security fears on women's travel.</u> Universities Transport
Studies Group Conference, Sheffield University.

Maccoby, E.E. and Jacklin, C.N. (1974), <u>The psychology of</u>
<u>sex differences.</u> Volumes 1 and 2. Stanford University
Press: California.

Mackenzie, S. (1988), 'Balancing our space and time: the
impact of women's organisation on the British city, 1920-
1980'. in Eds. Little, J. and Peake, L., <u>Feminist</u>
<u>perspectives in geography.</u> Macmillan: London.

Mackinley, A. (1987), Personal communication.

Madden, J. (1981), 'Why do women work closer to home?'
<u>Urban Studies</u>, 18.

McDowell, L. (1981), 'Capitalism, patriarchy and the sexual
division of space.' Paper presented to the Conference on
the Institutionalisation of Sex Differences, University
of Kent.

Martin, C. and Roberts, C. (1984), <u>Women and employment: a</u>
<u>lifetime perspective.</u> Office of Population Censuses and
Surveys / Department of Employment: London.

Massey, D. (1985), 'New directions in space'. in Eds.
Gregory, D. and Urry, J., <u>Social relations and spatial</u>
<u>structures.</u> Macmillan: London.

Maxfield, M.G. (1984), <u>Fear of crime in England and Wales.</u>
Home Office Research Study, No. 78, HMSO: London.

Meyer, M.D. and Miller, E.J. (1984), <u>Transportation</u>
<u>planning: a decision oriented approach.</u> McGraw Hill:
New York.

Mintzberg, H. (1973), The nature of managerial work: folklore and fact. Harper and Row: New York.

Mitchell, J.C. (1969), 'The concept and use of social networks.' in Ed. Mitchell, J.C., Social networks in urban situations. Manchester University Press: Manchester.

Mitchell, (1981), The use of local bus services. Transport and Road Research Laboratory, Report L 923: Crowthorne.

Morgan, D.H.J. (1979), 'New directions in family research and theory'. Sociological Review Monograph, 28, pp. 3-18

Morris, C. (1984), 'The permanency principle in child care and social work.' Social Work Monograph, 21, July.

Morris, L. (1987), 'The no longer working class'. New Society, 3.4.1987.

Mount, F. (1982), The subversive family. Cape: London.

National Childrens Bureau (1978), 'Patterns of foster care.'October, National Childrens Bureau: London.

National Childrens Bureau (1980), 'Fostering disturbed and difficult children: some local authority and voluntary agency schemes'. Fact sheet No. 11. National Childrens Bureau: London.

National Childrens Bureau (1980), 'Short term respite care schemes for mentally and physically handicapped children'. Fact sheet No. 13. National Childrens Bureau: London.

National Consumer Council (1987), What's wrong with walking? A consumer view of the pedestrian environment. HMSO: London.

National Foster Care Association (1987), Personal communication. 3rd June.

Newman, O. (1972), Defensible space. Macmillan: New York.

Nissel, M. (1980), 'the family and the welfare state'. New Society, 7th August.

North Tyneside Community Development Project (1978), North Shields: women's work. North Tyneside Community Development Project Final Report, 5. HMSO: London.

Oakley, A. (1974), The sociology of housework. Martin Robertson: London.

Oakley, A. (1976), Housewife. Penguin: Harmondsworth.

Oakley, A. (1987), 'The woman's place: What has been the effect of the feminist movement on today's families?' New Society, 6.3.1987

Office of Population Censuses and Surveys (1978), The General Household Survey, 1976. HMSO: London.

Office of Population Censuses and Surveys Monitor (1982), 1981 Census. HMSO:London.

Parsons, T. (1949), 'The social structure of the family'. in Ed. Anshen, R.N., The family: its function and destiny. Harper and Row: New York.

Parton, M. (1986), 'The Beckford report: a critical appraisal.' British Journal of Social Work, 16, pp. 511-530

Pas, E. and Koppelman, F. (1987), 'An examination of the determinants of the day to day variability in individuals' urban travel behaviour.' Transportation, 14, No.1, pp.3-20

Perez-Cerezo, J. (1986), Women commuting to suburban employment sites: an activity based approach to the implications of TSM plans. Institute of Transportation Studies, University of California: Berkeley.

Pickup, L. (1981), Housewives mobility and travel patterns. Transport and Road Research Laboratory, Report LR 971: Crowthorne.

Pickup, L. (1983), Travel issues in women's job choice: an activity based approach. Ph.D. dissertation, Department of Geography, University of Reading.

Pickup, L. (1985a), 'Women's gender role and its influence on travel behaviour.' Built Environment, 10, 1, pp. 61-69

Pickup, L. (1985b), 'Women's travel needs in a period of rising female employment.' in Eds. Jansen, G.R.M., Nijkamp, P. and Ruijgrok, C. J., Transportation and mobility in an era of transition. Elsevier Science Publishers B.V. North Holland: Amsterdam.

Pickup, L. (1987a), Commuting: the European dimension. European Foundation for the Improvement of Living and Working Conditions: Dublin.

Pickup, L. (1987b), 'Commuting and its consequences in the European Community - setting the scene.' in Eds. Reale, C. and Di Martino, V., Il pendolarismo: studio del suo impatto sulle condizioni di vitae di lavoro. Istituto di Medicina Sociale: Roma.

Pickup, L. (1987/88), A study to examine the public transport needs of low income households, with reference to the impacts of the 1985 Transport Act on Merseyside. Transport Studies Unit, University of Oxford, Working Papers 400 and 410.

Pickup, L. (1988), 'Women's low travel mobility - a function of gender roles.' in Eds. Little, J. and Peake, L., Feminist perspectives in geography. Macmillan: London.

Pickup, L. et al. (1987), Commuting and its effects on living and working conditions: some results from a European wide study. Proceedings of the International Conference on Travel Behaviour. INRETS: Paris.

Pickup, L. and Grieco, M.S. (1988), In a changing transport world: social networks and the processing of transport information. Mimeo, Transport Studies Unit: University of Oxford.

Pickup, L. and Town, S.W. (1981), The role of social science methodologies in transport planning. Transport and Road Research Laboratory Report SR 689: Crowthorne.

Pickup, L. and Town, S.W. (1983), A European study of commuting and its consequences. European Foundation for the Improvement of Living and Working Conditions: Dublin.

Pleck, J., Staines, G. and Lang, L. (1980), 'Conflicts between work and family life'. Monthly Labour Review, pp. 29-31

Podmore, D. and Spencer, A. (1987), 'Gender and disadvantage among a professional elite'. in Eds. Lee, G. and Loveridge, R., The manufacture of disadvantage. Open University Press: Milton Keynes.

Potter, S. and Cousins, S. (1983), State subsidies and the corporate motorists. Proceedings of 11th PTRC Seminar M, PTRC: London.

Poyner, B. (1983), Design against crime. Butterworths: London.

Preston, J. (1988), The effects of bus deregulation on households in selected areas of West Yorkshire. Paper presented at UTSG Annual Conference, University College, London.

Quidort, M. (1987), Delinquency and vandalism in public transport. European Conference of Ministers of Transport, Economic Research Centre, Round Table 77.

Ramsey, M. (1982), City centre crime: the scope for situational prevention. Research and Planning Unit Paper, Home Office: London.

Rapoport, R.J., Fogarty, M.P. and Rapoport, R. (Eds.) (1982), Families in Britain. Routledge and Kegan Paul: London.

Rapoport, R., Rapoport, R.N., Strelitz, Z. with Kew, S. (1977), Fathers, mothers and others. Routledge and Kegan Paul: London.

Read, G.D. (1983), Vehicle availability and its effects on trip making. Unpublished M.Sc. dissertation, Postgraduate School of Studies in Civil and Structural Engineering, University of Bradford.

Reale, C. and Di Martino, V. (Eds.) (1986), Il pendolarismo: studio del suo impatto sulle condizioni di vitae di lavoro. Istituto di Medecina Sociale: Roma.

Roberts, E. (1988), Women's work, 1840-1940. Macmillan: London.

Rosenbloom, S. (1985), 'The growth of non-traditional families; a challenge to traditional planning approaches.' in Eds. Jansen, G.R.M., Nijkamp, P. and Ruijgrok, C.J., Transportation and mobility in an era of transition. North Holland: Amsterdam.

Rosenbloom, S. (1987), The transportation patterns and needs of salaried mothers: a comparative assessment. Final report to the Rockefeller Foundation, Austin, Texas.

Rosenbloom, S. (1988), 'The impact of growing children on their parents' travel behaviour: a comparative analysis.' Transportation Research Record.

Ross, E. (1983), 'Survival networks'. History Workshop Journal, 15, pp. 4-28

Rowe, J. and Lambert, L. (1973), Children who wait. London Association of British Adoption Agencies: London.

Rubenstein, M. (1984), Equal pay for work of equal value. Macmillan: London.

Sahlins, M.D. (1965), 'On the sociology of primitive exchange.' in Ed. Banton, M. The relevance of models for social anthropology. Tavistock: London.

Satow, A. and Homans, H. (1981), 'The nuclear family rules O.K.?' Journal of Community Nursing, 12.

Shaw, M. and Hipgrave, T. (1982), 'Specialist fostering: a review of the current scene.' Adoption and Fostering, 6, No. 4, pp. 21-25

Smith, D.J. (1983), Police and people in London: a survey
of Londoners. Policy Studies Institute: London.

Smith, R. (1979), 'The movement of women into the labour
force.' in The subtle revolution: women at work. The
Urban Institute Press: Washington, D.C.

South East Economic Development Strategy (1987) All change:
the effects of bus deregulation and privatisation.
London.

Southampton City Council (1987), Safety of women in public
places: results of the survey. Southampton City Council,
Directorate of Planning and Development: Southampton.

Starkie, D. (1982), The motorway age: road and traffic
policies in post-war Britain. Pergamon Press: Oxford.

Stedman Jones, G. (1971), Outcast London. Oxford University
Press: Oxford.

Steer, Davies and Gleave Ltd. (1985), Passenger security on
the Underground: exploratory research. Steer, Davies and
Gleave: London.

Steinbruner, J. (1974), The cybernetic theory of decision.
Princeton University Press: Princeton, New Jersey.

Stevenson, O. (1980), 'Family problems and patterns in the
1980s.'Adoption and Fostering, No.2

Stevenson, O. (1986), 'Guest editorial on the Jasmine
Beckford inquiry.' British Journal of Social Work, 16,
pp. 501-510

Stuart Chapin, Jr. F. (1974), Human activity patterns inthe
city. John Wiley: New York.

Sunday Times, The (1977), Sunday Times Poll on Family Life,
quoted in Oakley, 1987.

Tanner, J. (1983), International comparisons of cars and
car usage. Transport and Road Research Laboratory,
Report LR 1070: Crowthorne.

Thorne, B. (1982), 'Feminist re-thinking of the family.' in
Eds. Thorne, B. and Yalom, M., Re-thinking the family.
Longman: New York.

Thrift, N. (1983), 'On the determination of social action
in space and time.' Environment and Planning D Society
and Space, Vol 1. pp.23-57

Tilly, L. and Scott, J. (19780, Women, work and family.
Holt, Rinehart and Winston: New York.

Tivers, J. (1976), Constraints on spatial activity patterns
- women with young children. Kings College, Department
of Geography, Occasional Paper 5, University of London.

Torrance, H., Ahmed, R. and Bashall, R. (1987), Free to
move: women and transport in Southwark. Campaign to
Improve London's Transport: London.

Transport and Environment Studies (1984), The company car
factor: a preliminary study of company assisted motoring.
London Amenity and Transport Association: London.

Transport and Environment Studies (1985), The accessible
city. Campaign to Improve London's Transport: London.

Transport and Environment Studies (1986), Changing to
green.Campaign to Improve London's Transport: London.

Trasler, G. (1986), 'Situational crime control and rational
choice: a critique.' in Eds. Heal, K. and Laycock, G.,
Situational crime prevention: from theory into practice.
Home Office Research and Planning Unit, HMSO: London.

Turner, P. and Macfarlane, A. (1985), 'Relationships in the long term foster home', Foster Care, October.

Turner, P. and Macfarlane, A. (1986), Letter to Foster Care, March.

Vincent, R.A. and Wood, K. (1979), Car sharing and pooling in Great Britain: the recent situation and potential. Transport and Road Research Laboratory, LR 893: Crowthorne.

Wachs, M. (1982), 'Social trends and their implications for transportation planning methods.' in Urban transportation planning in the 1980's. Special Report No. 196, Transportation Research Board, National Academy of Sciences: Washington, D.C.

Wainwright, H. (1978), 'Women and the division of labour.' in Ed. Abrams, P., Work, urbanism and inequality. Weidenfeld and Nicholson: London.

Warren, D.I. (1981), Helping networks: how people cope with problems in the urban community. University of Notre Dame Press: Notre Dame.

West Yorkshire Low Pay Unit (1986), On the breadline: the low pay crisis in West Yorkshire. WYLPU: Batley.

West Yorkshire Low Pay Unit (1987), Unfair pay: wage levels in West Yorkshire, 1979-1986. WYLPU: Batley.

West Yorkshire Passenger Transport Executive (1987), Household panel survey 1986; initial results. WYPTE: Wakefield.

Whipp, R. (1987a), 'Calhoun, kinship and community.' International Journal of Sociology and Social Policy, Vol.7, No.1, pp. 1-12

Whipp, R. (1987b), 'A time to every purpose: an essay on time and work'. in Ed.Joyce, P. The historical meanings of work. Cambridge University Press: Cambridge.

Whipp, R. (1987c), 'Women and the social organisation of work in the Staffordshire pottery industry, 1900-1930'. Midland History, Vol. XII, pp. 103-121

Whipp, R. (1988), 'Work and social consciousness: the British Potters in the early twentieth century.' Past and Present, No. 119, pp. 3-24

Whipp, R. and Grieco, M.S. (1985), 'Family and the workplace:the social organisation of work.' Management Monitor. Jan.pp. 3-7

Williams, J.H. (1977), Psychology of women. Norton: New York.

Wistrich, E. (1983), The politics of transport. Longman: London.

Women and Geography Study Group of the Institute of British Geographers (1984), Geography and gender: an introduction to feminist geography. Hutchinson: London.

Womens Safe Transport Group (1987), Guidelines for developing women's safe transport schemes. London Community Transport Association: London.

World Bank (1986), Urban transport: a world bank policy study. World Bank: Washington, D.C.

Yans Maclaughlin, V. (1971), 'Patterns of work and family organisation: Buffalo's Italians'. Journal of Inter-disciplinary History, 2, pp. 229-314

235

Zaretsky, E. (1982), 'The place of the family in the origins of the welfare state.' in Eds. Thorne, B. and Yalom, M., Rethinking the family. Longman: New York.